DATE DUE

FEB 1 1 2008	
FEB 2 9 2008	

Cat. No. 23-221

BRODART.

COMPLEX IT

16 PROJECT

Steps to
Success MANAGEMENT

COMPLEX **IT**
16 **PROJECT**
Steps to
Success **MANAGEMENT**

Peter Schulte

AUERBACH PUBLICATIONS

A CRC Press Company
Boca Raton   London   New York   Washington, D.C.

Library of Congress Cataloging-in-Publication Data

Schulte, Peter.
    Complex IT project management : 16 steps to success / Peter Schulte
        p.   cm.
    ISBN 0-8493-1932-3 (alk. paper)
    1. Information technology—Management. I. Title.

T58.64.S38 2003
004′.068′4—dc21   2003052318

Visit the Auerbach Publications Web site at www.auerbach-publications.com

© 2004 by CRC Press LLC
Auerbach is an imprint of CRC Press LLC

No claim to original U.S. Government works
International Standard Book Number 0-8493-1932-3
Library of Congress Card Number 2003052318
Printed in the United States of America 1 2 3 4 5 6 7 8 9 0
Printed on acid-free paper

Contents

Chapter 1   A Project Is More Than Its Technical Deliverables............ 1
1.1 Provisioning ISDN 1
1.2 How Did We Do? 2
1.3 The Project in Context 2
    1.3.1 Assumptions 3
    1.3.2 Disconnects 4
    1.3.3 Issues 4
    1.3.4 Obstacles 5
    1.3.5 Agendas and Personalities 5
1.4 The Big Thirteen 5
    1.4.1 What Is to Be Done? 5
    1.4.2 What Are the Benefits? 8
    1.4.3 Who Benefits? 11
    1.4.4 Who Is the Customer? 11
    1.4.5 Who Is the Sponsor? 12
    1.4.6 How Will the Deliverables Fit in the Legacy
            Environment? 12
    1.4.7 How Much Will This Cost? 15
    1.4.8 What Is the Timeline? 15
    1.4.9 What Are the Key Dependencies? 16
    1.4.10 What Is the Risk? 17
    1.4.11 What Are the Success Metrics? 18
    1.4.12 How Will We Support This? 20
    1.4.13 What Is the Shelf Life? 21
1.5 Discovery Techniques 22
1.6 Interviewing Techniques 23
1.7 Conclusion 25

Chapter 2   Learning Requirements Is Our First Priority 27
2.1 The Trouble with Requirements 27
2.2 ISDN Case Study Requirements 28
    2.2.1 What These Requirements Show 29

Contents

2.2.2 What These Requirements Do Not Show............................ 30
2.3 How Requirements Are Derived................................. 30
2.4 An Airport Is Born 31
2.5 Applying the Big Thirteen..................................... 32
2.6 Develop an Issues List................................... 32
2.7 Eliminate as Many Issues as Possible 32
2.8 Assign Real Issues to the Right Party................... 33
2.9 Why You Assign Issues...................................... 34
2.10 Turning Issues into Assumptions 36
2.11 Socialize Your Assumptions 37
2.12 Analyze and Incorporate Feedback............................ 37
2.13 Get Universal Sign-Off on Requirements.................... 38
2.14 Address the Feasibility of Implementing Requirements........... 39
2.15 Turning Requirements into Specifications 40
2.16 Mapping Requirements to the Project Plan 42
2.17 Workflow Analysis 42
2.18 Conclusion.. 43

Chapter 3   Using Technologies to Meet Requirements 45
3.1 Why Technologies Should Be Used............................... 45
3.2 How Technologies Really Get Used............................ 48
3.3 How Technologies Fail 49
     3.3.1 What Do You Mean by "Fail"?........................... 50
     3.3.2 What Do You Mean by "Technologies"?.................... 50
     3.3.3 Don't You Mean "Why Do Projects Fail"?............... 51
3.4 How to Determine If It Is Going to Work 53
     3.4.1 Listing Target State Elements........................ 53
3.5 Understand Your Technologies............................. 54
3.6 Review Validation Plan.................................. 56
3.7 Review Risk.. 57
3.8 Review Potential Integration Issues 58
3.9 Review with Customer and Beneficiaries 59
3.10 Submit to Technology Review Board if Required 59
3.11 Commence Validation Processes and Adjust as Required 60
3.12 Proceed with Rollout, Invoking Your Plan Bs as Required........ 63

**Chapter 4   Devising an Implementation Strategy Precedes
               Scheduling** 65
4.1 What Is an Implementation Strategy? 65
4.2 That Was an Implementation Strategy....................... 67
4.3 Why Do I Need an Implementation Strategy?................... 68
4.4 How Do I Use This Implementation Strategy?.................. 69
4.5 Building Your Implementation Strategy..................... 74
4.6 Finding Gaps with the Implementation Strategy 74
4.7 Implementation Strategy Components 75

4.8   An IT Implementation Strategy Exampl 75
4.9   A Vendor Management Implementation Strategy...................... 77
    4.9.1   Facilities.. 79
    4.9.2   Operations.. 79
    4.9.3   Technology... 79
    4.9.4   Customer-Facing Processes 80
4.10 Conclusion.. 81

Chapter 5   Plan B Is an Integral Part of the Project Plan 83
5.1   What Is a Plan B? 84
5.2   A Word about Risk... 85
5.3   When Is Risk Really Risk?.. 86
5.4   Identifying Risk 87
5.5   Murphy's Law... 89
5.6   Uncovering Project Risk 90
5.7   Uncovering Beneficiary Risk.. 91
5.8   Uncovering Corporate Risk.. 92
5.9   What to Do with These Questions 92
5.10 The Cost of Risk Management 95
5.11 Next Steps in Risk Planning.. 97
5.12 Plan B Strategies.. 97
5.13 Plan B Triggers... 97
5.14 Sample Trigger 99
5.15 Pulling Your Plan B Together 101
5.16 Sample Plan B: A Not So Wide Area Network....................... 102
5.17 Conclusion... 104

Chapter 6   Writing the Plan 105
6.1   Planning Process Objectives.. 105
6.2   Six Steps Toward Successful Planning.................................. 106
6.3   Starting the Schedule Build.. 107
6.4   The Project Pyramid 110
6.5   How to Use the Pyramid 111
6.6   Getting Serious about Your Schedule 115
6.7   Drafting the First Master Schedule 115
6.8   Selling the Critical Path 117
6.9   Getting Ready for the Detail 119
6.10 Finally, Your Project Calendar.. 120
6.11 Managing Team Lead Plan Detail... 121
6.12 Pulling It All Together 124

Chapter 7   How to Status Your Project 127
7.1   Rules of Engagement.. 127
7.2   The Politics of Bad News and Escalation 128
7.3   The Answer Man.. 130

7.4 Raising a Project "Jeopardy" 132
7.5 Checking Status against the Project Plan 135
7.6 Status Report: Smooth Sailing...................................... 137
7.7 Status Report: Rough Waters Ahead 139
7.8 Handling Challenges to the Schedule........................... 140
7.9 Generic Reactions 140
7.10 Adjusting Your Schedule... 141
7.11 Issues List 143
7.12 When Late Matters 146
7.13 Quality of Deliverables... 147
7.14 Conclusion 148

Chapter 8   Managing Project Information.. 151
8.1 Documentation Guidelines 151
8.2 What You Should Document.. 151
8.3 Communications Strategy 153
8.4 Meetings... 155
8.5 Conclusion 158

Chapter 9   Manage Your Dollars 161
9.1 Where Did the Number Come From?........................... 161
9.2 Budgetary Assumptions 162
9.3 Budgetary Source Data 164
9.4 Creating Estimates.. 169
9.5 Budget Laundry List 171
9.6 Things Can Look Odd under the Budgetary Microscope 172
9.7 Handling Prospective Shortfalls 173
9.8 Service Delivery and Cost Recovery............................. 174
9.9 When Is an Approved Expenditure Approved?........... 175
9.10 Where Does the Money Go? 175
9.11 Tracking Expenditures 176
9.12 Overruns 177
9.13 Conclusion 178

Chapter 10   Understanding and Managing Vendors............................ 179
10.1 About Vendors 179
10.2 Existing Vendors 180
10.3 New Vendors 182
10.4 Vendor Selection Process 183
10.5 Doing RFPs Right 187
10.6 Thirteen Steps of Vendor Management 190
10.7 Conclusion 193

Chapter 11   Manage Your Turnover.. 195
   11.1 The Handoffs.. 195
   11.2 Production Support Models... 197
      11.2.1 Historic Mode 197
      11.2.2 Emerging Model... 197
   11.3 Understanding the Model... 198
   11.4 Support Requirements... 198
      11.4.1 BAU Support Requirements 199
      11.4.2 Customized BAU Support... 199
      11.4.3 Totally Customized Support 200
   11.5 Runbooks 201
   11.6 Negotiating Support.. 201
   11.7 Conclusion... 204

Chapter 12   Handling Your Team... 205
   12.1 Working with People as a Manager 205
   12.2 Leadership... 206
   12.3 Your Role versus Theirs 206
   12.4 Decision Making.. 209
   12.5 Infighting... 211
   12.6 Coaching and Mentoring 211
   12.7 Ownership 213
   12.8 Follow the Bouncing Ball.. 214
   12.9 Project Team Table Manners 214
   12.10 Conclusion.. 215

Chapter 13   Managing Customers and Beneficiaries........................... 217
   13.1 How It Is Supposed to Work.. 217
   13.2 The Customer May Not Always Be Right 219
   13.3 Lead, Follow, or Get out of the Way 219
   13.4 Speeds and Feeds 220
   13.5 The Dynamics of Public Presentations................................... 222
   13.6 Managing Objections 222
   13.7 You Can Run, but You Cannot Hide.. 226
   13.8 Evaluating Beneficiary Risk.. 229
   13.9 Recognizing Scope Creep 229
   13.10 Reacting to Scope Creep.. 230
   13.11 Joint Planning with Beneficiaries 232
   13.12 Roles and Responsibilities 234
   13.13 User Acceptance Testing.. 234
   13.14 Service Levels 235
   13.15 Through the Looking Glass from the Other Side.................... 236

Contents

13.16 Bearing Bad News 238
13.17 Negotiations 238
13.18 Conclusion 239

Chapter 14   Handle Your Management 241
14.1 How Much Autonomy Do Project Managers Have? 242
14.2 Be on the Lookout for Specific Management Traits 243
14.3 Management Style 244
14.4 Problem Solving 245
14.5 Your Manager's Political Tendencies 247
14.6 Procrastination 248
14.7 Conflict Avoidance 249
14.8 Risk Aversion 250
14.9 Grasp of Theory and Details 251
14.10 Communications Skills 252
14.11 Basic Rules of Boss Management 253
14.12 Conclusion 253

Chapter 15   Lessons Learned 255
15.1 How Do People Learn? 255
15.2 Setting the Goals for Your Lessons Learned 257
15.3 How Well Was Scope Implemented? 257
15.4 Positive Contributing Factors 259
        15.4.1 We Developed Excellent Requirements 260
        15.4.2 We Got the Big Picture Early 261
        15.4.3 We Understood Our Starting Point 261
        15.4.4 Risks Were Correctly Identified 262
        15.4.5 The Budget Worked Out 263
15.5 Negative Contributing Factors 263
        15.5.1 Missed Dates 264
        15.5.2 Missed Budget 264
        15.5.3 Missed Requirements 265
        15.5.4 Operational Handoff Miscues 266
        15.5.5 Ownership 266
        15.5.6 Culture 267
15.6 Gathering the Team Together 268
15.7 Samples 270
15.8 Example: SouthPointe Lessons Learned 271
        15.8.1 Wireless LAN 271
        15.8.2 IP-Based Video Conferencing 271
        15.8.3 Thin Client Computing 272
        15.8.4 Analysis 272
15.9 Conclusion 273

Chapter 16   Becoming the Project Adult.. 275
16.1 A Day in the Life.. 275
16.2 Becoming the Project Adult 276
16.3 What Makes a Great Project Manager? 278
16.4 Experience and Training.. 279
      16.4.1 Project Management Methodologies 281
      16.4.2 Technical Background 282
      16.4.3 Quality Orientation... 283
      16.4.4 Business Acumen 285
16.5 Professional Skills... 285
      16.5.1 Leadership Skills... 285
      16.5.2 Advocacy Skills 286
      16.5.3 Solicitation Skills 287
      16.5.4 Grace under Fire 289
      16.5.5 Relationship Building... 289
      16.5.6 Organizational Skills.. 290
      16.5.7 Attention to Detail 292
      16.5.8 Work Ethic 293
16.6 Personal Attributes 293
      16.6.1 Builder's Mentality 293
      16.6.2 Problem Solving... 294
      16.6.3 Common Sense 294
      16.6.4 Maturity 295
      16.6.5 Equanimity 295
      16.6.6 Tolerance 295
      16.6.7 Self-Confidence 295
      16.6.8 Energy Level... 296
      16.6.9 Goal Orientation 297
      16.6.10 Superman Factor 297
16.7 About Consulting Project Managers 298
16.8 And Finally... 299

Index 303

Preface

Some 15 years into my IT career, or 5 years ago as of this writing, I awoke one morning with a feeling that I needed to reassess the approach I took to being a technical project manager. By then, I had participated in dozens of projects and played nearly every role while doing so. I had developed and sold projects, provided technical design and implementation expertise, managed many initiatives, and held operational management responsibilities for technologies and processes that sprung from projects I alternately did and did not have a hand in.

I enjoyed a reasonable amount of success, at least enough to be winning assignments in increasingly complicated, expensive, and high-profile initiatives. To put this in perspective, the budgets of my projects went from six to eight figures, that is to say into the multimillion dollar range. Fortunately, along with that came a gratifying increase in my income and standing in the professional community, which itself had transitioned from Tampa to Dallas to New York City. These were the booming 1990s, when money flowed freely, projects were ambitious, and the belief that technology could solve all business problems was often advanced with an evangelical fervor.

Not that everything was a breeze, mind you. As projects increased in size, so did the challenges of dealing with multiple technologies, a much broader stakeholder base, and increasingly testy politics. What led to the decision to take a hard look at my own performance was the burgeoning discomfort I felt at work that my professional life was overly chaotic and difficult to manage. Although it was easy to blame the environment and the challenging individuals who always seem to pop up in it, I knew in my heart that the only thing I could make better was my own behavior. And that, I came to believe, could stand some improvement in its very nature.

Simply put, I decided that I was far too reactive. Perhaps it is equally accurate to say that I was too one-dimensional. I would take a project, get a sense of its mission, and barrel (and occasionally bully) my way toward the finish line. I believed that I was intelligent and aggressive enough to handle problems as they came up. I further believed that I possessed enough will power to steer any initiative back on course, no matter how close to the cliff's edge it got. The nature of reality is such, however, that no individual, not even the corporate CEO, in my opinion, can reasonably expect to be successful with this strategy. The business environment in which IT projects take place is far too complicated and unpredictable for that. Besides, as human beings, we are not always as alert or rational as we would like to believe, and certainly not as clever.

I promise not to turn this into the story of one man's personal journey, but I will share some observations that evolved into the ideas and practices that serve as the book's foundation, not to mention my professional behavior. To paraphrase the Declaration of Independence, which, if you think about it, was the scope statement for the project of creating these United States, I hold the following truths to be self-evident:

- All projects have a certain rhythm or flow from beginning to end, almost irrespective of the project's nature. This includes technologies, corporate culture, and the personalities of critical stakeholders.
- As a consequence, the project manager's challenge is to understand this process and be prepared with certain strategies or tactics to guide the project toward the most practical and realistic definition of success.
- A majority of the challenges to project effectiveness are not only predictable, but are to a large degree avoidable, or can be minimized, with the appropriate and timely application of these strategies and tactics.
- The project manager cannot guarantee the success of his or her project because, after all, this is not a perfect world. We can make sure that we understand our jobs, however, and do them to the best of our ability, thereby holding up our end of the bargain.
- Although we cannot force stakeholders and the environment to behave as we would like, we can anticipate the likely breakdowns that I, at least, seem to experience over and over again as I progress from one project to the next. Anticipating trouble, and knowing how to react to it, is a very powerful tool that is not as intuitive, or requires as much prescience, as some people think.

As you shall see, I love solving problems. My approach is to break them down into little pieces. Then I examine the surrounding or underlying assumptions that are the likely root causes of that problem, and I attack them methodically, even though patience is not my strong suit. The problem I took on in my own regard, and now present in this book, is how to be a superior project manager particularly well suited for guiding complex information technology (IT) projects from start to finish. I unearthed and examined myriad assumptions about project management that I would wager I shared with most, if not all, project managers. I invite you to look them over, and ask yourself whether it is possible that believing any of them has led you astray, and may in fact prevent that achievement of project management competency.

- Those responsible for deriving requirements and the subsequent technical designs will be sensitive to the business drivers that led to scope, and they will remain faithful to scope throughout the project.
- Beneficiaries (i.e., those persons targeted to benefit from the project) will be loyal, enthusiastic, supportive, and noninvasive project by-standers.
- The project manager will succeed to the degree that he or she has a proven track record and expertise with some, and preferably all, of the project technologies.
- Risk analysis is a sidebar to, not a core element of, the planning process.
- The project plan is the schedule of events leading up to completion.
- Your team leaders will put project needs ahead of their own agendas.
- You can expect respect and cooperation simply by possessing a leadership title.
- Senior management will move heaven and earth to nurture and protect your project, which they hold in the same regard and view in the same light as you do.

When I examined past projects from a lessons learned perspective (i.e., asking myself what could have been done better and how), I kept circling back to my own expectations about how stakeholders and beneficiaries should have behaved, but did not. The assumptions listed previously capture most, but not all, of these expectations. If you play this expectation game long enough, you eventually get around to asking yourself why you had a particular expectation and whether or not it was realistic.

Perhaps the first time I was disappointed by the disposition of an expectation of this nature, I faulted the individual who failed to meet it. This was not necessarily a derogatory thing. That individual may have been overloaded with tasks, poorly trained, or had troubles at home that clouded his or her performance. After the same expectation and others failed repeatedly over time, however, I started connecting the dots. I recognized that perhaps it was not the case that Jack and Marie failed to meet my expectations. What appeared more likely, on reflection, was that neither of them agreed with me on that expectation. More significant, it dawned on me that my holding these expectations of others in the first place might, in fact, be the real problem.

You may be scratching your head on this one, wondering how the failure of a reasonable expectation could be the project manager's fault. I submit that when you look at it long enough in this manner, it does make sense. If

I have a certain expectation, that quite naturally impacts my own behavior. If I think Joe is doing his job, I do not worry about the output of his job (i.e., whether the quality is good, deadlines will be met, and so on). In other words, I take it on faith that an expectation will come to pass, and I have no responsibility for it other than to give it a cursory inspection. On the other hand, if you have come to acknowledge that this expectation game is perhaps naïve, would it not be reasonable to ask:

- Why do I think Joe is doing his job?
- Do I know what Joe's job is?
- Does Joe know what his job is?
- Is Joe capable of doing his job?
- Is Joe motivated to do his job?
- Does Joe have the necessary time and tools to do his job?

I am not saying that if Joe fails, *ipso facto* it is my fault because I am his project manager. The challenges inherent in managing complex IT projects are more sophisticated and occasionally more sinister than that. By the way, I will not solve this problem of managing Joe in the preface of this book. What I will say is that this sort of thinking pointed me in the direction of the process I eventually concluded would successfully attack the problem of being an excellent manager of complex IT projects. Boiled down to its essence, the process looks like this:

1. I will understand the environment in which my project must operate because the project will be far more than the sum of its technical deliverables.
2. I will carefully develop the requirements. These are the conditions the project must create to successfully implement scope.
3. Technology is a wonderful thing, particularly if it is properly applied in support of these requirements.
4. Being able to articulate how the project will unfold is a prerequisite to scheduling.
5. I will identify the most disruptive risks and develop Plan Bs that indemnify against, or minimize, the deleterious consequence of any that come to pass.
6. Avoiding unnecessary or confusing detail while clearly outlining the critical path is the key to creating a great project schedule.
7. The right relationships, a great sense of anticipation, and speedy issue resolution skills are the critical success factors for managing the project once it is under way.
8. Managing project information through a formal documentation process with the attributes of brevity, timeliness, and veracity is important for many reasons.

9. Understanding and managing the budget involve politics as well as arithmetic and should be approached like any other potential risk event.
10. Leveraging vendors is not always easy, particularly if their participation in my project involves a key deliverable or represents a significant dependency.
11. Understanding the operations perspective is the first step of many regarding handoffs of my creation into the IT production world.
12. Similar to good parenting, project management requires the right blend of flexibility, firmness, and a curtailed ego when dealing with team members.
13. Objections and scope creep are two of the problematic areas for which one must prepare when dealing with customers and beneficiaries.
14. Understanding how and when to involve my manager requires savvy and tact and should be based on a realistic appraisal of certain attributes he or she possesses.
15. The reason why lessons learned are included in traditional project life cycle methodology is to continually remind me of the reflective and adaptive nature of my job.
16. Effective project managers possess certain attributes against which I can evaluate myself as well as the candidates I interview for project managers on my team.

These are the 16 Steps I follow with the intent of being that outstanding project manager and, coincidentally, represent this book's high-level outline. A chapter is dedicated to each step. I tried to follow the same format for the steps, in which each one is:

- Rationalized (i.e., connected to our overall goal)
- Illustrated with real experiences to show how to apply each step to best effect
- Explained, to show the value in each step and the downside to skipping it

Because the book is organized along the temporal lines of real-world project flow, the important ideas are carried forward and revisited often, as are many of the supporting examples. This mimics the iterative process of complex project management. So much of what we do, we redo. Initially, we seek definition, then clarity, then redefinition and validation when implementation cries out for mid-course corrections to accommodate the shifting realities of the complex project world.

I made one basic assumption about the readership I targeted during the better part of the 3 years it has taken to compile this book — a population, for your information, that I work with every day. I confess to a complete and total ambivalence regarding the value of project managers having considerable technical skills, no matter how current they might be. In my experience, the complex project manager is equally likely to have or lack a strong technical background. In fact, because organizational, communication, and relationship skills are so important in this job, it is not unusual to find that good management type leading a big project.

I also need to define complex projects as initiatives that have many of the following characteristics.

- Multiple technical disciplines are called for to deliver requirements.
- The budget well exceeds a million dollars.
- A half-dozen or more subteams are engaged for design and implementation.
- Dozens of timekeepers can charge significant hours to the project.
- The project addresses a broad-based, diverse, or highly dispersed beneficiary community.

I would not discourage anyone from reading this book, regardless of prior experience. I have consolidated a huge amount of information into useful strategies or tactics and look forward to learning more each day I start my predawn commutes to New York City. Having said that, I targeted this book, from an experience perspective, at those project managers who, although perhaps rookies in the Big Leagues, have served in the past as team leads or led smaller projects. That profile puts you somewhere near where I indicated I was along the career continuum when I began this narrative. Further, I assumed that you have some Project Management Institute (PMI)-type training or certification, or are degreed in project management. I tip my hat to you on your achievement, which I also mention to benchmark the level of terminology and project life cycle knowledge I believe your education implies.

Probably the most important driver for me as this book's author was observing so many project managers (besides myself) struggle with the job, and the gap between the realities we face and the project management methodologies we have been taught. One of my goals, therefore, was to produce a book that would facilitate a drill down into the practical aspects of implementing best practices in the workplace. I leave it to you, and I welcome your feedback to determine how well this and my other goals were accomplished.

The other kind of reader I targeted is anyone at the sponsor or senior management level who supports large projects within an organization with an interest in understanding the project management process, if for no other reason than to improve the ability to select project managers to handle these complex initiatives. To that end, Chapter 16 is particularly relevant because it highlights the attributes that strong project managers typically possess.

Finally, I must take a moment to offer my gratitude and thanks. Many individuals out there have taught me much, whether they intended to or not. That may sound like a backhanded compliment. Perhaps it is. I definitely wish to single out three people. The first is my wife, Carol, who provides never-ending support and joy. In fact, it was she who suggested I write this book and served as my barometer for lucidity, based on her superior command of the English language and her equally longstanding tenure in the IT world. I also acknowledge my parents, who encouraged me to question everything while simultaneously reaching for the stars.

I thank you for taking a peek at *Complex Project Management: 16 Steps to Success.* I have made every effort to make it worth your while to keep reading, so let us get to it.

Peter Schulte

Chapter 1
A Project Is More Than Its Technical Deliverables

1.1 PROVISIONING ISDN

In 1996, I managed a provisioning project for a telephone service provider. The business driver was to push Integrated Services Digital Network (ISDN) circuits out into the residential and small business marketplace in anticipation of increased demand for reliable, high-performance Internet access. At the time, public interest in the Internet was practically nonexistent but expected to blossom, as it certainly did. Besides, the ISDN technology permitted two channels, so that the subscriber could simultaneously make a phone call and surf the Internet or use a fax machine on the same line. Our project scope was to develop a software system that would "automate" the ISDN provisioning process from end to end as illustrated in Exhibit 1.

The system would:

- Be used by customer service representatives (CSR) fielding customer calls
- Validate credit of customers wishing to order ISDN
- Determine if ISDN is available at the customer site
- Issue (once the sale was closed) the necessary orders electronically to the workers who would physically upgrade telephone network components, and reprogram the huge central office switches that route voice and data packets around the public telephone network
- Have to create a billing record so that access and usage charges would appear on the customer's monthly statement

Exhibit 2 lists the proposed ISDN deliverables proposed by the team after months of analysis.

1

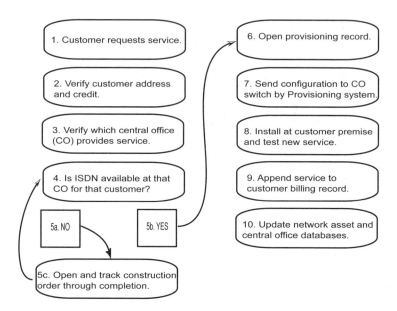

Exhibit 1. Workflow for Automated ISDN Service Order and Provisioning

1.2 HOW DID WE DO?

The project results were somewhat of a disappointment due to technical issues that were not anticipated, and that, once discovered, proved far too costly to overcome. The end result was a diluted sales order entry system that did not deliver workforce management or automated central office switch programming. ISDN was sold anyway, though not in the volumes predicted by the marketing department. By the way, the engineering group I worked with on this project was simultaneously piloting a Digital Subscriber Line (DSL), and, eventually, rolled it out in numbers far exceeding those forecast for ISDN.

1.3 THE PROJECT IN CONTEXT

Reflecting on this and other experiences taught me to be proactive from my first day on the project, in terms of getting the whole picture and looking for signs that might foreshadow complications, if not failure. As project manager, I take it as my responsibility to anticipate, plan for, and react professionally to all discovered impediments. I believe it makes sense to prepare for that. Much of that preparation is based on assessing potential risk factors. Deploying technology is tough enough, but, for some reason, we tend to start each new project as though the environment itself will not present issues and problems, even though it always does.

Exhibit 2. ISDN Provisioning Project Deliverables

- A client–server system that provides sales order entry, work order generation, and project tracking functions.
- A link to customer and central office databases to validate locations and billing information.
- A link to network asset inventory to check the availability of ISDN at any address.
- A set of tables correctly populated with the data required to set up any given circuit with a user-selected version of ISDN.
- A tariff for these services to be written, and submitted to the public utilities commissions in each of the states served by the telephone company to get approval to provide and bill for ISDN.
- Upgrades to the central office switch software to enable ISDN services.
- Upgrades to the central office switch ports to enable ISDN services.
- Upgrades to the work force management software to allow the dispatch of ISDN certified technicians to perform installations and maintenance.
- A handoff to the billing system to issue proper customer invoices.

The process I adopted, and have since validated many times, is a discovery process based on finding answers to the following open-ended questions. For simplicity's sake, this process will be referred to as the Big Thirteen. Do not expect to get the final answers the first time you ask each question. You may get conflicting answers. You may change your own opinions as you meet new people, gather more information, or uncover significant nuances that color known facts. The questions are listed in Exhibit 3.

I am no longer amazed at the wealth of information this process reveals, nor suffer embarrassment when stakeholders give me grief for my persistence, or the wonder I may express at unclear responses. Obviously, there is a little stealth embedded in this process. These questions are deliberately open-ended and politely asked even though the intent is aggressive and focused. The purpose is to:

- Uncover hard facts
- Assess the maturity of the project
- Get a feel for the positions and agendas of stakeholders with whom these conversations are held

In particular, this process provides the opportunity to uncover the following:

1.3.1 Assumptions

People on projects assume a lot, much of which gets passed around and adopted as wisdom if not "the design." This can be very dangerous if assumptions are left untested. It turns out that getting people to verbalize assumptions is the best way to air them out. Errant thought processes can

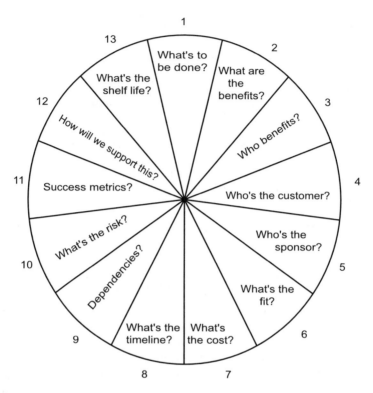

Exhibit 3. Big Thirteen Interrogatory

---

revolve around deliverables, dates, budgets, roles and responsibilities, or risk; in other words, everything.

1.3.2 Disconnects

This is also known as "following the bouncing ball." As you solicit and review various opinions, you might experience that somewhat odd feeling that things just are not adding up. At this point, it does not make sense to challenge anyone on these irregularities. Do, however, make note of them for future elevation and discussion as requirements, implementation strategies, and critical path elements start to congeal.

1.3.3 Issues

I listen for phrases like "We could do this, but (or 'if', or 'when')." Projects are highly dependent on time, resource, budget, and concurrent events in the business or infrastructure portions of your world. Ask enough "what if" questions, follow up with common sense, and you will uncover most if not all potential show stoppers.

1.3.4 Obstacles

The phrase "It is not going to happen" is a signal that further review of the topic is in order. This might be anything from a need for clarification all the way to a quid pro quo such as "What is it going to take to enlist your support and participation?" Other obstacles may not appear as blatant, but they are sure to come. For example, Chapter 13 studies in great detail the resistance from the end user communities you can look forward to.

1.3.5 Agendas and Personalities

Most of your team leads have control over the resource performing the actual tasks, such as router configuration, desktop computer deployment, or application code development. This is because team leads are typically managers of existing work groups with daily responsibilities in development, operations, maintenance, or support. They often feel overworked, underappreciated, and probably understaffed as well. In today's cost-conscious business culture, they may also feel under the gun to protect or justify their turf. As you listen to their views of the project, reflect on the possibility that they have personal issues or professional agendas that could temper their answers and possibly their behavior and performance as well. Knowing this about your stakeholders is always a good thing, by the way, and can be used to your advantage.

1.4 THE BIG THIRTEEN

What I would like to do now is cycle through the Big Thirteen in detail. You will note references to subsequent chapters where individual subjects are expanded.

1.4.1 What Is to Be Done?

This is your project scope. Scope describes the key attributes of target state. It should only take a handful of declarative sentences to fully describe. Think about NASA's project Apollo. Its scope was to slingshot Americans to the moon, and bring them back alive with a bag of rocks and some medical and scientific data. The scope was that simple, although, obviously, the project was unbelievably complex and brazen, given the timelines and challenges associated with implementation. It is that complexity that makes Apollo an excellent sample for this section. I would like to use it to clarify what scope is, and is not, and identify the confusion commonly associated with the hierarchy of scope, requirements, and specifications. We would be fine if we saw:

- Scope as the vision or target state
- Requirements as the conditions the project creates to achieve that target state

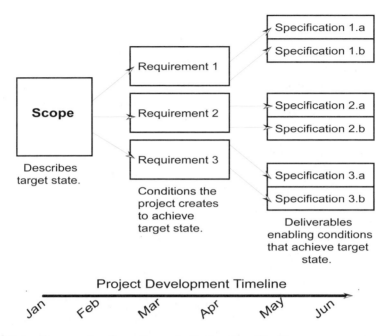

Exhibit 4. Progressing from Scope to Design Specifications

- Specifications as the deliverables enabling the conditions that create target state

Pictorially, we could represent this hierarchy as illustrated in Exhibit 4.

By applying this approach, Exhibit 5 illustrates how I would view Apollo.

It is important that you understand the following things about scope and the two subsequent generations of offspring (i.e., requirements and specifications).

- When NASA engineers sat down with the project manager to figure out how to implement scope, they first had to discover and validate the requirements, which are listed in part in Exhibit 5. In other words, the requirements elements displayed were the conditions NASA believed necessary to achieve scope, which again was getting the men to the moon and back with souvenir rocks and data.
- Once these requirements were validated, they began looking at what it would take to implement them. Eventually, the elements associated with the specifications listed in Exhibit 5 were developed.

You can think of requirements as the "what" of the project, and specifications as the "who, when, and how" of the project. From a technology per-

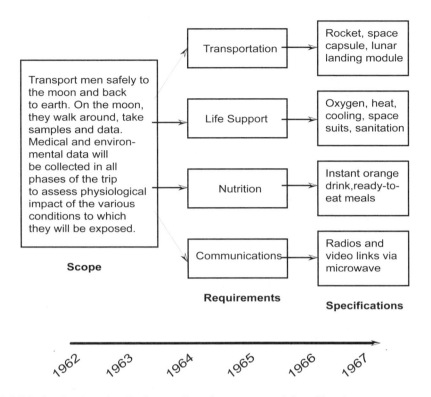

Exhibit 5. Project Apollo Scope, Requirements, and Specifications

spective, there were many challenges associated with cramming reliable equipment that could withstand a wide range of operating conditions into an unbelievably constrained space. Many of you have undoubtedly heard of all the wonderful technologies that were created or significantly enhanced as a result of the space program. Probably the most well-known offshoots of this project are the silicon chip, microwave technology, the liquid crystal display (LCD), and a commercially marketed instant orange drink. If you look at Exhibit 5, you can see how these "products" would end up as specifications in that they served as the means of enabling the conditions required to achieve scope.

The mistake that too many project teams make in the information technology (IT) world is to confuse requirements and specifications with each other and with scope. Put bluntly, it is as though the NASA Apollo team made the invention of an instant orange drink a project requirement, or even part of scope. The consequence of this common but egregious misstep is to make the invention of the drink a project dependency. Put more deliberately, the project team in this case would have decided that if a "just add water" orange drink could not be invented, no one was going to the moon!

The important lesson here is that to meet scope, these guys had to be brought home safely. Because this trip would take a week or so, clearly food was in order, thus the requirement for nutrition as Exhibit 5 shows. What that turned out to be was almost inconsequential, at least until the nutrition subteam was turned loose on the requirement, and they devised menus that would be ready to eat and take up as little space as possible.

All too often, in the IT project world, we see people take specifications and treat them as scope (i.e., the details of meeting requirements become the project). The danger is that people often rush to specifications without going through the flow described in Chapter 2 and, in a sense, ignore scope and requirements. It would be akin to Project Apollo becoming all about instant drinks, not about getting astronauts to the moon and back alive.

1.4.2 What Are the Benefits?

In other words, why are we doing this? What value is received for the investment in financial and human resource made to implement scope? Laudable government projects like Apollo or the magnificent but lamented World Trade Center are poor examples for this discussion because public projects do not normally have the same goals as IT projects. Most IT projects are largely, if not exclusively, driven by business objectives that typically are to:

- Solve problems
- Increase productivity by making data and IT processes more available
- Increase productivity through error reduction or automated audit trails
- Automate manual processes or streamline existing automation
- Consolidate processes through platform integration
- Lower costs by replacing costly-to-maintain legacy hardware and software
- Leverage newer technology for one or more of the preceding reasons
- Increase revenues and margins by improving the customer experience

This book is aimed at complex IT projects, which typically require dozens if not hundreds of team members, and cost upward of $100 million. They tie up resources for months and years. They drain corporate cash for that same timeframe, or longer, because project costs are absorbed long before benefits are realized.

As project manager, you must understand the benefits expected from the project you have taken on, because you are accountable for delivering those benefits. It is very easy to get caught up in the technology issues that naturally dominate the physical aspect of any IT project, whether it focuses on systems, networking infrastructure, desktop computing devices, and so on. Unless the development, procurement, integration, deployment, testing, and documentation activities undertaken to deliver these benefits actually do so, however, what have you accomplished? If that new payroll system you rolled out does not make the process any more efficient or useful than the 20-year-old mainframe system you replaced, what new doors has your project opened for the corporation, or for you and your key team members?

Think of it this way. Some high-level executive signed off on your project, probably after having been asked for similar or larger sums for other projects at the same time. After a while, they must get pretty tired of these requests, and ask some pretty hard-nosed questions to justify an investment they too will be accountable for, at least theoretically. If I had to go before a CIO of a Fortune 100 company or the governor of a large state, I would definitely be prepared to explain why that $50 million should be given to me over any of other supplicants lined up outside that executive's door. Throughout the book, particularly in Chapter 13, the importance of understanding and being able to articulate the benefits of your project in the most practical business sense will be put in context.

When I took on the ISDN project described earlier, I asked and was given the following intended benefits expected from that implementation. Just as a refresher, we were tasked with creating a system that supported the end-to-end sales and implementation of a specific public telephone network service. The intended benefits were:

- Support an aggressive sales campaign by making the process of installing circuits, always a challenge in the telecom business, more efficient.
- The customer was intended to benefit from the automation through a drastically reduced circuit installation time.
- Internal work groups were expected to benefit from the automation through higher productivity, lower error rates, and access to real-time data, including the status of any given circuit installation.

You must understand and become facile at proselytizing your project's benefits. They should guide how you interact with project stakeholders as discussions and documentation emerge in terms of designs, schedules, funding issues, and risk management. This is best illustrated with the following story. Suppose you are asked by a manufacturer of modest quality watches to manage a project where the scope is to design a new watch that falls in the high end in terms of price, elegance, and cache. When you ask about this clear departure from the standard product set, you are told that the benefits your employer seeks are:

- The right design will allow the manufacturer to break into the fancy watch market.
- Sales in that market enjoy much higher revenues with increased profit margins than the company currently generates.
- The company would be less reliant on the more volatile and competitive low end it has traditionally targeted.
- Existing customers can be "up sold" to the higher-priced model instead of losing them to the competition.

You put the team together, you hire consultants and engineers, and you labor mightily. Just before the deadline arrives, you go before the CEO and present your design for that new watch, and a factory in which it can be produced! The CEO is relatively satisfied with the watch design, but is stunned that you have also created a factory design she would have to invest hundreds of millions of dollars to build. When she asks about the factory, you say:

> Well, we think we came up with an excellent watch, as you can see. Upon further investigation, however, we determined that our current manufacturing processes cannot produce this design at a profit. In fact, no one in the world could, so we went ahead and figured out the best way to produce the timepiece!

I think it is reasonable to say that you completely missed the boat. There was no mention of creating a new factory as part of scope. Plus, the proposed factory cannot be associated with any of the professed benefits, and, in fact, violates the intent to enhance company profitability. Too many times, we see this happen in real-world IT projects, although it is not usually this easy to see through the thick clouds of techno-babble hanging over complex projects, particularly at the beginning. What happens is that designers get so far into innovation that they lose site of the intended benefits. The project manager should have asked, in the watch scenario, if we could produce it at a profit in our current factories. Once told that was impossible, the design should have been scrapped, and the designers instructed to come up with something that could be profitably made with legacy processes.

If the design is so innovative despite the manufacturing issue, it might make sense to go back to the CEO, early, and tell her about the exciting new product that would require a new manufacturing process. Perhaps she would buy into it, though she probably would not.

This common project "flight of fancy" can be detected and deterred many ways, but keeping project benefits in mind is perhaps the best one. Remember, the initial presentation of this benefits question is: "Why are we doing this?" Proposed requirements, designs, and future state operating models, all normal components of the design process, must always be vetted against scope and intended benefits, among other things, to keep this sort of debacle from happening. Brainstorming is great, but someone has to apply the rules of logic and common sense, no matter how complex the project is. That person is you, as project manager. Understanding your intended benefits, and using them to "sanity test" emerging design proposals, is an extremely powerful tool.

1.4.3 Who Benefits?

If we follow up on the previous question, quite naturally we want to know who is targeted to receive these benefits. In complex projects, there may be multiple beneficiaries who are variously intended to receive some or all benefits, so using a precision questioning technique is imperative. Do not stop asking questions once you learn, for instance, that the finance division, or manufacturing plus the European sales force are the beneficiaries. Find out what they do so you can get a context for how these benefits fit into their legacy worlds. We will develop these thoughts in later chapters, but it is not too early to start getting a feel for what these folks do and how they do it so you can begin attacking the planning tasks coming your way.

Be aware from the outset that beneficiaries cannot be assumed to be passive, willing to participate, or enthusiastic about your project. They will eventually reveal their intent to be active players in your complex project and will probably try to dictate the final shape of the project, up to and including major changes to scope and the project calendar. They are also likely to feel inconvenienced by the changes you will impose on their world. Not that it is easy, but you should make the effort to turn them into partners. Do not allow them to maneuver themselves into the position of project victims, a common tactic to be examined later. Should they do so, you are looking at costly and possibly very damaging scope creep.

The actual beneficiaries may surprise you, and for any number of reasons. I participated in a project that connected an existing transportation system at an airport to nearby commuter rail lines served by two railroad agencies. They turned out to be the most vocal of beneficiaries, even though the traveling public was considered the real beneficiary.

1.4.4 Who Is the Customer?

The customer funds the project, although in major projects the customer is generally not the beneficiary. This is because big initiatives are usually dictated from on high to support strategic business objectives that the end user or beneficiary plays little part in determining. This could be the result of a consultant's recommendation, or the way a committee determined how to address an issue like Y2K, which in many instances was akin to swatting flies with a sledgehammer. Suffice it to say that understanding the relationships between customers and beneficiaries will go a long way toward helping you filter out the noise and negotiate your way through the swamp of scope creep. See Chapter 13 in particular for additional information on this fascinating group of topics.

1.4.5 Who Is the Sponsor?

This person is often called the "program manager." Regardless of title, it is best to consider it a political position, not a turbocharged project management slot. Sponsors typically have many projects on their plate that may comprise a program, even though the projects may have few interdependencies or other familial linkages. Normally, you would expect the sponsor to be motivated to evangelize your project. You might ask this individual to smooth ruffled feathers for you when organizational boundaries are compromised, or beneficiaries or customers start flexing their muscles. The sponsor would normally be your first point of escalation for challenges to your scope and budget as well.

I would consider all these expectations as the best-case scenario when it comes to sponsors. Due to the position's political nature, minimizing bad press is usually the sponsor's biggest concern. That is followed closely by juggling moneys among his or her various projects as contingencies and other misfortunes arise. Ensuring that the results of your initiative are picture-perfect will, of course, be important to your sponsor, but to what extent your sponsor will go on your behalf is largely dependent on how visible your project is relative to the other initiatives on your sponsor's plate. Having said all this, does it not make sense to check out your sponsor in this regard to understand how solid his or her support will be? Chapter 14 contains tips on how to do this.

1.4.6 How Will the Deliverables Fit in the Legacy Environment?

It is quite possible that your rollout will raise compatibility concerns or other potential conflicts within the legacy environment. In the ISDN project, our software development manager decided to build the system using a client–server architecture. This made sense because the back-end processing was on mainframes, and, in 1996, this was how such things were done. Our problem was that we were ultimately forced to replace hundreds of desktop personal computers (PCs) for employees using the new system because their legacy PCs had less processing power than today's cell phones and were, therefore, incapable of handling the demands of the proposed system architecture. So, while the choice of client–server was an enlightened design decision, it resulted in the budget taking an unplanned and significant six-figure jolt. This made the system design a not-so-welcome choice from a project management perspective.

Perhaps you have experienced more current but similar fit conflicts with desktops, operating systems, browsers, or emulation packages. The point is not to disparage any product, but to alert you to the common project challenge caused by the churning of technologies that sometimes creates design or integration issues. Do not fail to ask this question many times because the fit issue can show up embarrassingly late, and require significant money and too many meetings to resolve once it lands on your doorstep.

If you recall the watch design project mentioned in Section 1.4.3, you can see how the logic applies to the question of compatibility, too. Sure, the new watch design is dynamite and perhaps breaks new ground, but we have no way to produce it without building a new factory. It sounds like a poor fit, does it not?

However, do not be cowardly on this issue. Some projects justifiably push the envelope in terms of fit, whether or not that was the intent. In other words, the challenges of working around fit conflicts may well be justified by project benefits. This is, of course, why we must understand presumed benefits before looking at fit. It could turn out that our hypothetical watch company CEO becomes enamored of the groundbreaking watch design and decides to invest in the new factory based on the enormous potential the CEO sees in your watch. One does not expect the corporate world to be that entrepreneurial, but it does happen.

If potential fit issues come to light, you, as project manager, are obligated to capture and analyze them. They are likely to emerge in the following:

- *Usability.* On one of my projects, the programmers chose to use a certain browser technology that best suited our needs. It turned out that this particular brand (and revision level) was not as ubiquitous in the global environment into which our application was to be deployed as we initially thought. The expense of upgrading the whole environment could not be cost-justified by the benefits of our initiative because we were talking about having to upgrade tens of thousands of desktop computers. Instead, we had to rework our system architecture using the legacy product that was back-revved practically to the level of obsolescence. This caused us a great deal of trouble because the functionality we were tasked with delivering was far more difficult to achieve with the older technology.
- *Compatibility.* Historically, when manufacturers upgrade their operating systems (OS), backward compatibility (i.e., the ability of older applications to work flawlessly in the new operating environment) cannot be assumed. If your rollout is based on using the latest and greatest OS or other base workstation client applications or tools, significant investigation, testing, piloting, and rework should be anticipated.

- *Business considerations.* Business as usual (BAU) activities that your project has zeroed in on may be extremely complex. In another project, we were tasked with converting call detail reporting (CDR) from paper to CD-ROMs and an internal Web site. CDR is a process whereby outbound long distance calls are captured from individual site telephone switches so that the cost center associated with the originating caller can be charged for each call. This was not a trivial task given that the volume from the hundred or so in-scope sites was millions of calls per month! Plus, there were other uses for this data, including budget forecasting and fraud investigation. The legacy process from which we thought we were converting was far more complex than we understood, so simply converting the publishing process from tons of green bar paper to the electronic media of CD-ROMs and the new Web site was just a third of the total work effort we should have examined.
- *Support.* The question of support is number 12 of the Big Thirteen, but deserves mention in the Fit area. With complex projects, the ability of your organization's BAU support infrastructure to absorb your deliverables is a concern you should proactively eliminate rather than assuming it to be a nonissue.
- *Calendars.* There will be times when your project calendar is your most important reality. Never assume that it will synchronize with the environment in which your project is gestating, however. I once had to delay one of our significant deliverables by 3 months because the e-mail infrastructure of the whole company was undergoing a significant change. The nature of this upgrade required that we delay the changes to the corporate network we were about to make. Making matters worse was our learning of this conflict at practically the last minute. This led to some tricky recalibrating of our timeline, as well as a few tweaks to our design.

Although you are no doubt cognizant that a lot of projects are going on in your shop, never assume that there is a really smart person sitting atop the heap who understands the potential conflicts that can result from all these concurrent activities. Not that those at the top are not smart, but it is fair to presume that they are not technically savvy enough to look down at all these activities and recognize pending issues that can derail one or more of the multimillion dollar changes that are constantly under way.

As a good project manager, you should be on the lookout for this risk. As you go through this book, you will read of many such instances and the lessons learned. The bottom line is that, once educated on fit, you may need to ensure that the appropriate changes in plans, schedules, budgets, and possibly even scope are made in consultation with stakeholders and executives. These changes may be required in other projects as well. Naturally, you will be tempted to lobby for your own needs to the detriment of other initiatives. There is no good answer as to whether this understandable parochial behavior will work out for you. You need to elevate these kinds of issues, but be prepared for the eventuality that your project winds up taking the hit and you are forced to make changes. Competing cliques, technologies, and calendars are usually resolved politically. These outcomes are unpredictable and most certainly beyond your control.

1.4.7 How Much Will This Cost?

The bigger the project, the stranger the stories behind the formulation and funding of its budget. Be that as it may, understand what commitments have been made to the project in terms of funding. Keep a running tab on estimated costs that will surface as your team develops designs and implementation plans, and compare that sum with the budgetary bottom line. Later, when you start analyzing risk, of course you will recognize that deflecting or responding to potential risks can become extremely expensive, so you need to bounce those potential expenses against the budget as well. See Chapter 5 for additional information on risk funding.

Unless you have just completed a major project with the same players, make the effort to divine how procurement works. Your organization's procurement procedures are bound to change, particularly in the fiscal fourth quarter when executives are looking to eliminate costs, or at least push them out to next year. This can obviously impact your schedule if not your ability to render scope, so take nothing for granted in this area. Be advised that original budget approvals may disappear the first time you cut a requisition for anything over, for instance, $100,000. You can take a peek at Chapter 9 for additional information on budget management.

1.4.8 What Is the Timeline?

During this discovery phase, what you are looking for is key dates we often refer to as milestones. Individual task dates can come later, so, for now, you want to focus on major events. Think of these milestones as the stepping stones one uses to traverse the creek without getting wet feet. Even the largest project has only a half dozen or so. These would typically be things like site availability, network turn-ups, software releases, User Acceptance Testing, and production-ready dates. This question is one of the Big Thirteen for two reasons:

1. Obviously, you are trying to understand what dates are critical to the corporation. Many dates are somewhat arbitrary, but you need to understand the expectations surrounding them nonetheless. In the case of projects like Y2K, or those mapped to specific business cycles or events, however, key dates are nonnegotiable, and have that "must finish by" quality about them. As you proceed with your

analysis, some dates are going to appear impractical for any number of reasons. The sooner you understand the original schedule, the sooner any issues or conflicts can be uncovered and addressed.

2. Second, as you begin meeting with your project team, customers, and beneficiaries, it is quite important that you understand the project's key dates. The user community has their own business rhythms or cycles that could pose conflicts with your dates. Typical user constraints are accounting closes and manufacturing cycles. Most organizations prohibit changes to the network or to network-attached devices at year-end. Mergers, acquisitions, new product rollouts, and other business events may also create issues that make your project's favored dates problematic, to say the least.

1.4.9 What Are the Key Dependencies?

Every big project has a handful of events or conditions beyond your control, upon which you depend to happen on time and meet other requirements to achieve your project goals. These are project dependencies. They can come from any part of the corporate world, including IT, finance, marketing, and so forth. Do not overlook potential dependencies from the outside world, such as vendors or external customers.

I did a Web project a few years back that relied on a separate middleware project to complete so we could use that new service to draw data our project needed from the mainframes. Our programmers provided specifications that I verified with the middleware project manager as being available once that project wrapped up. Her intended completion date was far enough ahead of our "must have by" date that we felt comfortable this was one dependency we should not lose sleep over.

Had our technical requirements not matched up with the middleware project, however, I would have been tasked with negotiating those changes with the other project. Were that the case, I could not fault the other project manager if she reacted to our request for changes to her project as forcing scope creep on her, and would have subsequently expected a whole round of talks between us as well as at the technical and management levels to clear that up.[1] Although we got lucky in this specific instance, I have gone down the road of trying to change the deliverables or calendar of other projects and can testify as to the difficulty of getting the job done without causing a great deal of unhappiness.

In a new construction project, availability dependencies can be extremely critical. I have had to manage around conflicts over when:

- Data center grade electrical power and air conditioning is available.
- Circuits linking the site to the corporate backbone are up.
- Elevators can be used to haul a hundred servers up to the fifth floor.

Some dependencies will require considerably more research and analysis than others. At the very least, you need to dig long enough to ascertain how a late or subpar occurrence of that dependency could impact you, and how reliable the execution of that dependency will be in terms of timing and completeness. Once you have identified the critical dependencies, plan on circling back to their owners as many times as you deem sufficient to ensure that your understanding of their progress remains current.

If that dependency is, itself, the planned output of another project, keep in mind that, as a project, it is as vulnerable to delays, funding lapses, resource constraints, and all the other project risks that you have to deal with in your initiative. What you thought was true and wonderful in July regarding the status and timing of that dependency may be radically different by the Fall. Experience tells us that change is more likely to be for the worse, so be sure to stay in close touch with that other project team. If possible, touch base with the sponsor or senior manager in that group, or have your manager do that for you, so there is some agreement or sensitivity at that level that the dependency exists and will be bird-dogged.

1.4.10 What Is the Risk?

This is somewhat of a tricky question because the answer you are looking for will change as the project transitions from vision toward implementation. When first handed a project, I have two questions:

1. The more obvious question is: "How hard will it be to get this thing done?" This is a question you will revisit many times, and is covered in great depth in Chapter 5. These discussions will revolve around proposed technologies, the environment into which your project will deploy, and so on.
2. The second question I have, and the one that is more useful at project start up time, is: "What happens if this thing fails, if we cannot get it done?" Responses to this question might reveal:

   - Regulatory or other business issues you should be aware of
   - That your project is a stopgap (see Section 1.4.13, "What Is the Shelf Life?")
   - The need to develop an alternate solution if the risk is highly probable

Suppose, for instance, the assumed means of meeting scope are based on a very iffy dependency, such as an unproven technology, or an acquisition or merger occurring (or not). Should this risk happen and essentially render the original project solution unworkable, you need to go on the attack immediately by crafting a detailed "Plan B." That means, in addition to getting used to the current thinking, you need to start hunting for additional political cover, funding, and quite possibly, a most senior technologist to formulate a clever alternative solution.

I sometimes believe one needs to have suffered a disaster or two to appreciate how important it is to be skeptical and proactive in this regard. Projects are not always well vetted at the time they are proposed, funded, and handed to someone like you to midwife into reality. How many times have we seen projects, which have good purpose and appear to be workable, turn out to be incredibly difficult if not impossible to deliver? If this new project of yours is a big one, you should satisfy yourself that the project can be done well with the resources at your disposal. Should you find gaps in this regard, it is wonderful that you identify them at the outset, when you and the sponsor can devise the best means of accomplishing your goals. For instance, I can recall many projects that were thrown out to vendors, and others brought back in-house, for this very reason.

In a general sense, when you are chasing down risk, you are looking for things that can go wrong and how to indemnify against such misfortune. I recommend during this discovery process that you also evaluate the risk of not getting certain things done at all. Big projects have multiple deliverables, some of which may not truly be needed on Day One. Identify these, and hold them as possible things to delay or delete later on when time, resource, technology, or budgetary pressures make delivering them as originally planned not the most desirable of circumstances. This information can prove to be a real lifesaver. Look to Chapter 5 for much more about risk.

1.4.11 What Are the Success Metrics?

I have heard pilots joke that a good landing is "any one you walk away from." When you ask the typical project manager what makes for a successful project, you will probably get the old "deliverables on time and at budget" cliché. In truth, projects are usually declared complete when the clock runs out or the money well runs dry. That sounds more like a timed sporting event or a trip to Las Vegas than good project management to me.

Initially, I like to kick off the process by asking stakeholders what results they believe would deserve high fives, a free golf outing, or getting that consulting contract extended 6 months. Although I am kidding a little, in truth, defining success metrics is not a simple exercise. Most people resort to anecdotes, such as "the new network screams," or "the customer did not go postal on us." The bottom line to success metrics is:

- Being able to articulate your benefits
- Finding relevant ways to describe how well you delivered them

Whereas this may have soft components (e.g., "the new network really does scream"), look to include hard metrics, such as:

- Average processing time is reduced from 3 days to 7 hours.
- Peak hour wide area network (WAN) latency is less than one millisecond.

Over the past several years, quality assurance methodologies such as Six Sigma have found their way into project management to support the thought process I call "success metrics." This is a welcome development so long as its use is tempered with business acumen and cognitive skills. It any case, it is good practice to develop your success metrics during the planning stage. Doing so puts the team on notice that effective implementation is expected and will be measured and published. After all, putting in a new payroll system on time and at budget that missed three key requirements and is a slovenly performer does not sound like a job well done.

It is a clever idea to identify what would constitute a good job long before the real work begins. It also helps to keep the project focus on benefits, which presumably led to the project being approved and funded. I was once tasked with helping reduce the error rate in provisioning voice mail for retail customers. There was too high an incidence of these mailboxes not being available to customers within the time frames dictated by the service level agreement (SLA). As a result, there were an awful lot of meetings about process, technology, and so forth held in an attempt to fix this very serious problem. The team came up with several proposals that would cost millions of dollars through the following typical process reengineering paradigms.

- Training
- Upgrades to network elements
- Standardization of nomenclature
- A new asset management system

This was all great stuff and not without merit, but my supervisor and I were getting increasingly frustrated with the whole business. In truth, we just could not see how the commitment of constrained resources to this degree would guarantee that a single minute or penny spent on these solutions would actually deliver the benefit of a significant reduction in the error rates plaguing our BAU processes.

During this time, I noticed that one of the key operations managers, to whom I shall refer as Mike, had stopped participating in these unproductive planning sessions. Having perceived Mike to be knowledgeable and conscientious, I took his withdrawal as evidence that he agreed with us that the project team had gone into that dreaded "solving world hunger" mode, that is to say, was losing touch with reality. Mike's job was overseeing the "back end" piece of the voice mail provisioning process. This clearly identified Mike as a key stakeholder, so his self-imposed exile from the project suggested to me that something was definitely wrong, not only with the project, but also with the systems he was stuck with operating.

Throughout the book, I emphasize the value in developing relationships beyond the setting of meetings, so I reached out to Mike. He was not all that approachable; but once he came to believe that I was trustworthy and could possibly help him, he gave me a pretty useful education regarding the issues as he saw them. He gave me access to the systems so I could poke around the error logs that I eventually downloaded to the tune of nearly one hundred thousand error records and ported into a tool I was able to use for statistical analysis.

The technical implications of the resulting frequency distributions were not readily apparent to me, but thankfully the charts and graphs meant something to the engineers. It turned out that approximately 90 percent of the errors could be traced to a manual data entry process that we could repair with nineteen thousand dollars in programming. So, after 5 months of project dithering, 3 weeks of mindless number crunching revealed an answer that barely took a month to implement and test.

The moral of the story is this. Had we begun the project with a reasonable success metric like "lower the error rate to 1 percent," and stayed focused on that metric, chances are we would not have looked to reengineer the whole environment at a cost of millions. Instead, we would have done the analysis I stumbled through much sooner, and identified the correct solution with a price tag that was, as they say, "chump change."

1.4.12 How Will We Support This?

Virtually any project creates some new support wrinkles, the most likely of which are:

- Staff headcount
- Staff skill sets
- The ability of the help desk to absorb a significant increase in user calls
- New conditions that the fault management team must monitor for and respond to
- Introducing new products or vendors to the support culture
- Introducing more rigorous service levels
- Disaster recovery
- Business continuity

Based on my own experience, effecting stellar results in this area will challenge your negotiating skills. Designers often ignore this requirement, leaving the project manager to clean up the huge mess this oversight can cause. That being the case, it is best to get this problem, which it is, in front of everyone early. Keep as many stakeholders as possible involved in its resolution. Understand how your support organization assimilates new responsibilities, no matter how disinclined they may be to do so.

The term "support" has many interpretations based on your specific corporate culture. I use it in the broadest sense, and pose it as the following question: "What has to be done, both on a regular and periodic basis, as well as in a pinch, to keep project deliverables functioning once they go into production and the project team moves on?" Besides the areas listed or implied previously, do not forget to consider backups, password and license administration, security, and anti-virus protection. Another potential challenge in this area, if you are dealing with applications and servers, or network elements like switches and routers, is transitioning your gear from the lab into the data centers or computer rooms across your enterprise.

Chapter 11 is dedicated to this somewhat Machiavellian topic of operations turnover.

1.4.13 What Is the Shelf Life?

The answer to this strange-looking question creates potentially life-saving value to the savvy project manager. Either by design or serendipity, one or more of your "deliverables" may actually represent a short-term solution to a long-term problem, i.e., whatever you are building will be undone or replaced in the foreseeable future due to business conditions, a pending merger or divestiture, or product life cycles.

This is a direct means of testing whether a proposed deliverable, as inferred from scope, does not truly deserve the full-court press you and your team think it would take to accomplish. I have been on projects where certain components were either diluted or jettisoned, despite loud protests from those clinging to design elements being exiled, because:

• Something better loomed on the horizon.
• The original "solution" was not worth the fuss its rollout would create.
• Excluding it would not impact scope that badly, if at all.

Because every complex project I have been on has had one or more original requirements tossed aside, delayed, or neutered, I go into new projects wondering aloud which assumed deliverables are likely prospects for the axe once reality sinks in. An interesting image to use in this regard is to ask yourself whether discarding a requirement, or even a few of them, will make little more difference to the project than the effect of throwing a deck chair of the Queen Mary ocean liner would change its level of flotation.

1.5 DISCOVERY TECHNIQUES

Now that I have talked about what to look for, it should be useful to spend a little time talking about how you go about getting this information. The following discussion is not limited, however, to the Big Thirteen process because the skills or techniques invaluable to developing useful information work in all matters of inquiry, not just this one. For starters, you need a game plan:

1. *Determine what information you need.* When you begin the discovery process, you will probably feel there are many gaps in your knowledge base. They are quite easy to identify by asking yourself two simple questions.
    a. What project matters confuse me, or seem to lack organizational clarity or consensus?
    b. What project matters just seem too unclear or undeveloped to allow me to make any significant decision, whether for design, risk, scheduling, or operational considerations?

2. *Determine the best source.* There may be multiple sources, with varying gravitas or credibility, or there may be just one. If the item in question is important enough, I like to sample multiple sources, so I can then play competing sets of data against each other. This makes the process more efficient and accurate. Do not hesitate to ask many people how to get specific information. The standard approach here is: "If you wanted to find out about X, who would you call, or where would you look? Who is the keeper of that information?"

3. *Get access to that source.* The source could be:
    a. An online database
    b. Documents such as contracts, white papers, or operational runbooks
    c. An individual or team you need to query or interview

4. *Develop the information.* Get what you need. You may need passwords or come bearing gifts for the gatekeeper to your Holy Grail.

5. *Review and analyze the information received.* Completeness, accuracy, relevance, and timeliness of information must be assessed along with the content itself. Be highly suspicious of census, asset, or demographic data (i.e., detailed information about users, computer assets, network components, circuit lists, and software licenses). In large corporations, this information tends to be old, incomplete, and occasionally guarded for strange reasons.

6. *Corroborate the information if significant.* Even if the matter at hand is not controversial, you are going to make decisions based on significant information, so validate it. Sometimes, the best you can do is to get others to review what you have learned and be told,

"Sounds about right." I have been led down the garden path enough times to let my scepticism force me to check out everything I am told. My favorite technique is conversational (i.e., "Did you know that …?") instead of skewing the inquiry up front with, "Can you believe this stuff?" If you have not adopted a good deadpan delivery yet, perhaps now is time to start practicing.

7. *Follow up on potential consequences.* Some information you learn may be not only significant, but possibly shocking as well. Project scope may have assumptions embedded in it which do not withstand scrutiny, or feasibility tests, for that matter. Most of us can cite instances where documented information could not be verified through physical inspection or consensus, so be sure. Try not to consistently believe the last person you speak with on any given topic, because life does not always work that way.

1.6 INTERVIEWING TECHNIQUES

Other than demographic data, most of the information you seek will be collected from one-on-ones or meetings with the owners or gatekeepers of that sought-after knowledge. Project managers tend to be single-minded and rushed, so we forget that information is a form of corporate currency. Thus, you cannot assume that people will readily part with it just because you ask for it, with nothing offered in exchange. Although some people will gladly tell you everything you need (and much, much more), others will be suspicious of your inquiries. Some are guarding or hiding information, whereas others simply do not share.

In Chapter 13, I will confess to having considerable experience in technical sales and sales management as a prelude to exploring many of the customer management skills I was taught or developed in those days. In this section, it should be useful to spell out the interview strategy I learned during that period. I hope it will assist you in the verbal part of the discovery process. This is my approach:

- Learn about the individual and his or her function, plus their organization's role, prior to the interview. I like to know if they are "connected" to any well-known or notorious players I may be familiar with, or should be.
- Recognize that people are different, so find out what you can about your quarry. I like to know if the subject is open, friendly, and generous, or if other personality attributes are more dominant.
- Prepare in advance the questions you need answered.
- When scheduling the meeting, explain your mission in general terms so they can prepare, arrange for the right people to be there as well, or allot enough time.

- Begin the meeting with a general overview of your mission and how you feel they can help you.
- Keep the discussion as conversational as possible. Work in your questions.
- Let the interviewee talk. Avoid interrupting him or her; circle back for clarification.
- Provide information if asked, but make it seem like they are getting the inside scoop.
- Gently steer the interviewee back to your flow when he or she gets off topic.
- Summarize what you think you heard, and ask for confirmation.
- Ask whom else you could benefit from talking to (and why).

I do not know about you, but I am a poor note taker, and my mind wanders. Sometimes, I try to finish other people's sentences for them. All this leads to ineffective interview results. Guard against any such tendencies you may exhibit. Keep summarizing what you think you heard until you are comfortable that you and the interviewee are communicating. After the meeting, write it up in an e-mail to this individual, and send copies to others as appropriate. Among other things, this establishes your seriousness, and puts them on notice that they are being quoted publicly.[2] I always include a standard line soliciting corrections for errors or omissions. If referred to other individuals, I follow up with them, making sure to mention that, "So-and-so thought I should speak to you about the such-and-such." And do not forget to thank anyone who gives you his or her time, even if it was a waste of yours.

Not everything you learn during this process will turn out to be true or relevant. In fact, you may miss things that indicate hidden issues or pending risk. Ralph may tell you how important he and his department are going to be to your project, when, in fact, Ralph tells everyone how important he and his department are. Still, handle everyone with tact and respect, because you just do not know what tomorrow or next year will bring. Ralph might have struck you as a bit pompous, or steered you in the wrong direction, either wittingly or otherwise. Corporate realities are such that Ralph may also be a gatekeeper who can clog your critical path somewhere down the road. So, even if your Ralph "experience" was unproductive and annoying, chances are that Ralph is here to stay. So, it is best to slap a smile on your face and get on Ralph's best side, if you can find it.

1.7 CONCLUSION

I could have included more than 13 categories in the interrogatory. I did not because, at this point, you are still trying to become familiar with this topic, not memorize the encyclopedia. You want to press the particular areas that are included in the Big Thirteen so you can get the lay of the land. The remaining fun facts about the world you have now entered will become apparent soon enough. Throughout this book, the Big Thirteen will occasionally reappear, particularly in the next chapter, to illustrate its use and reinforce its value.

Notes

1. Viewed from this perspective, not all scope creep is "bad."
2. Unless, of course, the information is truly confidential or potentially inflammatory.

—

Chapter 2
Learning Requirements Is Our First Priority

The two things that should drive your project are requirements and deadlines. The calendar tends to take care of itself, although there will be those white-knuckle moments every now and then. As for requirements, with the possible exception of hosting productive meetings, the single most difficult challenge facing the project manager is ensuring that the right requirements are derived from scope.

2.1 THE TROUBLE WITH REQUIREMENTS

People generally take one long look at scope, jump to conclusions regarding "the solution," then rush off to build it without adequate analysis and planning. We can illustrate this natural tendency by reflecting on the Integrated Services Digital Network (ISDN) project presented in the first chapter. The scope was the creation of an automated process for selling and installing circuits on the public telephone network. The assumption was that this new system could be constructed with a few menus linking the user to legacy information technology (IT) infrastructure, thereby drawing on the existing processing power and knowledge base to streamline the ISDN provisioning process.

In essence, what happened was that the requirements, if you will, were never fully examined. We were well into the coding process and holding meetings with many of the targeted beneficiaries long before the feasibility of our basic assumptions had been properly vetted. Theologians call this a "leap of faith." Good project managers call this "dumb."

Another common defect in technical projects is the comfort zone issue, wherein designers specify products with which they are most comfortable, and hope or assume that the selected product will satisfy requirements and be readily assimilated into the legacy-operating environment. This is understandable and hardly a capital offense, but it is putting the cart before the horse. Requirements should drive specifications, not the other way around. Remember that requirements describe what the project will accomplish, and that specifications state how those requirements will be implemented.

Finally, we must acknowledge that gathering requirements is a daunting task to the degree that multiple parties must be consulted, conflicts resolved, and compromises made. There is an old engineering joke about a camel being a horse designed by committee. I suspect that too many project managers shy away from a rigorous requirements process for fear of creating a beast that has no resemblance to the original assumptions made about scope. In truth, creating an honorable consensus on requirements can be as rough as getting legislation through Congress without painful bickering, Frankenstinian mutation of design elements, or the forced inclusion of deliverables supporting extraneous agendas. As our ISDN example suggests, however, if you do not follow the requirements process faithfully, the results may be far more disastrous than the confusion inherent in the democratic process of building consensus.

2.2 ISDN CASE STUDY REQUIREMENTS

Requirements are the conditions one must create to do justice to project scope. Another way of looking at requirements is to say they are the descriptors of "target state." In the ISDN case study in Chapter 1, we listed some of the desired features of target state. Let us restate them in a way that more properly supports the concept of requirements gathering. Please note that, for the sake of brevity, some detail has been omitted. If system design or telecom provisioning do not happen to be your cup of tea, instead of focusing on the detail, make note of the liberal use of declarative sentences.

- Sales order entry module
  - Customer service representative (CSR) can interact with the customer and the system "real time."
  - CSR can validate the customer account, credit worthiness, and site address upon entry of customer-supplied name, address, or telephone number.
  - CSR can ascertain availability of ISDN to customer site.
  - CSR can provide the customer with future availability of ISDN at the customer site, based on system forecast.
  - CSR can provide technical details on types of ISDN[1] offered at that time, and commensurate charges.
  - CSR can initiate an order based on the customer acceptance of prospective installation date, charges, and the specific ISDN service to be installed.
- Construction module

- Request to provide service not currently available is routed to outside plant engineering (OSP) assigned to the central office serving the customer for that order.
- OSP uses the system to issue construction order to legacy workforce system.
- OSP uses the system to track each project.
- CSR can access the construction module to provide customer updates as required.
• Provisioning module
  - Upon automated validation of service availability, the system shall send appropriate codes to the central office switch to program assigned port with customer-selected ISDN service features.
  - Any error codes on provisioning failure will be sent to legacy switch maintenance queue.
  - Successful provisioning causes notification to the billing system that the service is turned up for that customer account.
• Customer site dispatch module
  - System will initiate dispatch record in legacy workforce system to dispatch an ISDN technician to customer site for final installation.
  - System will receive updates from the legacy workforce system so the sales CSR can status site installation as required.
• Reporting module
  - All data generated by this system shall be available for canned reports and ad hoc queries showing detailed and summarized reports of sales and construction activity that can be broken down by ISDN service types, serving the central office, and other means to be determined.

2.2.1 What These Requirements Show

• *Detail.* In a perfect world, a requirements document should tell you exactly what the target state looks like. Put another way, we should know exactly what we are trying to accomplish. We do that by carefully building a detailed requirements document.
• *Workflow.* Requirements are descriptors of target state. In this case, project scope dictates the creation of an automated toolset, so it makes sense to describe each task the system must enable the end user to perform.
• *Key features.* Phrases such as "legacy system" are used to indicate that the new system shall interact with existing systems or processes. Phrases such as "real time" and "automatically" indicate whether or not the user has to initiate certain system events, as well as the availability of data sets.

- *Reserved requirements.* Requirements for the reporting module has both specificity as well as the dreaded "TBD" (to be determined). Although it is not a welcome term in a requirements document, "TBD" is acceptable only to the degree that it is unavoidable.

2.2.2 What These Requirements Do Not Show

- *System design and architecture.* Nothing is mentioned about which hardware and software platform will be used. In 1996, the mainframe or client server would have been the likely candidates, but from a requirements perspective, that was not important, nor was the method for linking to legacy systems, even though required links were defined.
- *Timelines.* Timelines were not mentioned because they were not critical to requirement. In many projects, milestone dates could merit inclusion. In the Y2K project world, for instance, one particular date was essentially the key requirement.
- *Product identification.* Many projects are product-based. In the ISDN project, there was no need to mention any, but in others it may be appropriate to name names. For instance, if the scope is to upgrade the local area network (LAN) operating system on 500 file servers, chances are the change is to the incumbent manufacturer's latest release, rather than a migration to a competing product. Common sense must prevail when articulating requirements. If Product X must be used, say so.
- *Rationale and other rhetoric.* Requirements are requirements. Why they are significant, and how they evolved, can be important for any number of reasons, but those stories normally do not warrant inclusion in your requirements document.

2.3 HOW REQUIREMENTS ARE DERIVED

The process, albeit somewhat nonlinear, looks something like the illustration in Exhibit 1.

Keep in mind that, as the project manager, you are driving the bus, but you are not the mechanic. Although your prior experience or expertise may add value to the shaping of requirements content or detail, your focus must be on ensuring that the right people are engaged and that ideas are circulated and openly debated. No matter how ribald these conversations become, you must keep everyone headed down the road of adequate specificity with a high level of consensus. Even if you do not agree with each emerging point, so long as the team does, and the process is thorough and professional, your opinion should fade into the background. Not that you should not make yourself heard, but in this context your voice should be just one in the crowd.

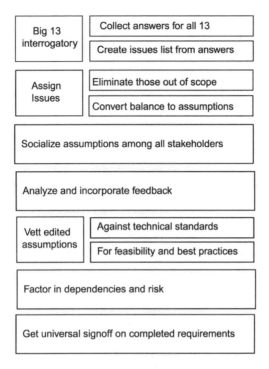

Exhibit 1. Requirements Development Process

Look at it this way. Your job is to lead and to induce consistent buy-ins from stakeholders. Even though you think something should be one way, if the consensus heads elsewhere, you must go with that, because they are tasked with making it happen, not you. If you force your preference on them, chances are their effort will lack the thoroughness and enthusiasm you need, and in the end everyone looks bad, particularly yourself. This guideline has exceptions, but be very certain you are doing more than advocating your personal prejudices before making the ill-fated "my way or the highway" speech. This is one performance that is not likely to raise calls for an encore!

2.4 AN AIRPORT IS BORN

Suppose your next project is to design and build a new international airport.[2] You have been given 1000 acres, $12 billion, and a half-decade before the first "wheels up." Here is your scope:

> *The Greater Palumbo Port Authority will design, build, and operate the Jaime Stetweiller International Airport to be located in the Farminghaven Region (County Parcel 102.2.1.A1C). The airport will be capable of sup-*

Exhibit 2. Big Thirteen Interrogatory Applied to the Airport Project

1. What is to be done?	• Build international airport with shopping mall and links to local mass transit.
2. What are the benefits?	• Locals will not have to drive 120 miles to nearest airport. • Thousands of jobs.
3. Who benefits?	• Local businesses. • Local labor pool. • The traveling public. • Airlines. • Various bureaucracies. • Financial underwriters.
4. Who is the customer?	• Port Authority in proxy for taxpayers.
5. Who is the sponsor?	• Governor.
6. Fit?	• No local mass transit to link to. • Inadequate water, sewer, and telecom facilities at site.
7. How much will this cost?	• $12 billion budget.
8. What is the timeline?	• Year 1: studies. • Year 2: designs complete, bids let. • Year 3: construction starts. • Year 5: open for business.
9. What are the dependencies?	• Regulatory approval. • Funding. • Operating model. • Linkage to off-site mass transit.
10. What is the risk?	• Environmental impacts.
11. Success metrics?	• Positive cash flow by third operating year.
12. How will we support this?	• Operating model TBD (to be determined).
13. What's the shelf life?	• Need to commission study of future capacity requirements.

porting current and future generation commercial aircraft serving domestic and international air routes.

Transportation support systems shall be in compliance with FAA [Federal Aviation Administration] regulations. Rapid transit rail will provide easy access to parking, car rental, hotel, and off-site mass transportation to be coordinated with local, state and federal agencies. Extensive and attractive retail space shall be provided to provide patron convenience and significant revenue to the Port Authority. Security shall be in compliance with all pertinent local, state, and federal regulations.

2.5 APPLYING THE BIG THIRTEEN

Once you recover from the excitement over receiving this plum assignment, it is time to pull out your Big Thirteen cheat sheet and start digging. Let us say that, after contacting everyone you thought you should speak to regarding the new airport, you came up with the results listed in Exhibit 2.

Exhibit 3. Airport Project Issues List

- Financing: how does that play out?
- How do we handle the politicians?
- Do we have staffing to provide environmental studies work?
- Airlines: how many, gate assignments, and features?
- Catering, plane cleanup, fueling, and plane maintenance?
- How many terminals, what style, and how many floors?
- Runways: how many, how long?
- Luggage handling and tracking.
- Fire department, public safety, and security.
- Bathrooms, garbage, and other health or sanitation requirements.
- How do you hook up to mass transit, and what will that be?
- Shops, hotels, restaurants, VIP lounges, and bars.
- What about air freight?
- Where do smokers go?
- Pay phones, arrival/departure displays, etc.
- ADA (Americans with Disabilities Act) requirements.
- Grounds: landscaping, public park, or other "features."
- What do the FAA (Federal Aviation Administration, Customs, and INS (Immigration and Naturalization Service) need?
- Private aircraft and charters.
- Internet kiosks for travelers?

2.6 DEVELOP AN ISSUES LIST

Now, we have already accomplished two things. We have uncovered some serious issues. For example, there is no mass transit to link the airport to, and no water, sewer, or telecommunications infrastructure at the site. Second, we know with some specificity how much we do not know. This we can document as an issues list that will be circulated relentlessly. With a little common sense, we can build an airport issues list that probably would look like Exhibit 3.

Of course, this is just the beginning of the fun. You need a game plan to deal with these issues. I recommend the following strategy:

- Eliminate as many issues as possible, particularly if they do not impact scope.
- Those issues that cannot be eliminated get assigned to specific individuals.
- Issues assignees must convert issues into assumptions by a specified date.
- Assumptions are then circulated for refinement and acceptance.
- Only upon sign-off does an assumption become a requirement.

2.7 ELIMINATE AS MANY ISSUES AS POSSIBLE

You want to do as good a job as possible, to think of everything in advance, and cover your flanks. This is a good thing. What this leads to, however, is you, as project manager, taking ownership for everything. This is a bad thing. True, it is tough to figure out what is on your plate, and what is not, from a project perspective. The only way I know how to solve this riddle is to ask two questions regarding each issue that finds its way onto my list.

The first question is: Does this issue impact scope?[3] If the answer is no, then I take it off my list. For example, issue number 16, "ADA (Americans with Disabilities Act) implications" is not an issue I need to resolve. The architects who will design the facilities are bound by law to ensure compliance, and thus it is they who own any ADA issues. I would certainly like to convince myself that the architects will do their jobs; but, other than looking over their shoulders every now and again, the ADA issue is not a requirement for me to fret over and track.

2.8 ASSIGN REAL ISSUES TO THE RIGHT PARTY

The second question is: Who owns this?[4] I am the project manager, not the architect, the operations manager, or an airline CEO. It is not my job to define the requirements. It is my job to see that the correct ones are identified and implemented. My challenge is to see that the right individuals take ownership for examining issues and turning them into requirements, or eliminating them, if that is the correct call. Based on my limited exposure to airport management, I would assign issues like numbers 5, 10, and 20 to the operations representative on the project team. If you examine these issues, you will probably conclude, as I did, that those are items that will impact how the airport operates. As the project manager, I want to be supportive of these issues being turned into requirements, but not own the process for doing so. Operations may go elsewhere for direction on some of these items. If that, in turn, requires my involvement, my role should take on the air of quality assurance,[5] instead of having to drive, document, and guarantee the resolution.

2.9 WHY YOU ASSIGN ISSUES

It is a bad idea to use team meetings to resolve specific issues. Solving multiple issues in a group setting is normally a waste of time and can do more harm than good. For some reason, people do it anyway. Let us examine this a little more closely.

A portion of airport scope dictates creation of a people mover that will carry airport patrons and employees between terminals, rental car sites, and parking lots. Also, the people mover must link up with local mass transit. During the Big Thirteen process, we learned that there is no local mass transit. If you follow our advice, you get this assigned to someone as an issue to be worked offline. Because it is rather significant, you should get a verbal update at your regular team meetings along with the other major

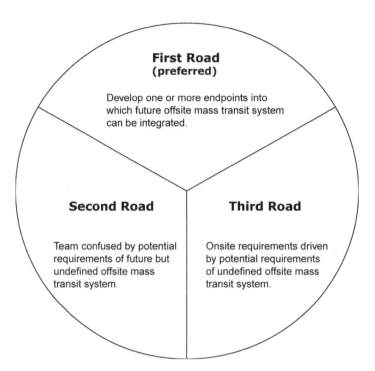

Exhibit 4.   Airport Wheel of Dependency

---

items. If, however, this "missing link" becomes part of ongoing group concern, you will find yourself going down one of the three roads depicted in Exhibit 4:

- *First road.* The team decides to develop one or more "end points" on the airport perimeter that allows linkage to whatever the future holds in terms of mass transit coming into the airport from the outside world. This choice was actually made at the Newark Liberty International Airport in Newark, New Jersey. The real Port Authority built a monorail system on the airport grounds that interconnected key airport facilities, with an end point at the airport boundary into which a future local mass transit could "plug in." Five years later, it was connected to the Amtrak Northeast Corridor commuter rail line. This came to life as a totally separate project, although obviously there was significant carryover in the ranks of stakeholders and contractors.
- *Second road.* The airport project team starts out following the previous strategy, but gets so wrapped up in what the link to the offsite

mass transit system could be that we cannot decide what kind of people mover to build on the airport proper.

- *Third road.* The airport project team gets drawn into countless meetings with various local and state agencies regarding the planning of potential mass transit systems that could link to the airport. Once we engage all the political, governmental, financial, environmental, and citizen groups that claim an interest in the off-site transportation system, the potential requirements for that external transit system end up driving the on-site people-mover design.

Clearly, the top wheel segment is the preferred outcome, although the other two are equally probable in the absence of good leadership. In our example, the correct move is to keep your team focused on the airport project, not the regional mass transit project. In other words, stick to your knitting. Cooperate with other projects, but do not do their work. That is counterproductive and generally ends up making more enemies than friends. In other words, do not let a dependency turn into a deliverable. Minimize its impact on your requirements to the best of your ability, because this is a great opportunity for "scope creep" to find its way into your project.

2.10 TURNING ISSUES INTO ASSUMPTIONS

Your next step is getting assigned parties to turn their issues into assumptions. Instead of asking "How do we know how many arrival–departure gates should be built at the airport?" we say, "Let us assume a reasonable number of gates and see where it goes." The reason you do this is to curtail the endless churning of issues without resolution. Your project documentation would reflect that particular decision in the following manner:

> *It is assumed that each of the 20 airlines will require 15 gates apiece, for a total of 300 arrival–departure gates at the airport. Fred Smith will validate this with the Airline Task Force by March 1.*

We may not be too sure about this, but we do it anyway. Once statements are made and circulated properly, people will react. Obviously, you would like to make any such "stakes in the ground" reasonable and rational, so research may be in order. Look for design documents, white papers, or other work that was done when the project was in its "preapproved" state. They might provide some decent baselines. Alternatively, look for similar projects. For instance, if it appears that the airports in Tampa or St. Louis have demographics similar to yours, check out their gate infrastructures.

What you are looking to accomplish is to drive the process off dead center and facilitate timely resolution. Unmanaged issues can take up far too many cycles while remaining open, so that in the end, you are forced to accept anything because you have allowed this part of the project to enter crisis mode. Allowing this to happen, as a project manager, is called procrastination.

2.11 SOCIALIZE YOUR ASSUMPTIONS

Now that you have identified your issues, assigned owners to each one, and turned them into assumptions, you should publish them on a regular and periodic basis with their status updated. You want people to keep moving on them. Using this public forum also provides the opportunity for appropriate stakeholders, some of whom are possibly unknown to you, to weigh in. Again, if meetings are required to "drill down," make sure that only those who are truly players participate. It seems like there are always team members with opinions on everyone else's problems.[6] As a rule, this type of person adds little value and is noisy enough to impede progress as well.

End users, or beneficiaries, should be included in this process for most projects, with the possible exception of hardcore infrastructure initiatives such as network upgrades. It is my observation that many project leads fail to do this. In fact, there appears to be a tremendous amount of laziness and arrogance in this area. It seems as though people either feel they know better than beneficiaries how things should be, or they cannot be bothered to find out. Understand that taking this step with an empathetic ear is one of the smartest moves you can make. Even if the users take a lot of time and create extra work, it is far better to engage them early and give them a voice in the process. The alternative is politically naive and can lead to serious trouble later. Chapter 13 takes a hard look at the perplexing world of customers and beneficiaries.

2.12 ANALYZE AND INCORPORATE FEEDBACK

Our terminal gate assumption stipulated 20 airlines needing 15 gates apiece, for a total of 300. Your feedback will range from "How do you know how many airlines will use the airport?" to "PuddleJumper Airways could not possibly need more than five gates." Stay with the process. Your goal is to come up with as many "hard" assumptions as possible. Once you have established a ballpark number, the right stakeholders will more or less be forced to take ownership for telling you the right number. You have made the number of gates negotiable and opened the door for practical forces to come into play, instead of being driven by opinions that might be uninformed, if not worse. In this case, that process will begin after the architects complete a draft design and cost estimate. That will show that each gate costs, for instance, $1 million to build and $25,000 an hour to operate.

This is really where you want to steer the debate because that is where it is going anyway. People float off into the ether with so many issues that, experience should tell you, will eventually be solved by practical matters like dollars and sense. As project manager, your goal should be to get there sooner than later.

We are going to leave the airport now to look at another example from one of my previous projects. In this one, I watched for weeks as the engineering group agonized over which of two servers to specify for a thin client application servicing several thousand users. We were fast approaching the "must order by date," and I still had no specs from these guys. Finally, frustrated, I sat down with the team lead to understand what their problem was. He was a good guy and all that, but he lacked management experience, so I walked him through the decision points gently.

In short, as he saw it, the only differences between servers were physical size and user capacity. One server was three times the size of the other, but could support twice the number of users as the smaller one. Physical size was not a factor because while we needed dozens of either type, there was adequate rack space in the data center. Both servers appeared to offer the same throughput per user even though the number of users per box was significantly different, as noted earlier.

Finally, I asked one simple question: "How do the two servers compare on a cost-per-user basis?" The engineers had not taken this into account, so we did the math on the spot. We were immediately able to conclude that on a cost-per-user basis, the larger, higher-capacity server was 15 percent cheaper per user than the smaller alternative. Because the design scaled to thousands of users, this delta was significant, and made the choice rather simple, all other things being equal. When you drill down with the right attitude and approach, it is amazing how frequently you can squeeze decisions out of folks who have been wringing their hands over something for weeks, if not longer. This story provides insight on the value you can provide as project manager. Let the experts be expert. Stick to your role as facilitator and provide closure to the open issues swirling around you. In other words, keep everything, and everybody moving.

2.13 GET UNIVERSAL SIGN-OFF ON REQUIREMENTS

The term "universal" is key, because it implies that people outside the project team, such as beneficiaries and customers, should have sign-off responsibilities. Requirements are descriptors of end state that will impact beneficiaries, even though projects typically treat beneficiaries the same way as a benevolent despot would rule the kingdom. This lack of empathy and respect can backfire. Beneficiaries, in my experience, are very good at disrupting if not sabotaging projects if they feel they were not given their due during the planning phase.

There are legitimate reasons behind this behavior. Each project takes on a gestalt or a life of its own to the point that the vision starts to make sense to you and your team. Outsiders, particularly beneficiaries, however, are likely to see things quite differently. What makes this difficult is that while they may raise objections, you cannot always tell right away whether they are valid or just the symptoms of change-resistance behavior.

I used the word empathy in the context of engaging beneficiaries and others who may be impacted by your project during this requirements phase. Having empathy in this case means that you understand that the target beneficiaries:

- Have little precise knowledge of your initiative
- Do not care to pay, or may not get budgetary relief, for project costs directly accruing to them
- Are unfamiliar or uncomfortable with the new technology you are rolling out
- Find your timetable disruptive to their business cycles
- Reject your goals for other reasons that may not appear rational to you

In the real world, these conditions are commonplace and, if observed, can flag serious trouble headed in your direction. I have seen worthy initiatives diluted if not killed by beneficiaries who behave in this manner after being offended that they were kept out of the loop during the project's requirement-gathering phase. As a client of mine once said of his environment, the instant a major project was announced, targeted beneficiaries formed committees to create "workarounds" to the project's presumed deleterious impact on their business-as-usual practices.

2.14 ADDRESS THE FEASIBILITY OF IMPLEMENTING REQUIREMENTS

As was stated elsewhere, this whole process is iterative, or nonlinear. In some cases, it will feel like you keep going around in circles while postulating requirements, getting a cacophony of response back from the stakeholder community, revising the requirements, and going through all this again. There is no way to avoid this if the degree of proposed change or level of complexity is high.

From a management perspective, it is also not easy to state categorically when certain things should happen. Evaluating the feasibility of a requirement certainly falls into this category. For instance, looking back at our hypothetical airport project, saying we need 300 gates may be acceptable to those who want that many people coming and going, but the cost, or working that many ports into a physical plant constrained by budget or other issues, may force a significant reduction in the number of gates later on in the discussion. Of course, such a change can have a domino effect and can force a review and rework of other design elements as well.

Having said this, however, does not excuse you from asking the feasibility question early and often. Let us go back to the ISDN project in which we were unable to deliver the fully automated provisioning system once envisioned. As the project progressed, we stumbled across a few showstoppers. For brevity's sake, I will look at just the worst offender. The most critical assumption we made was that three legacy production databases could be leveraged to:

- Automatically populate new orders with data
- Query network assets to validate service ability
- Initiate the Central Office switch port configuration process

What we learned, however, was that the data rules were divergent enough from one database to the next that we could not use data pulled from one table to query the next one for additional information. Simply put, a customer address could be entered several ways, none of which could be accurately resolved with clever programming (i.e., artificial intelligence). Because the address was the key field in the majority of planned searches, the most important assumption underlying the system design was invalid.

I was made aware of this disconnect after I drew up the proposed system flow and e-mailed it to the project team. Unbeknownst to me, someone shared it with a database administrator. She sent me 20 pages of database printouts to document the problem. This is mentioned to reiterate the value in socializing key project data like dates, assumptions, risks, and dependencies because you never know what will pop up, or from whence it will do so.

During the initial requirement phase, no one ever challenged the assumption that the quality of the databases was such that we could not leverage them. So, of course, we did not look and, therefore, did not know that our cornerstone assumption was flawed. This, in turn, meant that the vision of a "down and dirty" implementation creating seamless and error-free automation was virtually impossible. Although our budget was not paltry, it was not elastic enough to address these issues in any meaningful way.

2.15 TURNING REQUIREMENTS INTO SPECIFICATIONS

If requirements are the project's "what," then specifications are the "how." In our ISDN requirements review, it was noted that how systems linked, how they were coded, and on what platform they ran were irrelevant from a requirements perspective. As we completed the design work, it was time to specify how to link our new system to legacy databases, and whether to base the new system on local area network (LAN)-attached personal computer (PC) workstations to the mainframes using client–server technology, or go "3270" all the way.

Building the right requirements makes the specifications process far easier. We are not going to go into much detail on this, because the process is highly dependent on the technology involved, whether you build it in-house or outsource it, and so on. There are a couple of general points I would like to make, however. As you go through this process, the following dynamics can be anticipated to impact one or more of your deliverables.

- When a requirement is analyzed, it may turn out to be too costly, risky, disruptive, resource intensive, or take too long to implement given other pending events, such as corporate mergers, server operating system upgrades, or year-end accounting closes. In other words, a feasibility review could lead to scope tweak or schedule changes.
- The best specification may be out of step with corporate standards. Suppose rolling out browser X to twenty thousand desktops fits your project's requirements better than browser Y. The trouble is browser Y is the standard on 100,000 desktops throughout your organization. A lot of existing applications are compatible with Y, but might require customization to perform as well on your project-preferred browser X.
- Suppose UNIX boxes from Vendor A are better suited to your requirements than Vendor Bs, but the corporation sources all central processing units (CPUs) from Vendor B, who is firmly entrenched in your information technology (IT) culture.
- Chances are that standards exist, whether or not they are documented, for all technologies in your environment. Somewhere out there, possibly in procurement or product management, lurk the "standards police." Their mission is to keep you from buying anything "out of spec." The trend in today's business world appears headed toward more standards with ruthless and inflexible enforcement. We will examine this subject in greater detail in the next chapter.

The significance of existing standards is the potential divergence from them with your solution. This can happen because the designers select products they find compelling for whatever reason, and are content to let you handle any compliance issues the standards police may choose to raise. Although this may sound awkward, and can be, it is also the way a lot of folks do business.

When there is a standards conflict, common sense and possible political considerations will dictate whether or not you fight the standards police or your own designers. Before you take on the possibly Herculean task of requesting an exemption from the standards police, ask yourself whether your experts have thought everything through, and beyond, their own parochial interests. I have had the pleasure of overcoming that many times, as well as enduring designers' adamant refusals to acknowledge what even I could divine — that their proposal introduced unacceptable implementation or operational risk. Because of standards, compatibility, and politics, it is not always practical to have requirements drive specifications, but that should be your goal. Make exceptions only when necessary. When specifications are made without validating requirements, bad things will happen.

2.16 MAPPING REQUIREMENTS TO THE PROJECT PLAN

One of the worst duties of a project manager on these big initiatives is to create detailed project plans that are both accurate and relevant. Whereas this is the subject matter of Chapter 6, it deserves a word here. Having detailed requirements and subsequently derived specifications makes planning and risk avoidance far easier when it is time for those activities to kick off. Why is that? Because generating the appropriate level of detail and discussion on deliverables now will concurrently surface most of the sequences, dependencies, and risk that you will need to run through the planning process later. These latter bits of data are the natural offshoot of the requirements development process and can be swept right off the floor into the planning hopper when the time is right. By the way, this is just around the corner from where we are right now.

2.17 WORKFLOW ANALYSIS

Before moving on to the next topic, I want to take a moment to tout workflow analysis as a wonderful tool for project managers, particularly for the requirements definition portion of the project. If you have never personally invoked this process, either in the privacy of your own office or on a white board in front of the crowd, let me assure you that nothing stimulates good thinking and participation than jumping to your feet with a felt marker in one hand and exclaiming, "Let's see how this works!" It does not take long before the people you really want to contribute to the discussion either chime in or grab the marker from you and start going to town.

A workflow is just the way it sounds — the graphical depiction of a business process your project is creating, supporting, or replacing with one or more IT deliverables. You should consider incorporating two excellent workflow opportunities into your requirements development activities:

1. A proposed layout of a project deliverable — the ISDN provisioning process drawn up in Chapter 1 is a good example of this.
2. The exposition of an existing process that is a project dependency

The latter is particularly useful for the requirements discovery process that has been the focus of these first two chapters. In fact, you should attempt to make liberal use of it, and encourage everyone else to do so as well. What is interesting is that people can sit around a table for hours chatting or arguing about existing processes, or how a proposed process should work; but until someone starts drawing pictures, these conversations tend to go around in circles as everyone gets lost in the verbosity.

The other advice I would like to impart is that your workflow drawings should find their way into electronic form, be distributed as part of your normal correspondence, and be followed up. I cited an example of the benefit of this a few pages back. I studiously avoid mentioning products throughout this book to avoid the inference of approving or disapproving of any particular one, and will likewise remain mum on preferred products for drawing process flows. Chances are, however, that both your work and home computers probably have at least one program you can use to create this kind of document. All you really need is the ability to:

- Create and label boxes
- Move them around
- Draw arrows or use some other obvious means to show how the boxes interact, whether these dependencies are temporal or logical

Exhibit 5 is an example of a useful legacy from the voice mail provisioning workflow tale told in the success metrics section of the Big Thirteen in Chapter 1. You may recall that the crux of that project was minimizing provisioning errors. We eventually isolated the error source as nearly exclusively occurring in Step 8 illustrated in Exhibit 5. This was when the sales CSR manually entered information about the customer and the central office from which their new service would originate.

Although I did not understand all the technical ins and outs of this process, having investigated it to the level of detail described eventually facilitated development of the proper and cost-effective solution.

2.18 CONCLUSION

Thorough requirements derivation is very interesting to me, but something that is generally rushed through by most project managers. This is a terrible mistake. I once worked for a gentleman who subsequently rose to an impressive level of success and notoriety in a major corporation. He told me that the secret to project management is to steer the stampeding herd in the preferred direction, then slow it down before getting everyone moving forward in single file. How true that is. Approaching the requirements phase as outlined in this chapter has many benefits, not the least of which is getting that project stampede heading toward the right finish line!

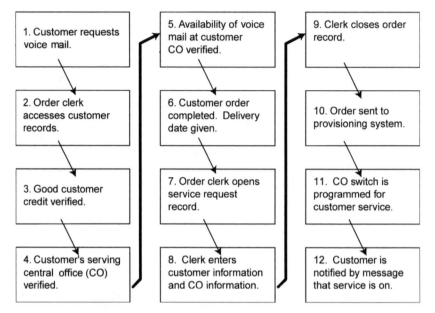

Exhibit 5.   Voice Mail Provisioning Workflow

Notes

1. At the time, the plan was to implement 6 of the 72 ISDN "flavors."
2. I am using this project to make a few points because if we go into detail on hardware or software I might lose half of you. Besides, many IT projects have this level of complexity and confusion even if they lack the glamour of building a huge transportation facility.
3. Alternately, you can ask if it really is an issue.
4. Your alternate question here is: Why is this my issue?
5. Quality assurance meaning: are we defining the requirements the right way with the right parties?
6. Try telling them their business!

Chapter 3
Using Technologies to Meet Requirements

Whatever your background, eventually you will manage a project where one or more technologies are unknown to you. The worst-case scenario is to be assigned to a project calling for multiple technologies with some links or dependencies with each other. Your team may be adequately staffed with experts, but it could turn out that only one team member worries about the whole implementation being seamlessly integrated. That person would be you because each expert can be assumed to worry solely about his or her piece to the exclusion of their peers' work efforts, or the whole package for that matter. This chapter's purpose is to illustrate workarounds to this predicament.

3.1 WHY TECHNOLOGIES SHOULD BE USED

In the last chapter, it was stated that technology should be specified to implement the requirements, which, in turn, are dictated by project scope. Further, it can be assumed that real-world business needs actually drive projects. One of the results of adequately applying the Big Thirteen interrogatory technique introduced in Chapter 1 is to understand these drivers. Always keep these in mind as technology issues arise during the planning and design phases of your project. You must do so because technologies have lives of their own that do not necessarily lend themselves to easy implementation and support. Worse, complex projects can easily become obsessed with the technologies themselves to the detriment of scope, beneficiaries, schedules, and budgets. In other words, if the technology or technologies themselves become scope, I can guarantee you nothing but pain and heartache, not to mention a highly probable state of defeat for you and your team. So, although it is natural and important to worry about technologies working, it is far more important to keep asking whether the technologies are delivering requirements, assuming you and your team know what they are.

Exhibit 1. Business Drivers and Their Technology Enablers

Business Driver	Technology
Provide new product or service.	Although the beneficiaries could be internal (i.e., workers) or external (i.e., customers or trading partners), this is likely, today, to be connectivity or "Web-based" products or services.
Consolidate facilities by relocating users to new building.	Latest LAN and WAN connectivity options such as routers, LAN switches and cabling, and multiplexers.
Make business application available "anywhere, anytime."	Convert mainframe or C/S applications to browser-based applications (e.g., HTML/XML or thin client).
Enhance user productivity.	Upgrade hardware, add functionality to legacy software, or replace legacy software with a newer product.
Maintain currency with technical advancements.	Upgrade to latest hardware or software release for operating systems, packaged productivity tools, etc.
Consolidate costs.	Consolidate and downsize computing platforms (e.g., migrate processing to midrange or LAN-based platform from mainframe or midrange). Outsource support or maintenance.
Improve network security.	Upgrade firewalls and proxy servers, or roll out encryption.
Leverage Internet connectivity.	Increase bandwidth (e.g., upgrade T1s to T3s), and incorporate SONET, WDWM, or DSL technologies.
Implement or upgrade DR or business continuity processes.	Build out new disaster recovery or business continuity site. Centralize server management and tape backup infrastructure.

The key to doing that is to keep project scope on the front page at all times. Perhaps it is easiest to do that by continuously reminding stakeholders of the answer to Big Thirteen question number two. This is the benefits question (i.e., "Why are we doing this?"). Again, the answer to this question should be some sort of business driver. Drivers that lead to technology implementations are too numerous to fully elaborate; the most common are listed in Exhibit 1.

Notice that each technology response to these drivers is pretty generic. For example, the initial response to the "Increase network security" driver is not "Install Vendor X firewalls," or "Add hardware encryption cards to edge routers." Instead, a rather prosaic solution is suggested, based on the general kinds of technology available to accomplish these different kinds of goals. This point is important enough that I want to pursue it. To do so, I will stay with the proposed opportunity to enhance network security.

Firewalls, proxy servers, and encryption increase security, but they do it in different ways:

- Firewalls provide security by controlling, to a certain extent, how people can get into, or go out beyond, the corporate Intranet, based on Internet Protocol (IP) addressing. Obviously, the primary goal is to keep prowlers from hacking into your internal network. Firewalls also perform other traffic access management duties.
- Forward and reverse proxy servers protect access into and out of your intranet as well, employing a totally different strategy and technology from the firewall approach.
- Encryption is yet another security enhancement that scrambles transmissions with the intent that intercepted data is undecipherable.

Therefore, each of these potential technical solutions differs from one another in terms of:

- The kind of protection provided
- Cost
- How it is integrated within the network infrastructure
- Functionality in addition to primary capability
- Potential (negative) impact on throughput, applications, or user satisfaction
- Skill sets required to design, install, operate, and maintain

Although "improve network security" is a reasonable statement of project scope, as a requirement, it is excessively vague. I managed a network security project where enhancing network intrusion safeguards was a key component of scope. The driver was to increase external access for thousands of users to more applications and data, particularly so that the mostly sales-oriented user base could be more mobile. From a technology perspective, this meant that the corporation was migrating the applications from a mainframe to dozens of Web servers. This change would significantly increase the amount of Internet Protocol (IP) traffic flowing in and out of the data center, which, in turn, exposed the company to significantly higher risk of being hacked, due to the nature of the Transmission Control Protocol/Internet Protocol (TCP/IP). The traffic load would increase dramatically as well. This was expected to stress the existing IP infrastructure (e.g., bandwidth, routers, proxy servers, and firewalls), with the resulting risk of frequent network outages. All this information needed to be considered as technology decisions were made.

To some degree, project output will be impacted by available technology. Therefore, part of the design process is reconciling requirements derived from scope with the potential technological solutions. This example is intended to demonstrate how important it is to analyze "Improve net-

Exhibit 2. Security Goals Mapped to Technology

Security Improvement	Technical Solution
Keep hackers out of your network.	Use firewalls to reject logins from prohibited external IP addresses.
Keep hackers from stealing internal IP addresses.	Use reverse proxy server to mask internal, originating IP address.
Block internal users from unauthorized Web sites.	Implement forward proxy server with site-blocking software.
Prevent hackers from stealing data transmitted from site to site.	Install hardware or software encryption.

work security" very carefully before getting on with the design. Exhibit 2 presents the most common or typical "security improvement" goals.

This table could have more rows, but there is no need to get into an extended conversation on network security as long as the point is taken that one must clearly define the requirements in terms that will facilitate the appropriate selection of technology.

3.2 HOW TECHNOLOGIES REALLY GET USED

Simply put, six processes are normally followed to select technology. In descending order, they are:

- *Basic needs.* Clearly, the key requirements will cause technologists to make certain design assumptions that (hopefully) are subject to further analysis. These assumptions can be based upon current practices such as the "buy or build" decision for a new software system. What is significant here is that if it is likely a new human resource package will be purchased and customized instead of built from the ground up, a different path will be pursued with subsequent requirements and, thus, technology decisions. This can include computing platforms and operating systems, workstations, the network, and disaster recovery or business continuity.

- *Corporate standards.* Many big projects are upgrades to, or extensions of, legacy systems or infrastructure. Adding a new site to an existing wide area network, or bringing local area network (LAN) server operating systems up to the manufacturer's current revision are typical examples. Standards can dominate nearly every aspect of technology, if for no other reason than to leverage cost savings through "single sourcing," and reduce confusion from installation, support, and compatibility perspectives. Exhibit 3 approximates what is undoubtedly in place in your organization.

- *Personal preference.* Quite naturally, people go with what they know when given the chance. If you could write new code with any one of three "languages," you are most likely to pick the one you have had

Exhibit 3. Typical Technology Standards

- For "Web" software, only Visual Basic (VB) and eXtensible Markup Language (XML) are permitted.
- All directory infrastructure shall be LDAP compliant.
- The e-mail client is Company D's.
- Only one brand of the UNIX operating system is supported.
- All routers and switches shall be provided by Z, Inc.
- All new cabling will be Cat. 6.
- Use only 1-gHz XYX laptops with 512 mb of RAM, infrared port disabled.
- HotSurf is the preferred browser.

---

previous success with, all things being equal. Unfortunately, comfort levels do not always lead to intelligent choices.

- *Evaluation.* I was on a project where the sponsor mandated the use of IP Telephone for a new site instead of the company's traditional choice of private branch exchange (PBX) telephony. Because IP Telephone was a new technology at the time, three products were evaluated in terms of functionality, performance, ease of use, and each manufacturer's support capabilities. This competitive analysis was backed up with a pilot of the selected product before the final decision was made to go forward with IP Telephone. In other situations where new ground is being broken, consultants are brought in to research the market place to see what other like-minded customers are doing, or to analyze potential solutions against requirements where in-house expertise might be thin. In the IP Telephone situation, we contracted with a firm who had successfully installed that product in a similar environment, thereby minimizing the risk associated with our dearth of in-house expertise for design, implementation, and support.
- *Fit.* This is the main reason that "fit" appears in the Big Thirteen interrogatory. In the present context, that tiny word expands into the following questions:
  - Do we know how to use this technology?
  - Will it cause any issues with legacy infrastructure, including existing applications, protocols, topologies, or monitoring tools?
  - Can the support infrastructure, including data centers, network management, help desks, maintenance or support vendors, and local support personnel absorb this new technology?
- *Cost.* Although this technology, once deployed, can be proclaimed as the best thing since sliced bread, will the accrued benefits turn out to be a smart, defensible investment?

3.3 HOW TECHNOLOGIES FAIL

If I walked into a room full of engineers and asked why technologies fail, I would expect them to immediately throw three questions back at me, namely:

Exhibit 4. Why Technologies Fail

- The technology did not support or deliver the requirements.
- The technology did not scale well to production requirements.
- The technology had interoperability issues with the legacy environment.
- The technology was "buggy," unstable, or intermittently inoperable.
- Manufacturer support was ineffective.

- What do you mean by "fail"?
- What do you mean by "technologies"?
- Don't you mean, "Why do projects fail?" because there is nothing wrong with properly applied technologies?

Each of these questions is somewhat rhetorical and contains the seeds of the answer we seek. Let us see what can be learned from walking through each of them.

3.3.1 What Do You Mean by "Fail"?

In the present context, technology is known or assumed to be the reason for unsatisfactory results. If this is the case, how specifically can technology be blamed? If you really think about it, technologies fail in just a few ways, as listed in Exhibit 4.

One would expect your project experts to indemnify against these conditions through experience, proper research and analysis, simulation, testing, and running a proof-of-concept scenario in any condition where the selection of the right technology is not a "slam dunk."

The eleventh question of the Big Thirteen stresses the creation of hard success metrics in advance of implementation, so that managing toward success has a more disciplined goal than "we got the system installed in time for quarter-end processing." To the extent possible, you should expect your technologists to agree with this approach. Ask them to incorporate it into their design process for those requirements that require customization, complete fabrication, or involve technology that is new to them, to your corporation, or to the marketplace in general. Do not assume that, in the absence of such a request, they will behave in this manner.

3.3.2 What Do You Mean by "Technologies"?

Ignoring the philosophical aspect that I am not qualified to discuss anyway, there is an interesting issue here. The IT world has come a long way in the past few decades. Still, no single type of technology, in and of itself, is a silver bullet, nor are they stand-alone. End computing devices, such as personal computers and hand-helds, local area networks (LANs) and wide area networks (WANs), host systems, and "the Internet" all must coexist in varying degrees of compatibility and productivity.

The complexities are such that unless everything is perfectly aligned, any system or application that you inject into the corporate environment can experience unstable if not unpredictable performance. The reasons are many and varied. The most significant is that you can never assume that everything you use works seamlessly with everything else you see, and cannot see, in your IT environment. For example, you can never assume that all servers are at the exact same level of operating systems. Anti-virus and server monitoring tools do not always integrate seamlessly. The way applications are distributed to the desktop can vary from site to site. In fact, you can never be assured that each and every desktop has the same "build," or that the local network behaves the same way from site to site or, in some cases, from one floor to another or even among same-floor cubicles.

The bottom line is that although new or significantly enhanced technologies come along every now and then, they will be applied on top of, or slipped into, a nonhomogeneous environment that already has indigestion. As companies struggle with mergers and acquisitions, efforts to transparently integrate different networks, systems, and platforms add enough complexity and uncertainty that any new technology rollout should be approached with some apprehension.

3.3.3 Don't You Mean "Why Do Projects Fail"?

Some would contend that it is projects, not technologies, which fail. I personally do not worship at the altar of technology, although I still get the occasional cheap thrill from new IT bells and whistles. More important, I believe that the ultimate outcome of technology projects will be hugely impacted by how well the technology rollout has been conceived, tested, and adjusted as you wend your way from start to finish.

This is a practical matter. A few years ago, I worked with several teams to move a complex architecture of application servers from one data center to another. The customer was driving the previous project manager so aggressively that we inherited a mess that was bumping up against some critical business deadlines. This was a financial application with "do or die" dates associated with its output.

One piece of the architecture included a half dozen Web servers frontending the application server, the purpose of which was to deliver data to global users. There was a need to load balance the Web servers, which meant that there was an agent embedded in the Web server software that made sure that as each new user logged in, he or she had a session established with the least-congested server. The obvious benefit was that not all 75 users were trying to access only one of the Web boxes.

COMPLEX IT PROJECT MANAGEMENT: 16 STEPS TO SUCCESS

When the servers were installed in the new data center, we were horri-fied to learn, at the eleventh hour of course, that load balancing did not work. Based on my peripheral knowledge of the network and blessed with personal relationships, I was able to get a quick diagnosis of the problem. The new data center had a more sophisticated, much faster network infra-structure than did the legacy site. That was the good news. The bad news was that the load balancing software that had worked so well in the legacy site, on older hubs made by a since-deceased company, did not work on the new gigabit Ethernet data center LAN we had so proudly constructed.

This tale illustrates why I maintain, with a touch of irony, that it is better to be lucky than good. It just so happened that one of the top network engi-neers and I were on good speaking terms. For that reason, I happened to know that he had in his possession switching gear the vendor had just brought to market that could be installed in our new data center switches and deliver load balancing. We swiftly engaged other engineers, the ven-dor, cable pullers, and the telecom switch management team to install and test this brand new technology. We made our deadline the same way some teams probably win the Super Bowl — on the very last play.

Part of our good fortune was the fact that the "add-on " equipment that saved the day was a brand new product. The only reason we had it was because the vendor gave us a set for evaluation, because our company was a big customer and they hoped we would find a myriad of uses for it. I men-tion this only because it would have cost over $100,000 to buy it. No one was funded for that, plus we were not positive in advance that it would work with the application.

This story illustrates many aspects of project management, but it partic-ularly goes to the heart of project failure. We narrowly avoided a disaster. The core project team, myself included, was clueless about the load bal-ancing issue. As project manager, I was fortunate to be able to reach out for help to folks who were astute and professional enough to pitch in when they could have sat on their hands. I have omitted several details to this story. Suffice it to say that many mistakes were made, not the least of which was the previous team wasted so much time that there was no opportunity to test until 72 hours before cutover date and end-of-month processing for a mission-critical financial application.

In other words, it was very poor project management. It was as though the driver steered into well-documented potholes instead of seeking the safer, easy way out. Unfortunately, although the details of this tale might be unique, the cause of this debacle is one I have seen over and over. This is why, no matter how technically astute you might be, even with the technol-ogy at hand, as project manager the most important question you must continuously ask is: "How do we know this thing is going to work?"

Exhibit 5. Vetting the Technology Plan

1. List target state elements.
2. Map proposed technologies to each target state element.
3. Familiarize yourself with proposed technologies.
4. Review validation plan.
5. Review risk and establish Plan Bs as required.
6. Review potential integration issues and mitigate as required.
7. Plan postimplementation support requirements.
8. Review with customer and beneficiary.
9. Submit to technology review board if required.
10. Commence validation process; review and adjust as necessary.

Exhibit 6. Sample Target State Chart

Deliverable	Description/Functionality
Telephony	IP Telephone
Applications	Desktop build v. 2.9, both "fat" and "thin"
Home and shared directories	Storage area network (SAN)
Application backup/archive	Daily backup of SAN using robotic tape unit
Disaster recovery	Data replicated to off-site SAN
LAN printing	IP-based, multiple LAN printers per floor
Video conferencing	IP-based, to the desktop
Mainframe printing	Print jobs rerouted to IP-LAN printers
Mainframe access	Client emulation via off-site gateways
Wireless LAN	Available Day Two[a]

[a]Day Two designates any deliverable that may be delayed.

3.4 HOW TO DETERMINE IF IT IS GOING TO WORK

Having a sixth sense about such things would be great, but prescience is in short supply in this world. On the plus side, you can and must take a couple of steps to ensure that the technologists have a sound game plan. These steps are listed in Exhibit 5.

3.4.1 Listing Target State Elements

As the design emerges from scope analysis and the requirements definition processes, you must generate and maintain a target state document. It should list each major deliverable and, at least, the key requirements of each deliverable. You should not get too detailed; I prefer simplicity. Your target state chart is not intended to replace in-depth design documentation, but should be similar to a project billboard you use to keep people focused on the main goals. Take a moment to review Exhibit 6, which is a diluted version of one we created for a project during which we installed many technologies in a new building before moving in thousands of users.

Exhibit 7. Useful Questions for Understanding Technology

What does it do?	IP Telephone provides traditional PBX or Centrex services, plus other features.
Why is it being used?	To demonstrate our commitment to new technology, and save money on infrastructure.
What are the key components?	Standard trunks to the public telephone network. Dedicated servers to route calls. Standard LAN switches and cabling. Desktop PC plugs into handset for LAN connectivity.
Will installing it be difficult?	We hired an experienced vendor.
Can Operations support this?	Installation value added reseller (VAR) will provide Tier II and Tier III support. Corporate voice help desk will be trained to provide Tier I support.
What is our Plan B?	We wired for a PBX as a contingency.
Do we have training requirements?	Training is planned to all users. Also, see Operations Support.

3.5 UNDERSTAND YOUR TECHNOLOGIES

Perhaps you do not, but I know a few snake oil salesmen masquerading as technologists. Even if that is unfair, I decided a long time ago that I should know something about the technologies the team wants to roll out, if for no other reason than I can engage them in productive conversations. That gets them to open up, share any misgivings they might have, and work with you on appropriate resolutions. Besides, it is a lot easier to gain their respect and cooperation if you act interested in what they are doing. You might even be able to help them, as we shall soon see.

Instead of obsessing over your presumed ignorance, ask yourself exactly what you need to know about a technology to project manage it into reality. I believe you can do this by answering seven questions. These questions and their answers are presented in Exhibit 7 using IP Telephone as the technology straw man. When we started the project, all I knew about IP Telephone was that it was a new, LAN-based way of providing the telephone services you would expect to find in any modern corporate site.

A simple sketch of this analysis would look like the one shown in Exhibit 8.

I deliberately focused on the pieces and parts relevant to the build-out. Exhibit 7 recounts cables, trunks, and circuits. It ignores the technologist's buzz, such as Lightweight Directory Access Protocol (LDAP), synchronizing with e-mail, and the alchemy of embedding one's mellifluous voice inside an IP packet and zipping it across a fast Ethernet wire between e-mails from the boss. Although that is fascinating to me, knowing it does not make me a better project manager.

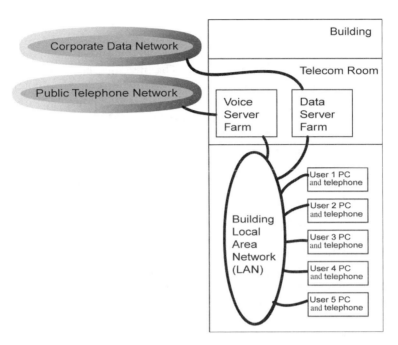

Exhibit 8. IP Telephone Site Architecture

Actually, I got the scoop on IP Telephone as shown in Exhibit 7 from the three project managers on our team who were responsible for product selection, telecom plant, and voice service rollout. Except for one glitch early on, this piece of a very complex and political project was one I felt comfortable with almost from the start. First of all, I had done a few voice and data projects before so, once I filled out the technology questionnaire for the IP Telephone, I felt I could deal with it. Far more important was the fact that these three project managers proved to me that they were up to the tasks at hand. That is a bonus of approaching the vetting process this way. It gives you the opportunity to evaluate technical people or managers while reviewing their technologies with them. It helps you determine who can be trusted and who just might require a little closer scrutiny.

It is also worth mentioning that the table holds project requirements, high-level tasks to rollout IP Telephone, a Plan B for the risk of it not working, and a postimplementation support strategy. That is not a coincidence, by the way. Requirements, tasks to accomplish them, task owners and dates, and real-time status are all you need to consider. If you decide, when the project is completed, that you want to become an IP Telephone guru, knock yourself out. But for now, stick to your job, which is making sure this thing is going to fly right side up and can land safely, too.

3.6 REVIEW VALIDATION PLAN

Just to recap, you now have a proposal that Requirement X will be implemented using Technologies A, B, and C. The obvious question is: "Can we build it in our environment in such a way that the requirement shall be met in an acceptable manner?" You are likely to hear "Of course," but unless you are also told, "We do this all the time," your retort should be, "Show me." That should probably be put more tactfully (i.e., "How do we validate the strategy?"). I have illustrated one approach with IP Telephone, which included a competitive analysis, a pilot, and a Plan B provision to fall back on proven private branch exchange (PBX) technology if our efforts to make IP Telephone work proved inadequate to match our success metrics.

Earlier in this chapter, I recounted the near-disastrous load-balancing escapade and acknowledged that some details had been omitted. I want to recycle the story, this time baring all, and what the approach should have been. This was a case begging for the validation of the proposed technical solution prior to the investment in time and money that was made. By the way, the application's high-profile user was exposed to significant risk because the output was subject to regulatory oversight with punitive sanctions for missed deadlines. First, let us look at the project's high-level tasks:

- Build a dozen servers in the new data center to replace the nearly obsolete ones at the legacy site. Production data shall be ported from legacy servers to the new farm for testing and refreshed immediately prior to cutover, with no loss of data.
- Migrate the multigigabyte database from a proprietary repository to the corporate standard for LAN-based database servers.
- Re-architect the application to add "thin computing" as a front end, so this pseudo-client/server (C/S) application can be launched at the user desktop anywhere in the world using common browsers.
- Replicate the load-balanced, Web browser architecture for global, casual users on new servers, too.

It is also important to look at this from a more anecdotal form, a process to be described in Chapter 4 as an implementation strategy. In this case, the story looks something like this:

- The processing site will be moved to a new environment.
- The application will be re-architected.
- The database technology will be changed.
- This would be done on new servers in a new environment.

- At nearly the same time, the key users will be moving into a new building as well.
- Their old personal computers would be replaced with faster ones using a more current operating system that also used a different strategy for launching applications.
- Their network logins, which this application used for authentication, would be moved to a new domain with new user IDs and passwords.

In other words, you would be hard-pressed to introduce more risk than what was already on the table. We were brought into the server side of this project at the last hour. Had I arrived during the planning phase, I would have urged the team lead to come up with a plan like this.

1. Validate that the new user LAN/desktop environment performed acceptably with the legacy application infrastructure at the legacy site.
2. Move users to the new site and new LAN/desktop platform and reconnect them to the legacy application platform.
3. Build out and test the new architecture, in the new site, in a carefully phased test to ensure that each possible risk point was isolated to facilitate troubleshooting, repair, and performance evaluation.
4. Test the new architecture from the new site with the new LAN/desktop platform.
5. Validate data refresh and data recovery.
6. Execute production cutover with the back-out "Plan B" of reconnecting to legacy site/infrastructure.
7. Sunset equipment at the legacy site.

Quite naturally, you would look for a lot of more testing detail, end user roles and responsibilities, and so forth, but this would be the skeleton to which that muscle and flesh would be affixed.

3.7 REVIEW RISK

Deliverables in any project have some risk. Chapter 5 is dedicated to the topic, but it is appropriate to take a peek at it here from a technology planning perspective. You should look for potential leaks and foul odors in a few places:

- What happens if this technology cannot deliver the requirement(s)?
- What are the chances that this works in the lab but does not scale to the 20,000 targeted beneficiaries?
- How can we validate that this will work in our real world?

You might find yourself getting booed off the stage, but you are not doing your job if you do not press the technologists to provide their own thoughts on these three simple questions. Most are honest and profes-

Exhibit 9. Plan B for Server Farm Migration and Relocation

Risk	Plan B
The re-architected database or application does not work.	It is thoroughly tested beforehand with user's legacy LAN/desktop.
The users' new LAN/desktop environment proves incompatible with the legacy application architecture.	We test well in advance of migration to the new LAN/desktop so any issues can be identified and repaired.
The new LAN/desktop environment does not work with the re-architected application at the new site.	Validate legacy LAN/desktop environment works with re-architected servers, then test new environment.

sional, but your job is to ensure thoroughness. The key is not being a topical expert, but dedicating yourself to sniffing out risk and inspecting for a good plan that will test for, and resolve, as many errors as possible. Because you are staking your own reputation on project output, this is not the time to give technologists the benefit of the doubt because you do not know their field, or you like them, or you cannot be bothered.

As for mitigation, once potential risk is identified, the task at hand is crafting good Plan Bs.[1] This is a relatively simple thinking exercise. Take a minute to review the server migration plan we presented earlier. If you notice how it is crafted, you can see that risk mitigation is built right into the test and implementation plan. Exhibit 9 gives an appropriate summation.

In summary, the idea is to know where to look for risk, understand the impact of any significant risk, and have a plan ready to overcome or avoid those undesired consequences. In this case, our risk strategy assumed the worst-case scenario — that the re-architected application would not work on the new desktop in the new site on the date set by business cycles and move schedules. We recognized the need for a multiple fallback strategy so that we can run the old application from the new site on the new desktop in the event that target state, running the new application on the new desktop from the new site, was delayed. If you review the last table, you will find those steps are documented.

3.8 REVIEW POTENTIAL INTEGRATION ISSUES

This load-balancing tale is a superior example of project-driven technology that did not integrate well into the target environment, and is presented to stress the value in making Fit a primary target of your technology vetting process. Thoroughness is the only trick here. We once had a situation where the engineers wanted to roll out the most current version of the LAN authentication process. This software is part of the LAN operating system, and manages a database that tracks user identifications (IDs) and network resources such as shared printers and servers. The engineers wanted to use the new version because, although radically different, it was the next step for the global network, and they wanted to use our project as a test bed within the production environment. At first that seemed all right, until I got tipped off that the new system was incompatible with the company's Domain Name System (DNS).[2] This meant that if the upgraded authentication software does not interoperate with the DNS system, users could not log into and utilize network resource without manual intervention. Needless to say, this was a less than comforting prospect.

When confronted with this concern, the engineers came up with a workaround that sounded strange to me, although technically I was way out of my league. Still, as project manager, I was unhappy with how all this made me feel, so I asked the engineers to meet with our security and operations people. These folks did understand the issues and they quashed the initiative on the spot for a whole peck of reasons. We went with the older, DNS-compatible system. Within 6 months, the two systems became compatible through vendor revisions, but that half-year wait was out of the question as far as our project schedule was concerned.

3.9 REVIEW WITH CUSTOMER AND BENEFICIARIES

Neglecting to engage your customer and beneficiaries in technology design reviews can be politically suicidal. If you accept that as a basic rule, then the real issue is timing. If you wait too long, the beneficiary will probably be annoyed at being kept out of the loop. If that happens, you can expect them to raise objections, some of which may be red herrings (i.e., false). If you approach beneficiaries before your plan is adequately vetted, you have given them the opportunity to poke holes in it, and then you face a credibility battle that can be tough to win.

A related consequence of premature disclosure is beneficiaries seizing the opportunity to sneak requirements into your plan, and begin driving you. This is where a lot of scope creep comes from, by the way. Although you need to form a partnership with these people, if the balance of power shifts their way, your ability to manage the project is significantly weakened. Chapter 13 covers this complex subject in more detail.

3.10 SUBMIT TO TECHNOLOGY REVIEW BOARD IF REQUIRED

You may not think there is a formal review process in your company, but there may be de facto ones. I have seen them embedded in budget or funding reviews, where an architect on the chief technology officer's staff shows up asking questions with the intransigent air of a department of motor vehicles clerk. I have also known product managers who tell you that, as of last week, your specified server or software technology has moved onto the corporate "endangered species" list, and thus requires signoff from someone who is on maternity leave in Nepal and cannot be reached for some time. In other words, weighty objections to your design can come out of left field at the very last moment.

Again, the timing of exposing your design to public scrutiny can be tricky. Some projects shoot straight down the middle in terms of technologies, but for some reason I end up on projects where new ground is broken. Once your design sees the light of day, it is possible that procurement, vendor management, product management, data center operations, network management, help desk, and accounting will be looking for you to justify selected technologies.[3] If this surveillance occurs too early, it can put a damper on the creative process. If done at the last minute, however, you are much more vulnerable to the tendency of such arbiters to object to, if not forbid, certain design characteristics.

The best approach is to invite representatives of these groups to join your project at startup. Copy them on minutes, and share emerging design documentation with them. If you make them feel as if they are a part of the team, they are more likely to forewarn you of possible compliance issues. Further, you would look to them to run interference with their supervisors in the event that you start drifting out of spec. Be prepared to rationalize technology choices in a way that benefits the corporation. I have seen temper tantrums work in this regard, but sooner or later that approach backfires, so be prepared to do battle with as many good thoughts and supporters as you can muster. If you have maneuvered beneficiaries into a similar alignment, they can lend muscle in this regard as well. Instead of panicking, remember that the objections you face might be political, bureaucratic, or simply one more instance of a person in power flexing his or her muscles. In other words, their motive may have nothing to do with the technical or business-oriented merits of your technology decisions.

3.11 COMMENCE VALIDATION PROCESSES AND ADJUST AS REQUIRED

Exhibit 10 presents an appropriate validation procedure.

The key thing to remember is you want to get into the production environment well in advance of cutover or rollout time, so you can discover and react to any problems that may crop up. In the previous load-balancing example, the incompatibility of the legacy load-balancing software with the new network switching was not anticipated. Because the user acceptance testing (UAT) ended up running late, we had very little time to react once the issue surfaced.

When planning this validation process, you need to look for potential failure points and have a remedy scheme prepared to the extent possible. If we revisit the load-balancing scheme one more time from this perspec-

Exhibit 10. Technology Validation Process

Validation Step	Rationale
Proof of concept (alpha test)	In laboratory environment, validate functionality and that components work together acceptably.
Stress test	Simulate production load via scripting, "packet flooding," or other relevant techniques.
UAT	Turn test environment over to beneficiary for testing. This is a dress rehearsal, and should be run in the production environment with adequate safeguards, or in isolation if testing in production is not feasible.

Exhibit 11. Test Plan Document Review

Document	Contents
System architecture drawing	Shows hardware and software components and inter-connectivity.
System architecture description	Describes applications, tools, and services, and how they interact.
Draft runbook	Required for operations turnover. Indicates how services and application are started and stopped, how users log in, user functionality, backup and disaster recovery schema, and other connections (e.g., File Transfer Protocol [FTP]).

tive, load balancing should have been identified as a test item. How? It should have been quite simple. During the test planning meetings, several documents, as presented in Exhibit 11, should be reviewed.

A diagram, such as the one displayed in Exhibit 12 detailing system architecture, would clearly have identified load balancing, as would system documentation that lists each hardware component and identifies applications or services running on each platform.

A draft runbook, which is normally required by operations, would also have flagged load balancing as a piece of system architecture requiring specific configuration, as well as an escalation list for support in the event of an outage.[4]

Again, as project manager it is not your job to write detailed test plans or come up with clever solutions to tricky problems. It is your job, however, to insist that such work is done. The best way to ensure compliance is to schedule meetings to review the plans. Network and operations personnel should be present in addition to implementers, software developers, etc. The intent is to focus the right eyes on the technology game plan

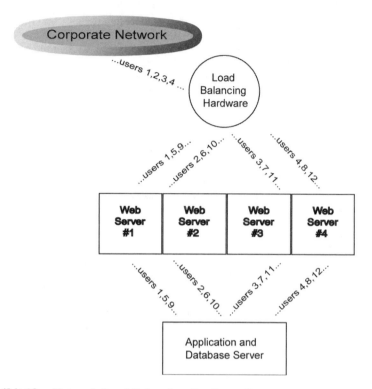

Exhibit 12. Network Load-Balancing Configuration

so that any gaps or potential points of failure can be identified and resolved.

The last action item in this piece of the project is addressing risk, performance issues, or unfulfilled requirements. You can also expect that, once the user gets involved, new requirements will mysteriously arise. Although you may or may not know why new demands come to light at this stage of the game:

- It could be the fault of the analysts who developed your requirements.
- End users might have done a poor job of articulating their needs.
- A new requirement may spring from a recent change in the business environment.

Hopefully, you can see why this process should be agreed to and scheduled well in advance of any production dates. Also, you should consider planning this in phases. In other words, have a first UAT in June, a follow-up in July, and so forth even though production turnup is not scheduled until October. You know things take time to get ironed out, so be realistic, and be sure your plan reflects that reality.

3.12 PROCEED WITH ROLLOUT, INVOKING YOUR PLAN Bs AS REQUIRED

Managing project implementation is the subject of Chapter 7, so we will not spend much time on it here other than to close the loop on validating your technologies. The original premise of this chapter was that, as project manager, you are the sole individual tasked with worrying about everything coming together because your team leads are "smokestacked" with their individual enterprises. Keep in mind that everything may not come together. Delays and their causes are explored later in this book, too.

You do need to begin preparing for that eventuality, however, and think about how to manage around that — now. Some deliverables are truly stand-alone, so if they are late or prove to be unwieldy, you should understand what position you may be forced to take. For example, our target state chart earlier in this chapter suggested the potential rollout delay of certain deliverables. The only one so noted was wireless LAN. When I researched that technology, I could see two major problems with the maturity level of the product. The first was that the 400 kilobytes-per-second throughput compared very poorly with the 100 megabyte house network users could access in cubicles, offices, and conference rooms.

The other drawback was security. At the time, wireless LANs were not that hard to hack into, even from cars on the street, using off-the-shelf hardware and software. The nature of this client's business made that exposure unacceptable. As a result of these deficiencies, wireless LAN moved from Day Two to Day One. That was one of the few noncontroversial calls we made on this project because there was not much pent-up demand for the service anyway. Still, just to cover ourselves, we had the contractor install antenna cabling throughout the site so the infrastructure was in place. Whether wireless LAN gets turned up in this particular location remains to be seen.

You may feel obligated to make other technology adjustments as well. If, unlike the wireless example, your problematic technology remains compelling even though its rollout is not shaping up, you may need to dilute its intended rollout or slow it down. You may need to beef it up, such as adding servers if capacity or speed is not scaling as you had been led to believe that it would. Other tactics can be invoked as well, depending on the technology and the problems you are having with it. I must say, however, that none of these potential adjustments should come as a surprise. The preemptive testing strategy outlined in this chapter should be rigorous enough to suggest the probability of disappointing performance. If that is the case, and a quick fix does not appear likely, you must initiate damage control with stakeholders. Whether it is to dumb down expectations, or to perform other undesirable political acts, keep in mind that bad news is much better received early than late. There is no applicable "just in time" paradigm associated with project management, especially when it comes to blowing the whistle on unrealistic or uninformed expectations.

Notes

1. See Chapter 5 for more detail on risk analysis and mitigation planning.
2. DNS resolves IP addresses.
3. And/or brands.
4. See Chapter 11 for details on runbooks.

Chapter 4
Devising an Implementation Strategy Precedes Scheduling

Years ago, I sat next to a gentleman who had a big sign in his cubical that urged him to "visualize success!" With my projects, I like to take this one step further by visualizing the steps taken to successfully implement project requirements. I call this process "devising an implementation strategy." Although I long since abandoned my first career as a boat builder, I remain an avid house remodeler. I do my own plumbing, cabinetwork, wiring, and so on. One has to mentally prepare when switching from one of these trades to another because each requires different skill sets, tools, materials, and processes. I do this by imagining each step required, for instance, to install a light fixture or build cabinet drawers. This helps remind me of what materials or tools I may need. It also minimizes mistakes and extra trips to the home improvement center by thinking it through before getting started. In this chapter, I want to show you how to apply this technique to project planning.

4.1 WHAT IS AN IMPLEMENTATION STRATEGY?

Simply put, an implementation strategy is the plan in anecdotal form. One could also reference this project management step as defining the approach to implementing project requirements, as opposed to planning the implementation. This latter duty is a subsequent step we will undertake when we are ready to schedule the implementation.

Once again, I will use a non-information technology (IT) example to introduce a significant thought process so as not to leave behind those unfamiliar with any particular IT discipline selected as the straw man. This time, the demonstration project will be the countertop we built at home for our new island cabinet — the last piece of a 2-year kitchen remodeling project. When my wife and I sat down to figure out this piece, our first task was to select a material for the top from the traditional choices of:

- Polished stone such as marble or granite
- Wood
- Plastic laminate
- A composite material that resembles stone
- Ceramic tile

We went around and around on this because many issues must be considered, including appearance, cost, durability, and ease of maintenance. Eventually, we decided to use a beautiful wood, Honduras mahogany, that we would stain and then coat with a clear, high-gloss protective finish. Although it did not unduly influence the final decision, labor was a consideration. Had we gone with marble, granite, or composite stone, we would have hired a company to measure, build, deliver, and install the top. If any other material had been selected, then I would be task owner. There is a long lead-time for outsourcing countertops in our area, which is in the midst of a building boom, meaning that contractors of any sort are difficult to engage. On the other hand, my professional workweeks are long and arduous, so scheduling my free time can be problematic as well.

The top is 9 feet long and nearly 4 feet wide. Along one long side, toward the middle, will be a four-burner drop-in gas cooktop. It will require a connection to the gas line running under the kitchen floor in the basement ceiling. It will also require two separate electrical branch circuits:

- One will power the electric ignition system for the gas burners.
- The other will electrify the pop-up cooktop ventilation system.

In addition to the pop-up vent, the ventilation system consists of a duct that runs from the underneath portion of the cooktop inside the island cabinet, down through the floor, across the basement ceiling, and out the foundation wall. This allows the cooking fumes drawn from the top of the stove to be blown into the backyard.

The countertop, along with the electrical connections and ventilation system, had to be fully completed by Thanksgiving, which was 2 months away when we kicked off this phase of the kitchen redo. Not only did I have to finish my tasks by the holiday, but the wiring and ducting also had to be inspected by the local building department. Also, we had to hire a plumber to make the gas connections. After thinking this through, we decided to have all the work we were doing completed two weeks prior to Thanksgiving. That way, the inspectors and the plumber would have an adequate window in which to complete their tasks, and we could serve Thanksgiving dinner from our newly finished, fully functional, certified kitchen.

4.2 THAT WAS AN IMPLEMENTATION STRATEGY

What you just read is an implementation strategy. This one forecasts how we intend to complete our deliverable. You should be able to identify its author as a project manager because in it you can find:

- Requirements including the integration of all components
- The design, including decision points and cost considerations
- Dependencies
- Approach; this is the logic driving the project plan (i.e., "how we will do this")
- Roles and responsibilities
- Milestones and time constraints
- Risk, including scheduling constraints and the possibility of inspections

Just to be sure everyone is comfortable with this concept, I will retell the countertop saga — this time couched in typical Project Management puffery.

The most important decision facing the prospective countertop user for island kitchen cabinets is material, features, and appearance because the large, flat surface will dominate the room and be used frequently. Available material types vary in look and feel, cost, and the ability to resist water, chemicals, stains, heat, and cutting or chopping. During the design phase, one solution will be selected from the available media of natural stone, simulated stone, plastic laminate, ceramic tile, and wood. The selection criteria shall be appearance, cost, ease of maintenance, and durability. Subsequent to that decision, color and detailing will be determined, and a purchase requisition will be issued. The top must be completely installed and user-ready in time for the upcoming Thanksgiving holiday.

The implementation tasks and owners are dependent on media selection. The in-house team can implement any media except natural or simulated stone, which would have to be outsourced. If done by the in-house team, work can progress immediately upon selection of media. Lead-time for the stone treatments is typically 4 to 6 weeks.

The top will measure 42 inches by 108 inches, with a nominal thickness of 1½ inches. A 30-inch drop-in, gas-powered cooktop will be installed 2 feet in from the south end of the countertop on the east side, with a pop-up ventilation system installed at the immediate back edge of the cooktop. Natural gas, electrical wiring, and ducting for the cooktop and downdraft ventilation system must also be installed.

The in-house team shall perform all such work except the gas work (that will be subcontracted to a plumber). To provide an adequate scheduling window for the plumber and inspections by the local building department,

Exhibit 1. Nine High-Level Planning Steps

Number	Step	Our Status
1	Define target state.	Complete
2	Define target state components and processes.	Complete
3	Define how these components and processes fit together logically.	Complete
4	Define the sequences in which those components and processes are built.	Not started
5	Define the sequences in which these components and processes are integrated together.	Not started
6	Transform these sequences into blocks of time.	Draft — high-level
7	Assign start and end dates to each block.	Draft — high-level
8	Assign an owner to each block.	Draft — high-level
9	Insert these blocks with sequences intact into a project-calendaring tool.	Not started

all other work must be completed no later than 2 weeks before Thanksgiving.

Outsourcing for the potential media choice of natural or simulated stone, and for the required plumber, will require vendor negotiations. Due to the estimated costs, bids from multiple vendors, and a review of terms and conditions of the potential vendors, will be required. Financing for a natural stone solution would be necessary due to the significantly higher anticipated cost of that option.

Once the top is fabricated, whether by the vendor or the in-house team, it shall be delivered to the site, installed securely to the target cabinet, and cleaned. Upon successful completion of inspections and user acceptance testing, the installation shall be turned over to operations, and vendor invoices will be processed for payment.

4.3 WHY DO I NEED AN IMPLEMENTATION STRATEGY?

Within the overall narrative this book has undertaken:

- We have now come to understand our project's goals and a lot about the team and the environment in which the project will be deployed.

- We know our requirements and most of our specifications because we have worked through the technical design process.

There is more heavy lifting awaiting the project manager before we start building and deploying, but we are definitely ready to commence planning. Exhibit 1 presents the flow of the planning process, and restates where we are along the project management continuum.

As we start this chapter, we are pretty much done with steps 1, 2, and 3. We probably are in decent shape with steps 6, 7, and 8, although they should be labeled "draft" at this stage (and not just because some detail

Design Details (items 1-3) Target state components and processes, and how they fit together.	*Implementation Strategy* the sequence in which components and processes are built and integrated	Implementation Details (items 6-9) Tasks to achieve target state with dates and owners.

Exhibit 2.   Alternate View of the Nine Planning Tasks

has yet to be derived and documented). Step 9 is certain to give us all headaches, so we will avoid this one for as long as possible. If you do the math, that means that steps 4 and 5 have yet to be touched, or at least articulated and documented in any meaningful way. Curiously enough, these two items can be best accomplished by using the implementation strategy tool under current scrutiny. To clarify this, let us first revisit the nine planning tasks from another view, as depicted in Exhibit 2.

If you have done any detailed project planning (i.e., juggled thousands of tasks), you understand from looking at the two blocks in Exhibit 2 that it is mind-boggling, if not impossible, to travel from the left box of design details to the right box of implementation details in any meaningful, practical, or useful way without a bridging technique of some kind. This is because design and implementation details do not necessarily map to each other, whether they are one-to-one, one-to-many, or many-to-one. I use the bridge or transforming tool of the implementation strategy to overcome this major disconnect, which, in truth, is far more than a presentation issue. The implementation strategy is largely represented by steps 4 and 5 in our planning table, and the two-headed arrow between the two boxes sitting atop this paragraph.

4.4 HOW DO I USE THIS IMPLEMENTATION STRATEGY?

The key to bridging the gap between design and implementation details by using the implementation strategy can be found in one of the characteristics presented in the review of the kitchen countertop story, specifically this one:

> *Approach; this is the logic driving the project plan (i.e., "how we will do this")*

I love the word "logic" in this context because it implies that we are applying some cognitive procedure to this process of generating a useful plan from the jumble of ideas and personalities that presently lie before us;

Design Details	Implementation Details

Countertop
  wood
  assembly detail
  size and location of hole for
    cooktop
  stain and protective finish
	Countertop
	  buy wood
	  machine wood and assemble
	  cut hole for cooktop
	  stain and finish
	  install on island cabinet

Cooktop
  appliance
  gas
  electric ignition
	Cooktop
	  buy cooktop
	  install in countertop
	  connect gas
	  connect electric
	  connect ventillation

Ventilation system
  appliance
  electric power
  ductwork
	Ventilation system
	  buy system and ductwork
	  install in cabinet and
	    countertop
	  install ductwork
	  connect electric

	Inspections
	  get permits
	  electric inspection
	  gas inspection
	  final building inspection

Exhibit 3.   Fill in the Two Blocks

however, I refer to this process as implementation strategy, not implementation logic, because there is more alchemy than science in this process, no matter how you cut it.

The one leap of faith I ask you to take is to agree that the implementation strategy must be created before you move toward scheduling the tasks that comprise your project activities. Final planning is the topic of Chapter 6, so this business of an implementation strategy is an interim step, but a crucial one. We take it to gain a full understanding of the attributes of the work to be performed, though not necessarily the detail of that work. In fact, other than the critical elements described in the countertop review, you need little else to construct your implementation strategy.

Our next step to see how the implementation strategy works is to fill in the two blocks (see Exhibit 3).

It is not always easy to decide how best to present a theory. What I generally do is show a process and its application before rationalizing it, so here we go again. Most project managers would look at the two boxes in Exhibit 3 and try to match them up into a plan, because there appears to be a one-for-one relationship between the boxes and their contents, save for the inspection box thrown in at the bottom of the right side. For instance, the wood countertop is detailed on both sides. The left side represents the key design elements, while on the right, the discrete steps required to get a finished countertop onto the island are documented. This is repeated for the other key design elements of that project: the gas cooktop and the ventilation system.

So, as was just said, we appear to have our plan, right? Unfortunately, that is not true. If you are not knowledgeable about kitchen building, then it would be understandable if you do not appreciate how unrepresentative the right side is of how this project would be executed by an experienced builder, even though the basic high-level tasks are accurately depicted. What is wrong or misleading about it, you ask?

What is wrong is what is missing, and this includes steps 4 and 5 from our planning review (i.e., those steps identified earlier in the chapter as the heart and soul of the implementation strategy), namely:

- The sequence in which those components and processes are built.
- The sequence in which these components and processes are integrated together.

In plain English, the issue is that, although the right side accurately captures the high-level tasks in sequence for implementing each of the three key deliverables, it does not show the actual flow of work that would lead to the successful implementation of the entire project.

Before I lose too many of you, let me jump ahead for a moment. Any complex IT project will probably contain design elements that are unknown to you. Even if you know everything, the shear volume of detail on complex projects is overwhelming. Therefore, no matter how technically savvy you may be, I ask you to consider that this parable of my kitchen remodeling nightmare remains compelling. If you must, think of the three key elements of countertop, cooktop, and ventilation as stand-ins for Web sites, data center moves, switched ATM networks, or whatever mush your complex project currently approximates.

Though running the risk of delving too deeply into kitchen construction processes, I would like to close this section by asking you to take a look at the following illustration. In it, the implementation detail boxes previously placed on the right have been moved to the left side of the page. In the

Implementation Details	Implementation Strategy
Countertop buy wood machine wood and assemble cut hole for cooktop stain and finish install on island cabinet	**Design** Countertop Cooktop Electric Gas Ventilation
Cooktop buy cooktop install in countertop connect gas connect electric connect ventillation	**Procurement** Wood Cooktop Ventilation components Electric components Gas (engage vendor)
Ventilation system buy system and ductwork install in cabinet and countertop install ductwork connect electric	**Scheduling** Gas My tasks Obtain permits Inspections for gas, electric, and final building
Inspections get permits electric inspection gas inspection final building inspection	**Implementation** Build and finish top Install electric, gas, and ducts Install countertop on island Install cooktop and ventilation Connect electric, gas, and ducts Pass inspections

Exhibit 4. Reflecting the Implementation Strategy

revamped drawing in Exhibit 4, the right side now reflects the implementation strategy articulated at the start of this chapter in a more graphic form.

Before ending this part of the discussion on implementation strategies, a few comments are in order:

- If we did a good job of devising an implementation strategy, then the boxes on the right that were derived from that strategy accurately reflect the upcoming flow of project work.
- All items listed on the left were transformed to the right using the implementation strategy-bridging tool.
- By no means does the right side substitute for the final plan, whether it captures all detail or not.

At this point, however, the level of detail shown is quite close to what you should shoot for when you create implementation strategies. For example:

- It would take pages and pages to write up the details behind the seemingly innocent item called "Install electric, gas, and ducts" that appears in the Implementation box at the bottom of the right side.
- Many more pages would be required to document other information, such as risk, that factors into the real implementation.
- Even though this was an implementation plan wherein I personally will own 95 percent of the tasks, all that detail was ignored as irrelevant when we devised the implementation strategy for this piece of our kitchen remodel.
- At that point, I was not scheduling anything, so I really did not care whether I needed just Saturday morning or the whole weekend to implement the wiring requirements.
- The fact that I was the task owner did not color my job as project manager to assemble the implementation strategy. If the line item was "Install and configure routers" instead of "Run electric," the story would not change.

There is no guarantee that when we build the final schedule, it will mimic the implementation strategy side of Exhibit 4. What is a sure thing is that it will be pretty close, whereas the boxes on the left are practically useless as the basis for a valid project calendar. This is why I urge you to use the implementation strategy as a transformation tool to get a leg up on approximating the real project schedule.

Two project views must be considered to capture this method:

- *Deliverable view.* If your project has seven major deliverables, such as systems, network infrastructure, disaster recovery, and the like, then you should have seven implementation strategies. Presumably, the appropriate team leads would create these, although it has been my experience that you should facilitate this process with them.
- *Roll up view.* In the end, you are far more responsible for the aggregated output of the various teams, so your personal focus should be on the overall strategy. This may seem strange if the deliverables are stand-alone, but you should create a strategy that covers all of them. Chances are that some dependencies or linkages do exist among your deliverables. Even if that were not true, you still need to sequence your own efforts as each deliverable moves through the process from the Big Thirteen to operational handoffs.

4.5 BUILDING YOUR IMPLEMENTATION STRATEGY

Now that time has been spent understanding the tool, it should be easier to understand how to create it. In Chapter 2, the idea of mapping out workflows as part of the requirements development process was commended to you. Basically, implementation strategies are built the same way. Ideally, you would start by leading a room full of individuals responsible for a deliverable and map out the process of implementing that deliverable. Verbiage should make its way on to the white board. When all is said and done, that should be drawn with a software package showing blocks of work and how they interconnect. Leave out the Gantt chart stuff until you have plowed your way through Chapter 6. I recommend capturing the strategy in text form as well.[1]

Roll-up implementation strategies get built the same way. Obviously, it is preferable that you have already gone through the exercise with major deliverables individually before building your overall implementation strategy. This way, you and your team leads are comfortable with the process. More important, individual strategies are already known and can be readily applied to the crafting of your roll-up strategy.

This process has many useful outcomes, most of which have been described and should not need revisiting. What is worth noting at this point is that gaps are likely to emerge in longstanding assumptions about various project components, milestones, and risk. This is most probable when you are building the roll-up implementation strategy, but can occur when drafting individual deliverable implementation strategies as well.

4.6 FINDING GAPS WITH THE IMPLEMENTATION STRATEGY

Finding these gaps is a somewhat intuitive process. Perhaps it is best described as the conductor listening for sour notes when the orchestra starts learning a new composition. The dissonance is initially visceral, at least until you hone in on it and discover that the trombone section is misplaying a note or misjudging the beat.[2] In IT projects, one should inspect for specific gaps. My favorites are:

- *Handoffs.* This can be in the form of output, such as data or process. The question to ask is whether given output meets all downstream project requirements, or just those of a parochial team.
- *Timeframes.* If Joe needs the network up by June, but it will not be ready until August, this disconnect should come to light (it better).
- *Duplication of effort.* Uncoordinated teams sometimes travel the same road. Team A produces ninety percent of that which Team B will produce at one hundred per cent a month later. Is this a useful condition?
- *Risk.* Does the output of one team actually increase risk that another team, or the project, becomes vulnerable to?

<u>**Exhibit 5. Implementation Strategy Components**</u>

- Requirements
- Design
- Selection of technology
- Costing
- Procurement resource considerations
- Build out
- User acceptance testing
- Handoff to operations
- Paying the bills

- *Rework.* Does a significant portion of Team A's output subsequently require changes by another team? Because, for instance, Team A creates a deliverable that, although functional, does not:
  - Meet production standards
  - Fit business requirements
  - Scale well when deployed into a nonhomogenous global environment

No hard rules can be applied to this process other than to reiterate that when your implementation strategies take shape, this is the perfect time to listen for those sour notes. At this stage of the game, it is a far easier task to bring the trombones back into line than just before opening night.

4.7 IMPLEMENTATION STRATEGY COMPONENTS

You might wish to refer to Exhibit 5 when building your implementation strategies to double-check that the final output will be complete.

The walk-through that leads to a summarized, anecdotal implementation plan can be done in meetings, with small groups, or by the owner of that particular requirement. Dependencies, risk, and even disconnects from basic assumptions will readily surface, particularly if you encourage the active participation of stakeholders and beneficiaries. If you use this process wisely, your planning and the management of the emerging plan will be far more effective.

4.8 AN IT IMPLEMENTATION STRATEGY EXAMPLE

We built a new campus in which the local area network (LAN) design called for switched fast Ethernet with several high-speed laser printers attached to the LAN on each floor. We were in the build-out stage of the project, with just ten weeks left before the first 300 tenants were due to move in, when I got bad news from one of my spies. The user requirements surveys had finally come in, albeit late. They revealed a requirement that, to be honest, had escaped my attention. Apparently, the survey team had discovered that at the sites the users were moving from, they ran hundreds of print jobs directly off the mainframe network, often using "mainframe printers" that had features like forms handling and huge cut-sheet capacities. Though chagrined, I immediately recognized two problems:

- The company was phasing out the dedicated mainframe network, so it was not extended to our new site.
- The printers we were installing in the new site did not provide these specialized features support forms, or high volume.[3]

In other words, our site technology could not meet a significant user requirement. Whether we should have known about this many weeks or months before was irrelevant at this point. So I scrambled around to understand this "new" requirement and identify someone who could help us. After a few false starts, the right experts were identified. Fortunately, I had enough networking experience to feel comfortable with these new team members and their approach. After a few more sessions with them, I was able to submit the following implementation strategy to management:

In the legacy sites, users print from mainframe applications to printers attached to the dedicated mainframe network. This infrastructure is separate and distinct from the Ethernet LANs constructed in legacy sites, and at our new campus as well. The corporation is phasing out the proprietary network, so it was not extended to our new site. Therefore, without an alternative plan, there will be no way to produce all the mainframe print jobs at the new site. What we will do is redirect all these mainframe print jobs to the LAN at the new site, where they will be output from the LAN-attached printers using Transmission Control Protocol/Internet Protocol (TCP/IP).

This will require changes to the print definitions in the impacted mainframe applications. It also may require installing IP-compatible, mainframe-style printers with continuous forms, high-speed or high-volume features that the LAN laser printers being installed at the new site do not have, but that meet the user requirements as their old printers at legacy sites do.

A team with experience in converting mainframe printing to the LAN/IP environment has been engaged to do the analysis, design, implementation, and testing. They will also provide project management, and coordinate any special purchases as required. The main project will pick up any labor costs associated with this conversion, but the customer will be charged for any new hardware or software if required.

This real-world implementation strategy identifies the requirements, issues, and plan components at a high level. This provides completeness and keeps it reasonably brief. That is important because what you just read is basically all I needed to know about mainframe printing for our project.

There is one last benefit of using implementation strategies. The project from which I pulled this example had a dozen or so other deliverables. Although I had to develop and understand 11 other implementation strategies, that was a lot easier than trying to carry thousands of tasks around in my head. It was also easier to speak with others about this project because I had crisp stories to tell, instead of having to memorize the Manhattan telephone directory and be able to pronounce all the names in it.

If this presentation has convinced you that implementation strategies have value, then you have just added a very powerful weapon to your arsenal. It is interesting to note that if you cannot recount a major project deliverable in this manner, then either you do not know enough about that deliverable, or it has yet to take shape. In either case, further action is necessary. Either you need to find out what is going on with that requirement, or it has not congealed to the point that it can be packaged in this manner.

The idea here is to craft implementation strategies before gathering all the associated tasks and populating the Gantt chart. Therefore, the strategy should include all relevant aspects of the plan. If you start early enough, requirements gathering should be included.[4] In other words, the implementation strategy is the game plan for successfully implementing that project requirement. Risk, dependencies, team or task assignment, procurement processes (e.g., a request for proposal [RFP]), and hiring consultants for design, implementation, and documentation should be included if relevant. Any postimplementation requirements, such as training and support, should be noted if a significant work effort is anticipated. This is particularly true if the deliverable or its implementation represents a departure from business as usual.

You need an implementation strategy for each major deliverable, plus a "rolled up" implementation strategy that shows how the all the pieces fall into place. This latter plan provides a higher-level story (i.e., the infamous 30,000-foot view). It should incorporate external events or dependencies. You should also identify whether or not key events are serial or parallel (i.e., sequential or concurrent, to give your anecdote a temporal sense). As is the case with individual implementation strategies, it is important that you can tell the whole story. Look at it this way; if you cannot tell it, you cannot manage or rally support for it.

4.9 A VENDOR MANAGEMENT IMPLEMENTATION STRATEGY

I was hired as a program manager for a company that was negotiating a contract to provide vendor management services for a large customer. This customer had a division that managed the delivery of approximately

2-dozen communications services to internal users. These services included:

- Voice (private branch exchange [PBX], long-distance, teleconferencing)
- Video conferencing
- Data circuits
- Telex (wire transfers)

Internal groups delivered some of these services, whereas others were outsourced. Within this context, the term "vendor management" referred to the end-to-end process of:

- Taking internal customer orders for any of these services
- Placing orders with the appropriate service providers
- Validating invoices against purchase orders
- Processing approved invoices for payment
- Assigning invoice costs to the user cost centers for cost recovery purposes

The key reason this customer was negotiating with the company I represented was to automate these procedures. The legacy processes were either manual or faced obsolescence issues, not the least of which was the pending Y2K rollover. The intended benefits of this project were to:

- Reduce error through the application of Six Sigma.
- Reduce order fulfillment time.
- Make all order status and fulfillment reports available on an internal Web site.
- Streamline the cost recovery process.

Soon after my engagement, my company was awarded the contract after a highly competitive RFP process. The two parties signed a letter of intent. Negotiations over the statement of work were about 25 percent complete. That document would contain all of the requirements and many detailed specifications as well. Once the technologists, business process owners and lawyers had signed off, the document was approximately 200 pages long. Completing this document took 3 months. While it was emerging, I developed the operating model for our target state, which included a call center and a staff of 75 split between two locations. The main location was proximate to the customer, while the other location was 300 miles away. This second location would also contain our disaster recovery site for the midrange and Wintel servers that provided the technology support for this endeavor.

In the following "rolled-up" implementation strategy, my company is referred to as "vendor." The customer is designated as such.

4.9.1 Facilities

The vendor shall retrofit two sites to support this contract. One site will be the main call and data center. It will be located within ten miles of the customer headquarters location, and contain the bulk of the support staff and technology. A secondary site will be located at the vendor headquarters and will contain the telecommunications vendor management group. It will also serve as the disaster recovery site for the vendor's main data center. Construction fit out will commence immediately and be complete within 60 days. The two data center designs will be complete in 60 days as well, and will be operational from an infrastructure perspective within 6 months. Disaster recovery testing shall occur at the beginning of the seventh month. Both centers will be fully staffed and operational at the end of 9 months.

4.9.2 Operations

An organizational chart and operations work flow will be submitted to the vendor's internal management for approval within 2 weeks.[5] This will delineate how scope will be honored from a staffing perspective. Once the vendor's management, including human resources (HR), has approved the model and operating budget, the chart will be submitted to the customer as a courtesy even though the customer does not have approval rights over the vendor's staffing model. HR will commence hiring staff and developing operating procedures as per the contracted statement of work. The vendor's program manager has also submitted requisitions to augment existing staff for project management and support, programming, network design, etc. Candidates for key positions are identified and will be hired upon management approval.

4.9.3 Technology

Based on the work invested in the original RFP response, the technology design is nearly complete, with some computing, network, and software components already in development, if not near completion. The missing design elements are subject to statement of work negotiations, but are detailed in nature instead of strategic, so technology work can proceed. Purchase orders for the baseline technology, including systems, communications devices, software, and consulting services have been prepared, and supplier negotiations are under way.

A service bureau has been identified and negotiations are under way to subcontract the call detail reporting component of the statement of work to them. This will greatly minimize the technology investment required of the vendor. This contract should be in place within 90 days. Initial testing of their deliverables is scheduled for the beginning of month seven, with user acceptance testing (UAT) later that month, and production cutover immediately thereafter.

The vendor is tasked with putting up two Web sites. The procurement site is still under requirements discussions with the customer. That should be completed by the end of month two. The initial customer test is scheduled for month six, UAT in month eight, and turn up into production at the end of month nine, as per contract.

The other Web site to be built will provide cost charge back history viewable by cost center, organizational roll-ups, and technology service type (e.g., voice, telex charges). It shall be completed by month five after internal development. Customer UAT is scheduled in month six, with final production scheduled for month eight.

The manner and means by which the system shall interact with the five key suppliers needs additional research and design, after consultation with these suppliers. While the ultimate goal is the utilization of an automatic order processing service, such as an electronic data interchange (EDI) service bureau, with the emergence of eXtensible Markup Language (XML) as a future Web-based data exchange technology, it is likely that automation will be deferred until year three of the contract. This decision will be made within 60 days, with appropriate staffing and technology plans laid out for the course of the contract to ensure that service level agreements (SLAs) are met and maintained within the contract budget, with the likelihood that the technology in this area will be phased in as it matures and is integrated into the vendor's base technology.

4.9.4 Customer-Facing Processes

Because differences exist among the 75 customer sites regarding the use of certain suppliers and legacy procurement procedures, some manual work is envisioned as the customer becomes aligned with the output of this project, and consolidates its supplier relationships in terms of coverage, cost, and service levels, all of which remain the customer's responsibility. The status of this aspect of the implementation, and its potential impact on staffing, technology, and budget, will be reviewed with management from the customer and vendor sides every 90 days.

This was an incredibly complicated project. It featured multiple customers and beneficiaries, too many technology issues, and a few challenges too obscure or painful to recollect. The implementation strategy, however, was sound despite the uphill challenges buried under some of the more optimistic statements it contained. Not the least of these were a general timescale, and the frank admission of unknowns, although they were assigned checkpoint or resolution dates.

Keep this project in mind. It will resurface in Chapter 6 when we get to the equally challenging project management task, which is the development of a truthful but useful project schedule.

4.10 CONCLUSION

If you think I got a headache as a result of figuring out that project, imagine what would have happened if I tried to schedule the tasks without having some ideas as to where we were headed and how we intended to get there. This particular project had a very unfortunate cast of characters from a communications standpoint, so my job of keeping everyone on the same page was extremely difficult and, at times, impossible. Quite happily, few projects are quite that extreme in this regard. It was this project that proved to me, once and for all, that getting agreement on an implementation strategy is a must before going forward with detailed planning. The latter should be pretty easy once everyone agrees on the approach.

Hopefully, the examples used in this chapter fully illuminate the value of developing as complete an implementation strategy as possible. It should be documented and circulated for review and critique because, although your story may originate as fiction, you want to make sure that it ends up as fact, with a happy ending to boot.

Notes

1. There is a forthcoming IT example, so we can finally escape the sawdust I keep throwing at you.
2. Of course, as a savvy conductor/project manager, you may expect this from the notoriously slow-learning trombonists.
3. We are talking about 1000-page long print jobs here!
4. As described earlier in this chapter with the countertop example.
5. This vendor was a small company capable of such decisions after a single meeting.

Chapter 5
Plan B Is an Integral Part of the Project Plan

If the goal of your project is to plant a cherry tree in your front yard, before you stick that shovel in the ground, do you pause to consider these questions?

- Am I digging in the right spot?
- Do I know how big the hole needs to be?
- Is this shovel the right tool, or do I need a backhoe?
- What if I hit a big root, underground utility line, or septic tank?
- What if the shovel breaks?
- What if I get blisters?
- What if the tree dies a week after I plant it?

If you are like most people, you generally think positively about the outcome of each project you undertake. We downplay the probability of mishaps because if we were convinced in advance that too many things will go wrong, who would get out of bed in the morning? In the project world, however, things can and probably will go wrong, so you want to flag the likely points of failure and be ready with a fix or a workaround should they transpire.

Of course, you cannot anticipate them all. We once had a truck with several hundred computers hijacked during its three-block journey across town. It took us 4 days to verify that the truck had been stolen,[1] and 2 weeks to get the personal computers (PCs) replaced. We took a lot of good-natured ribbing for this, but in truth the 2-week delay was nearly catastrophic. Did our risk plan address highway robbery? No, it did not. Did we ask Security to protect all subsequent shipments on this project? Yes, we did.

Nor can you avoid every dire consequence you did acknowledge as a possible project event. There is also a people side to this, as would be the case with unproductive or disruptive team members. Personnel issues nor-

Exhibit 1. Wedding Reception Plan B Options

Plan B Option	Upside	Downside
1. Have an alternate day if rain is forecast for the primary date.	Should allow total freedom of site selection.	Scheduling nightmare for guests, caterers, and the band.
2. Pick a site where you can move indoors if it rains.	Chances are you can stay outside, but you are covered if it pours.	May limit choices based on accommodations and cache.
3. Splurge for a nice big, white tent.	Should not impact site selection.	Tents are costly, can leak, and feel closed in.

mally do not have easy fixes in the current laissez-faire environment. Team management is explored in complete detail in Chapter 12, but is mentioned here to further illustrate the far-reaching effects of the project risk virus. Planning for things to go wrong is part of the job, so that is what this chapter is all about.

5.1 WHAT IS A PLAN B?

Let us say we are scheduling a wedding reception for which being outdoors is a requirement. Lost souls may ignore the possibility of inclement weather, but we take our wedding planning seriously around here. Therefore, from a Plan B perspective, we are faced with three logical choices:

1. Have an alternate date you can switch to if rain looms in the forecast.
2. Schedule the event at a site where you could move inside if necessary.
3. Put up a tent and consider the risk to be mitigated.

Exhibit 1 lists each course of action as a potential Plan B. Also listed are the merits and potential downsides to each option

The up- and downsides of each Plan B option are pretty easy to deduce and play out. The two swing issues are site selection and cost. If cost is no problem, putting up a tent makes the most sense, because you should be able to hold to your schedule regardless of precipitation, and site selection is not impacted. Well, it should not be. Honesty compels me to report that friends of ours had to take down a tree in their back yard to make room for a tent for their daughter's reception. They, however, fall into the "cost is not a problem" demographic, which is not the case for all families and information technology (IT) projects.

Our three Plan B options differ in whether they are contingent or not. The first two are, whereas the third option, erecting a tent, is not. By choos-

Exhibit 2. Variations by Plan B on Triggers, Schedules, and Work Effort

Plan B	Trigger Test	Lead Time for Trigger	Implications
1. Have an alternate day for wedding.	Based on forecast for primary date.	No more or less than seven days prior to wedding.	Scheduling nightmare. Must double book venue, travel arrangements, band, and caterer.
2. Pick a spot that is okay indoors or out.	Based on same day forecast and observations.	Two to four hours prior to reception.	Everything has to get moved indoors (band, bar, tables, and chairs) if it rains.
3. Rent a tent.	None required.	None required.	Hope no one slips and falls when running to the powder room if it rains.

ing this last option and implementing it as part of our regular plan, we pre-emptively eliminate rain as a risk. In contrast, the first two options are contingent. With these strategies, we decide to deal with rain if it becomes:

- Highly probable (option one)
- A reality (option two)

Exhibit 2 allows you to see that options one and two have a trigger underlined in the "Plan B option" column and a "go/no go" decision point underlined in the "planning issues" column. These triggers and go/no go decision points are key components of contingency planning. It is important to recognize that the choice you and your team make on Plan B can affect your schedule procedurally. By this, I mean that different approaches to mitigating a risk can create additional and diverse tasks for the team. Let us see if Exhibit 2 clarifies that point by using the wedding reception weather risk once again.

So far as I am concerned, Plan Bs are normal components of your regular project plan. Whether it is "built-in," as we did by renting a tent, or contingent on some trigger, will be determined by many factors to be discussed in this chapter. In either case, integrate the "built-in" Plan B and embed go/no go trigger dates into your project calendar as well, with back-up plans ready to go should that trigger get pulled.

5.2 A WORD ABOUT RISK

Conceptually this is a pretty straightforward process. The steps are to:

- Identify potential risks
- Determine which are significant enough to merit proactive planning
- Complete plans as appropriate
- Gain sign-offs

As you go through this process, keep in mind that you should inspect for three types of risk:

- *Project risk.* This class of potential calamities directly relates to the project's success. Emerging conditions or events can damage your deliverables, or wreak havoc with the schedule or budget. This class of risk generally includes missed dates or deliverables, plus dependencies that do not pan out for some reason or other.
- *Beneficiary risk.* Project activity can disrupt your beneficiaries' worlds. Cutting over to a new system may lead to loss of data or productivity. Technologically disruptive projects can generate costs the beneficiary must absorb without compensation, the risk being their reticence to produce the required funds. For instance, I worked a project where the beneficiary was forced to replace 2000 desktop PCs with laptops despite the fact that a few million dollars worth of depreciation remained on the books for these legacy PCs that had been purchased to satisfy Y2K requirements. Although this problem was eventually solved, until a "white knight" donated the necessary funds, a key attribute of target state was severely challenged.
- *Corporate risk.* Data integrity, security, and antivirus protection should all be on your watch list on behalf of the organization. Most of us can cite issues with the public, governmental agencies, vendors, and labor unions that created real or potential risk in past projects. I worked on a project where the productivity of a new Web site was critical to corporate well-being to the degree that poor performance would cause significant revenue loss. The nature of the business also dictated the highest degree of protection for data flowing in and out of the corporate intranet. From a project perspective, the beneficiary was the external sales force numbering in the thousands; but from a risk perspective, it was the corporation with the most to lose.

5.3 WHEN IS RISK REALLY RISK?

I can sit here all day and spout off nearly everything that could go wrong on practically any project, because, as we shall see, this is highly although not completely predictable, as the hijacked shipment mentioned previously demonstrates. All this really means, however, is that I am neurotic in the very best Woody Allen tradition. Seriously, in our business, risk is risk only if it is acknowledged as such by your project team and the likely "victims," or someone acting in their proxy. I can predict all the gloom and doom I want, but unless the potentially harmed parties agree on the likelihood of danger and a specific course of action, this exercise can be futile.

Why is that? Let us look at the likely outcomes of a meaningful risk analysis, and you will see what I mean:

- *Blowing it off.* A potential risk is discussed, and the project team and possible victims agree that there is no issue. An example would be that the customer cannot move to the new building as originally planned on July 1, but has to wait 2 weeks due to construction delays. It is conceivable that the move can be postponed without any significant impact.
- *Stacking the sandbags.* In this scenario, both the potentially impacted party and we agree that a glitch would be unacceptable, and jointly develop a good Plan B. Let us say that the potential construction delay in the previous example would cause unacceptable disruption in the beneficiary's world. The user states that they must move during the first half of the month because their busy time is the second half of the month when they close the previous month's books. We have multiple options, such as finding "swing space," rescheduling the move, or going to the whip on the contractors to guarantee the original move date. This last Plan B should probably be reworded as "going to the wallet."
- *Rolling the dice.* After detailed conversations, the potential victim acknowledges the risk and accepts up front the possible consequences without contingency. In the previous example, the customer may say, "All right, then we will have to work overtime to meet our business deadlines and move at the same time, if that is how it works out."
- *Going into denial.* The worst possible outcome is when you discuss a significant risk with the potential victim who dismisses the probability of its occurrence, or your forecast of dire consequences if it transpires. If improperly handled, this situation can explode at your feet. In this case, Murphy's law is reaffirmed and the victim not only blames you for the disaster, but will allege that you failed to yell, "Duck!"

5.4 IDENTIFYING RISK

It is therefore critical that you get a buy-in from the potentially impacted party or parties. This must include not just the probability of harm, but also the prognostication of impact. By the way, it is a politically beneficial move for you to induce them to come up with the potential consequences of risk. You do not want to be solely responsible for this risk assessment for two reasons:

1. You want them fully engaged in this process, preferably in partnership. After all, they should know their world better than you do and, therefore, be in a better position than you to determine the degree of risk associated with any issue you elevate to them. Further, once

engaged, they may come up with nuances, or worse, in response to your initial warning.

2. Should it be determined that an indemnification or remediation plan is appropriate, it will require logistics, resources, and funding your project may lack. The worst position in which you can find yourself is for the potential victim to say, "You are the one creating this mess, so you have to figure out how to fix it, pay for it, and get it done. Call me when you are finished." This condition only compounds the likelihood of damage, so it is one you want to avoid.

The point is made in Chapter 13, which is dedicated to handling customers and beneficiaries, that it is better to take your pain up front, when it is smaller, than to dodge issues until they become unavoidable. This is definitely one of those times. If you get any pushback at all, escalate your thoughts on the situation as far up both food chains (yours and theirs) as you dare and in very clear terms. Let them come back at you quibbling over probability and consequences. In fact, it is great if they do, because you have managed to drag them into the arena where they must negotiate.

However, do not make this a "gotcha" exercise. It is your obligation to educate the potential victim (who could be your own boss, by the way) and make sure they get it. I recently went through a server move planning session with a customer. Regarding the disaster recovery (DR) component of the application platform, there was a strong possibility that when the DR platform was moved to a data center in another state, the DR instance of the database could not be synchronized with the production platform for the better part of a week. It took an hour to walk the user through this, which is why I will not belabor the details The point is that our DR engineer took the time to make sure the customer really understood this scenario. As of this writing, we are waiting for the customer's response regarding the acceptability of this risk, so we do not know what the outcome will be. Still, we are comfortable that our warnings were heard, and are thus confident that whatever happens next, no one will be able to claim ignorance or surprise should that ship run aground.

It is not our decision whether or not the DR data lagging production by nearly a week is acceptable. We do know that the fix would be complex and, therefore, do not want to pursue that until the customer has the opportunity to analyze the risk. Most risks can be obviated by the generous application of money, but how many are worth unconditional exorbitance? As project manager, you definitely want to force the impacted party to make that call. That way, it is easier to ask them to dip into their own pocketbook for any additional costs. It has been my experience that perceived risk is indirectly proportional to the number of dollars the customer is on the hook for to make that threat go away.

In this DR example, the problem was caused not by the move but the manner and means by which the customer managed a several hundred-gigabyte database. In other words, their technology introduced most of the risk associated with the move. A more robust platform would not have created this exposure. As project manager, you must ask why you should take on a beneficiary's problem as your own when you were simply tasked with relocating their platform, not solving the shortcomings of their technology or process.

This is the kind of "scope creep" that frequently emerges from the beneficiary community. Simply put, the project manager exposes potential issues with the legacy environment, and the beneficiary expects the project manager to:

• Provide the resources to resolve those issues
• In essence, assume financial ownership for preexisting risk

The lesson to be applied here is the recognition that projects often accept these responsibilities long before the breadth, depth, cost, and pain of such a commitment is fully understood, at least by the project manager.

5.5 MURPHY'S LAW

Now that the process of identifying risk has been put into context, it is time to look at how you go about sniffing out these potential sore points in your project. Risk can be driven by the nature of your project, by your environment, or by the technology you are delivering. Risk can also come out of left field, as the stolen computer shipment proves. The September 11, 2001 tragedy hurt my project in several ways, some of which took months of recovery. Mother Nature chips in every now and then, too, such as the time I experienced a painful delay when a crucial shipment could not leave an airport socked in by a hurricane.

Having said all this, however, should not cause great alarm or a defeatist attitude. Being prepared to deal with risk is a state of mind. You know that troubling events or conditions are bound to emerge on big projects, and you want to be ready for them. This state of readiness includes crisp anticipation, reacting with alacrity, and having the confidence that you and your team will do the right thing, even if you have to think outside the box (i.e., get creative big time).

The key is to understand your exposures. No one, apparently, was in the position to predict the murderous destruction at the World Trade Center and the obstacles it immediately presented to those of us who were working projects in or proximate to that killing field.[2] As a professional worrywart, I have since added loss of existing land-based and wireless telecommunications as well as physical access to buildings and their computing

Exhibit 3. Questions for Uncovering Project Risk

1. What if the new deliverable does not work as advertised?
2. What if it works poorly?
3. What if I cannot deliver everything on Day One?
4. What if a key technologist or team lead becomes indisposed?
5. What if a key technologist or team lead is unproductive?
6. What if we do not have enough skilled resource?
7. What if we run out of money?
8. What if a vendor misses a shipment or some other key deliverable?
9. What if a vendor runs out of money?
10. What if a key vendor employee leaves the project?
11. What if a key new product or upgrade does not perform as advertised?
12. What if we cannot get access to a site whenever we need to?
13. What if we cannot get access to a process whenever we need to?
14. What if a dependency does not pan out?

---

devices as risks to investigate on all future projects. Downtown Manhattan was a mess for weeks after September 11. It is amazing how well thousands of technicians and engineers performed in those terrible days.

As stated, there are risks specific to the technologies. Their discovery was addressed in Chapter 3. In addition, I have a process for mining projects for risk. What I am doing, of course, is looking for things that could break. I go about this by asking "What if?" questions of myself and everyone else associated with the project. Risk has already been divided into the three classes of project, beneficiaries, and the corporation, so let us cycle through the categories before moving on to the next steps.

5.6 UNCOVERING PROJECT RISK

Project risk is defined as the class of events or conditions that can directly impact project success in a negative, if not disastrous, manner. Asking the generic questions listed in Exhibit 3 can expose the vast majority of them.

As with this class and the others, the questioning process does not end with a simple response to any of these questions. Having an open if somewhat skeptical mind and following up with common sense is very important. Refer to number nine in Exhibit 3, which ruminates on the potential consequences of a vendor running out of money. It happens. The scenario this question invokes is as follows.

You have assigned certain deliverables to Vendor X, who is small or unknown to you. Truthfully, you cannot guarantee that they have the muscle to hang in there with you should the project prove more complex or time-consuming than originally planned. If Vendor X disappears from the scene, how would you complete those deliverables? If they are proprietary, you face a different set of challenges than if Vendor X is basically providing staff augmentation services to free up your own experts or technicians in that particular information technology (IT) process or discipline.

Having gone this far, if I felt that the risk of this vendor's demise is severe enough, it may cause me to question the benefit in using them at all, or worse yet, wondering why we are using that particular process or technology they are allegedly providing to the project. If you take this approach, you may actually feel responsible for pushing back on the designers or other team members in such a way that the need for the vendor is eliminated, or the intended process is replaced or at least modified to the degree that the risk becomes far more palatable.

Ultimately, risk analysis, like practically every other cognitive duty on your plate, goes to the basic principle of examining assumptions to see how firm your foundations truly are. It is very important that you can envision worst-case scenarios such that you can:

- Honestly evaluate the deleterious impact on your project
- Accurately handicap the probability of such risk actually coming to pass

This can be quite gruesome. Few people I know savor the prospect of imagining dire circumstances dispassionately and coolly imagining how to bail themselves out. Unfortunately, I cannot think of any other effective way to do this. I recommend that you sit with the appropriate stakeholders for each potential risk, as outlined in this chapter, and ask them the questions detailed in this section and the next two.

5.7 UNCOVERING BENEFICIARY RISK

This class of risk includes those potential disruptions to the beneficiary environment caused by your project, or project dependencies driven from the beneficiary's end. Needless to say, when addressing customers and beneficiaries, you may feel the need to be a little more tactful with them regarding some of the following questions. Some of these may not be relevant, either; however, once the question gets asked, ensure that answers are commensurate with the perceived risk.

Before proceeding with this set of questions, I need to add a cautionary word. Be wary of responses from this constituency such as "We will take care of it," or "That is our problem." Although we all love it when others take ownership and thus lighten our burden, I would not take those answers to these questions as the final word on the topic. You may feel the need to be apologetic by following up on such statements, but it is very dangerous not to. I take such professions in this context as being blown off because the response suggests denial or lassitude, and does not prove to me that anything proactive will actually get done. So, if I believe a risk is sig-

Exhibit 4. Questions for Uncovering Beneficiary Risk

- What if the new deliverable does not work?
- What if it works poorly?
- What if I cannot deliver everything on Day One?
- What if the beneficiary provides inadequate data or requirements?
- What if we cannot access beneficiary resources whenever we need to?
- What if the beneficiary lacks funding for its project deliverables?
- What if the beneficiary has conflicting production freezes?
- What if the beneficiary has to change our schedule?
- What if a vendor controlled by a beneficiary does not perform?
- What if a key new product or upgrade does not perform as advertised?
- What if we cannot get access to a site whenever we need to?
- What if we cannot get access to a process whenever we need to?
- What if a dependency does not pan out?

Exhibit 5. Questions for Uncovering Corporate Risk

- What if network freezes or change control issues occur?
- What if required tools (e.g., virus scanners) crash new applications?
- What if our rollout creates security holes (e.g., open ports on servers)?
- What if our rollout introduces problems in the network?
- What if our rollout creates conflicts on the desktop?

nificant enough, I walk through them through the scenario despite their protests, perhaps softening my aggression by stating, "I want to be sure that everyone is comfortable with how we will all behave should this risk come to pass." Exhibit 4 lists effective questions to use for uncovering potential risks to the beneficiary community.

5.8 UNCOVERING CORPORATE RISK

This class of risks is associated with potential impact on the overall environment and associated processes as a result of your project. I have separated them from the other two classes because in the process of researching them you will probably get drawn into discussions with operations, security, or standards police who otherwise are unknown to you or not heretofore involved in your project. As project manager, you are likely unaware of, or at least unenlightened, in the technical, operational, or political issues revolving around these types of risks. The questions in Exhibit 5 lay the groundwork for discovering potential corporate risk.

5.9 WHAT TO DO WITH THESE QUESTIONS

I do not tout these lists as all-inclusive. Furthermore, I am confident you can think of additional or improved inquiries. That is fine with me. Some questions might not apply to your project, whereas others may be used several times when you have multiple deliverables, for instance, or have unconnected beneficiary groups to deal with. It should also be mentioned that these questions are generic, meaning they cover areas of concern that require specificity based on the project at hand. Also, an exhibit in Chapter 7 documents most of the common contributors to date slippage, which in turn is a key, if generic, risk. You might want to refer to that list before heading off on your risk scavenger hunt.

I need to make additional comments in this space. In the wedding reception scenario, everything was covered — everything except for the most important piece. This piece is the articulation of risk and why it must be avoided, which in this case is the fact that it is simply unacceptable to expose the reception to inclement weather. Many items need to be protected: outfits, hairdos, the wedding cake, table settings, and the band or DJ's expensive electronics. As you look for risk in IT projects, you need to understand how to imagine unacceptable scenarios, and work backward to the events that precipitate them, or at least serve as warning signs. With weddings, it is simple. A soaked bride, or Aunt Millie slipping on a wet dance floor and cracking her hip, are clearly unacceptable conditions that are easily prevented by indemnifying the venue, including its infrastructure and denizens, against rain, standing puddles, slippery grass, and spattering mud.

The best way to produce similar project analyses is to trace the project's critical path, or review the implementation strategy you built after applying the thoughts from the previous chapter. The critical path consists of a half dozen or so milestones with fixed dates. Once you identify the key deliverables that contribute to each milestone, you can examine each of these for potential "breaking points."

Looking at dependencies is another great way to uncover risk. In fact, it is my personal favorite. I have been on many projects where a risk was based on something beyond our control happening, or not happening, in a specific way, and by a crucial date. In one of my more complex projects, we built a new corporate campus. The company used two well-known operating systems for local area network (LAN)-based computing. The forward-looking engineers on our team wanted to eliminate the use of one manufacturer's legacy protocol in the new site. This LAN communications protocol was quite the thing in its day but was in the process of being replaced by Transmission Control Protocol/Internet Protocol (TCP/IP) in the normal course of product evolution. The problem was that many of the older applications in the environment resided on servers that used the older protocol. The risk was if we blocked the older protocol from entering the new site across the wide area network (WAN), users moving in would be unable to log into applications resident on the older-protocol servers at other sites. I should mention that this organization had many thousands of servers, many, if not most, of which could reasonably be assumed to still use this older protocol.

Therefore, I worried about disgruntled, unproductive users in our new site (i.e., those users at our new site wishing to log into one of these older servers found elsewhere in this corporation's far-flung network). Engineering informed me that there was another project afoot to update all servers to the IP version, and that this should be accomplished before our new site opened, so this protocol issue would be moot.

I said, "Great!" to their faces, but privately was not so reassured, because, quite frankly, I did not believe that this server upgrade project could possibly be completed worldwide before we opened our new site. My view of the risk was that an executive visiting our site would want to log into some legacy server in Geneva or Sydney and be unsuccessful. This is the very type of client you would not choose to disappoint. So, we took the coward's way out and allowed the old protocol in our new site. We received no complaints related to this protocol issue, so I was happy. Further, our conservatism was vindicated because as of this writing, some 2 years later, the protocol upgrade project had long since been cancelled, well short of completion.

As dependency risks go, this is not the most exciting story, but it is relevant when you consider how the issue came up in the first place. During the project design phase, we were having a technology review with the engineers. I mentioned having read somewhere that they intended to "turn off," or filter out, the old protocol at our new site. Having long since lost my aversion to sounding ignorant, I asked what the benefit was in doing this. The answer was that this legacy protocol tied up bandwidth with lots of network chatter, and the manufacturer was phasing it out.

That sounded good. Still, I asked what to me is an obvious project management question. "Is there any downside to keeping the old protocol out of the site?"

"Well," I was told, "Anyone at the new site trying to access a server using the legacy protocol somewhere else in the corporate world would be unable to do so. Unless, of course, they called the Help Desk, and a change control was issued for the router filter tables, a process that normally takes 3 to 5 days to complete."

I may be technically dense, but somehow this solution did not strike me as being wholly aligned with the customer service model, particularly when contemplating the aforementioned visiting executive needing access to a legacy protocol box on the far side of the globe.

5.10 THE COST OF RISK MANAGEMENT

At some point, risk planning needs a financial context. This can be played in two ways, assuming, of course, that the risk is significant to one or more project stakeholders.

- *Buy insurance.*You pay a premium, for instance, $1000 a year for full coverage of your automobile for liability, theft, collision, and medical risk that could cost you millions if you had to pay those bills out of pocket. In the project world, you may similarly decide to spend additional sums up front in the hope of avoiding a geometrically higher cost should that risk come to pass. Renting a tent for the wedding reception fits this category. In the real IT world, examples of this strategy include bringing on additional consultants to get a better comfort level that programming will be done in time or buying swing servers to make server relocation projects less prone to production outages than would be the case with "hot cut" moves.
- *Save money for a rainy day.*You may determine that the best way to deal with a risk is to allocate money to fix the problem should it occur, but do nothing else about the potential problem in the interim. That is an appropriate strategy under some conditions, but it would be great to have the money if you actually needed it for that purpose. You may get an increase in funding, or you may chose to cut back on discretionary expenditures to escrow those contingency funds. In one project, we did just that by canceling a "nice to have" deliverable. The savings were earmarked for loading up on temporary resources that we were pretty sure we would have to deploy at the 11th hour. Given that this particular risk was paying an enormous late penalty fee, reallocating funds to obviate that sanction was an easy choice to make.

Of course, by the time each person raises his or her hand for risk mitigation money no matter what its basis is, your budget is most certainly not up to the task. As a result, decisions must be made on which risks truly deserve funding, and which will have to be dealt with some other way should they come to pass. Years ago, I was exposed to an interesting, if simple, manner of evaluating risk from this perspective:

- Estimate the cost associated with remediation (or damage control)
- Multiply that by the probability of its occurrence

To illustrate this, suppose the remediation of an identified risk costs $100,000 for engineering, hardware, and software, and that the probability we would have to invoke that Plan B is 25 percent. Then, the risk value of this scenario comes out to $100,000 \times 25$ percent = $25,000.

You can perform this calculation for all presumed risks, then rank them against each other to help prioritize your risk planning, at least from a budgetary perspective. Of course, the problem with this approach is if you use it at the office but left your common sense and political acumen at home that day, you could make some very strange decisions. For instance, one could make a compelling case, particularly after September 11, that if the data center vaporized, we would lose a billion dollars of productivity and customer good will.[3] Quantifying this risk as being discussed would yield a risk value of $10 million ($1,000,000,000 × 1 percent). This number would no doubt be far higher than any other calculation for your project, even though its occurrence is unlikely, September 11 notwithstanding.

There is a more useful way to apply this algorithm. Let us look at the data center loss another way. Suppose, as previously alleged, that the "smoking hole" would result in a loss of $1 billion in productivity and customer good will (i.e., business), and that the probability of this happening is 1 percent. The math tells us $1,000,000,000 × 1 percent = $10,000,000.

Ask yourself if it is possible to provide disaster recovery for that data center for $10 million. In other words, could you build a mirrored site, rent processing power at a vendor site, or duplicate the mission critical applications several hundred miles away for that $10 million? The answer may be yes or no, but you can see how this clarifies the risk assessment conversation.

Maybe, once you drill down, it would cost twice that much (i.e., $20 million). So be it. Document the results of this analysis and hand it back to the potential victims. Let them decide whether kicking in an additional $10 million makes sense to them. Be sure they understand that without that support you are restricted in what you can do, and what the likely consequences would be to the user community. In other words, tell them what risk you could mitigate for $10 million or whatever number your analysis yields. Keep in mind that any significant risk ultimately belongs to the business, not the project, so there is no reason you should be left to tangle with this on your own. If the customer or beneficiary feels the project should carry the financial burden, then you need to draw on your management's ability to negotiate with their management, especially if this conversation turns ridiculous or nasty, which it often does.

Present your analysis and let them make the call, but do not do that by tossing it over the wall to them. Instead, I recommend the approach of saying, "Bill, I think if such and such is done, the impact to your organization is basically neutralized. The problem is that I do not have the $100,000 (or $10 million) it would take to make this problem go away. Can we talk further about the need to address this and how to make up any funding shortfalls that decision would create?"

This last statement falls in the category I call "chuck and duck," (i.e., something you cringe in advance of saying because you anticipate grief in return). This would be one of those times as a project manager that you get to tell a beneficiary that your project is going to cost his organization time, money, or pain. That may sound hypocritical if not mercenary, but these things happen in the corporate world every day. Besides, chances are that you personally did not create the risk and, further, that it is the tenuous or unforgiving environment in which your project labors that is largely to blame. Take the approach that you are the good guy trying to minimize collateral damage, not create it.

5.11 NEXT STEPS IN RISK PLANNING

One thing should be made clear at this point. Some risk can be identified and eliminated by changing your plans, be they technical (design), logistical (implementation strategy), or user-oriented (training). This is intelligent planning. Keep in mind that Plan Bs are usually but not always contingent actions that will be invoked under potential but not certain "wrong turns." You can also build some flexibility into the main project plan, such as doing a proof of concept pilot, or phased rollouts, as a means of ensuring checkpoints with adequate recovery time built into the plan should the undesirable or unthinkable happen.

Writing a Plan B should not be as tough as writing an essay good enough to get into an Ivy League university. It is a simple business proposal. Based on doing the legwork recommended to this point, you and the potential victim have:

• Identified a risk requiring action
• Described the nature and potential cost of that action
• Defined the event or condition that would trigger that action

5.12 PLAN B STRATEGIES

We will review the construction of Plan Bs in a minute. Before we do, let us take a peek at the traditional strategies used to prevent or react to Murphy's Law as presented in Exhibit 6. You are probably familiar with most of them.

Three things should be clear from this discussion:

1. In the complex project world, the cost of Plan Bs is quite dear.
2. All require detailed preparation.
3. Long lead times may be associated with them.

This brings us to the next important Plan B consideration.

5.13 PLAN B TRIGGERS

There must be a trigger, an event or circumstance, that everyone agrees causes Plan B to kick in. This is also known as the "go/no go" decision

Exhibit 6. Plan B Strategies

Plan B Strategy	Description
Pilot (proof of concept)	Instead of rolling out everything to 5000 Metro users or to all 200 sites, start out with a small, manageable sample. Set realistic goals and test parameters that allow you to gauge whether or not the implementation strategy works as intended. Engage beneficiaries from the planning phase forward.
Phased rollout	This is a natural extension of the pilot concept. Users are "converted" to the new network or application in measured segments or modules, not "flash cut." This gives you the time to measure success and react.
Day One versus Day Two	It makes sense not to rebuild the whole world at once. If you are remodeling your home, would you demolish bathrooms and the kitchen at the same time and try to live there? Identify any deliverables that can be pushed off until Day Two.
Backing out	In one major project, we rolled out laptops to hundreds of users, but left their old desktop PCs in place for a week while we tested new machine functionality. The thought was if we ran into issues, the old PC could be reconnected so the production user could carry on while the new laptop was reconfigured. Back-out strategies can be much grander in scope or scale, such as turning the old routers back on or reverting to the legacy payroll system.
Belt and suspenders	In the IP Telephone effort featured throughout the book, we wired the new site to accommodate both IP Telephone and traditional PBX voice technology in the event that the newer IP Telephone technology did not pan out. Although expensive, the cost was rationalized by the awful prospect of a voice outage impacting thousands of users.
Alternates	This strategy can be applied to facilities, computing platforms, network connectivity, resource, or vendors depending on the risk at hand. I once contracted a service bureau to process time-sensitive data to my specifications to meet a potential shortfall in the in-house development of an application to process millions of records as the front end to a complex mainframe accounting process. This was neither trivial nor cheap, but it was smart.

point. It can be as critical to Plan B as the actual planned actions. We exited the previous section with the phrase "long lead times." Suppose, as in the last strategy described in Exhibit 6 ("Alternates"), we need to consider engaging a different team, renting new space, or arranging for processing data a different way. These are practical and common alternate actions you find in Plan Bs. Invoking them probably adds expense, which you can thumbnail at a cost equal to the cost of the deliverable or condition being "replaced" before drilling down into the detail.

It takes time to get alternate floor space to address a data center or end-user facility issue, provision an alternate high bandwidth circuit into the site, or engage a service bureau. Lead times could be 3 months or more, particularly if the product, service, or resource is constrained, or contracts are required. That being the case, the worst thing about these types of "cures" is that once you think you may need to use one of them, you pretty much have to go ahead and implement them. This, in turn, could mean that you have to cough up hundreds of thousands of dollars months in advance of actually knowing whether you need to invoke that costly Plan B or not. If the lead time is that long, what choice do you have? Of course, that brings the budget back into play. If the financial hit is onerous enough, other harpoons may soon fill the air, but to avoid doing the right thing because you fear getting a bloody nose suggests that perhaps it is time for you to entertain a career change.

I previously alluded to the Plan B trigger as an event or condition that, once detected, "triggers" or kick starts a Plan B. This precipitating event depends, of course, on the project and the risk that your Plan B addresses. Nearly any such instance in the IT world can be tagged as "readiness," however, as in "If such and such is not complete by September 16, then we will invoke Plan B." Other instances may be cited as well. Testing may be a trigger if threshold levels are not met in terms of performance, throughput, error rate, and so on. Again, this will depend on the nature of your mission.

Suffice it to say that, similar to success metrics, Plan B triggers should be as clearly and finitely defined well in advance of the potential requirement to invoke them. There should always be a human fail-safe, of course, like that last finger on the ballistic missile launch button. In the absence of this precision, you will likely be faced with endless hand-wringing and debate down to the wire, particularly if the money has not yet been spent or weekend hours are at stake.

5.14 SAMPLE TRIGGER

One of the stories woven throughout the book concerns the implementation of IP Telephone we built out at a new campus. To summarize the roll-out from a Plan B perspective, there was concern that the technology that was relatively new at the time might not scale well to the campus. As a consequence, we decided to design and implement the infrastructure for both IP Telephone and private branch exchange (PBX) services, the latter being the telephone system technology normally installed in corporate sites. We developed a series of trigger test parameters and selected a date by which we had to decide whether to proceed with IP Telephone, or pull in our wings and implement the safer PBX platform. The go/no go decision would be based on several issues, including how several similar sites at other companies were faring, the results of our ongoing pilot testing, and so forth. As a result, the voice portion of our plan was akin to Exhibit 7. Notice how far the trigger date was in advance of "production day." Details will

Exhibit 7. Building a Trigger Date (i.e., Go/No Decision) into Voice Project Schedule

Oct.	Nov.	Dec.	Jan.	Feb.	Mar.	Apr.	May	June	July	Aug.	Sept.
					Trigger Date	Trigger tests false. Proceed with IP Telephony rollout.				Station reviews and testing	Turn up into production
IP telephony implementation for Voice services is under way, though PBX infrastructure is prepared should trigger test lead to cancellation of IP						Trigger tests true. Implement PBX in lieu of IP Telephony.					

vary from project to project, but this is an approach you should not hesitate to adopt on any high-risk, high-venture implementations.

5.15 PULLING YOUR PLAN B TOGETHER

It appears that now we have agreed on an action plan to address a risk that should be avoided at all costs or would, at the very least, need some deodorant. We have agreed under what circumstances we would bring that action plan to life, which implies a scenario with a date associated with it. Now we have to complete the plan. What is left, you ask? Why, the four worst pieces, of course, which are:

1. Who is going to write the plan?
2. What is the decision point, or trigger, that invokes Plan B?
3. Who is going to do what if the plan is invoked?
4. On whose nickel would this get done?

Funny, when you put it like that, it sounds like any other planning opportunity in the project world. That is what Chapter 6 is all about, in conjunction with Chapter 4, of course, regarding the crafting of the anecdotal implementation strategy prior to throwing names and dates at the wall. I do not want to steal my own thunder, but contingency planning has a funny little twist that deserves one last look.

As a carpenter, if I were asked to build a structure to provide weatherproofing and security for storing materials to be used at a construction site, obviously I would not build the Taj Mahal. Why spend the money and time making it bulletproof for the ages, right? Still, I would probably find its complexity would be uplifted by building codes, insurance and safety considerations, union work rules, site-specific issues (i.e., space and convenience), and so on.

Contingencies in the IT world are not much different. Presumably, whatever you are planning to do, even on a "maybe basis," will be shaped by your real world. Data will be passed across the corporate network, people whose safety is proscribed by corporate liabilities will be temporarily housed, vendors with existing performance clauses will be engaged, and other resources will have to be fed and watered as normal. In other words, from a planning perspective, you are not likely to be free from any of the constraints you would face were your contingency plan the real thing. That increases costs and timeframes, possibly well beyond the "for temporary use only" paradigm originally envisioned. There may not be adequate connectivity, power, or rack space in the computer room for those five extra servers. It may be Thanksgiving, and changes to the network are tough to get approval for because of that traditional year-end freeze; and on and on it goes.

The bottom line is that you will not be able to put off any detailed planning, or hide the potential need to invoke a Plan B from the managers and bean counters who will add many cycles to the process once you turn up the lights. Let us close this thing with an experience from my own recent past.

5.16 SAMPLE PLAN B: A NOT SO WIDE AREA NETWORK

We built a corporate campus that consisted of two buildings side by side with an access road between them. The design called for each building to be a separate node on the corporate backbone. Each site, in other words, was intended to have its own connection to the high-speed fiber optic corporate network, or cloud, to which the other corporate sites were attached. This is best practice for network design — the strategy being that each building has an independent WAN connection and thus is not dependent on the other building, in case its WAN connection dies for whatever reason.

The plan called for turning up the first building in late spring, with the "B" building coming online somewhere near Halloween. It was a good plan that suited the move-in schedules of beneficiaries quite nicely and gave the telecom teams adequate time to do all their work in both buildings. Building A came up quite nicely, in fact, a week ahead of schedule. Not long after that, we learned that there was absolutely no way that the B building would come up at Halloween due to issues beyond our control. In fact, our telecom team lead learned, after considerable investigation, that instead of coming up in early November, January was a far more realistic date for Building B. That slippage was totally unacceptable from the beneficiary relocation standpoint, because we needed a minimum of 45 days for network element burn-in between the day WAN connectivity was achieved and the first wave of new beneficiaries showed up in the lobby of Building B. Because the move-in dates were nonnegotiable, we needed to come up with a snappy Plan B, and pretty quickly at that, given the long lead times of this sort of work.

What to do? Given market conditions and existing contracts, we were precluded from going to an alternate vendor. So, it did not take us long to make the only sane decision available to us: to connect the two buildings by running some mighty expensive fiber underneath the street separating buildings A and B. We also had to add conduits in the second building so as not to hog the space required in existing pipes once the "real" network connection was ready to be made. Exhibit 8 is a very simple look at the story in pictures.

The network guys did a great job of coming up with a design that would support this "kluge" that had to transport LAN and mainframe traffic, IP

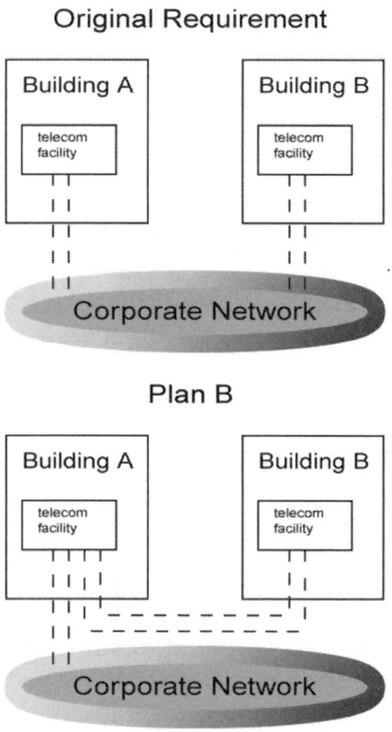

Original Requirement

Plan B

Exhibit 8. Wide Area Network (WAN) Connectivity

Telephone, satellite video, and security data for the turnstiles and end point devices between the two buildings.

We made these decisions in May and started in July because we had to jump through a few other hoops: for instance, street trenching to support the additional cabling required permits, and it had to pass through two other utilities other than the carrier because of right of way issues. Only so many feet of trenching could be dug each day for reasons I still do not comprehend. And, of course, the network and phone system had been designed and all components already bought, so we had to buy more switches and routers. Needless to say, we accrued significant incremental costs to implement Plan B.

This is a great example of the degree of difficulty associated with high-risk contingency plans. I would like to tell you that this Plan B had been cooked up a year before we needed it, when the project was in the planning phase. That would not be truthful. We did discuss this as a potential risk months before we had to react, however, so we can claim adequate prescience on this one.

Our Plan B worked. The move deadlines were met, so the outside world remained in the dark as to the effort and expense required to keep the plan whole. Eventually, we were able to implement the original design. We recovered most of the additional expense by "selling" the additional routers and switches to another business unit. That was a beautiful thing!

5.17 CONCLUSION

Large projects present many opportunities for failure. Keep referring to your target-state document and understand the business implications of each component being cancelled. Despite what some people might think, especially those project team members with a vested interest in any given requirement, the survival of your organization simply does not rest on all deliverables going in on time, if at all. If a rational analysis suggests that the implementation or impact of such a deliverable is problematic, try to delay or cancel its rollout with management's informed blessing. If I did not know better, I would guess that the phrase "Discretion is the better part of valor" was coined by a mortally wounded project manager.

I want to close this chapter by highlighting a point previously discussed regarding the specific risk of a vendor going out of business. It is probable that a thorough risk analysis will lead to some changes in your plan, whether the impact is on the target state or the schedule. One of the challenges in this business is that one can generally anticipate a huge gap emerging between the original assumptions made about scope and what the final outcome turns out to be. An enlightened project manager knows this going in, and leverages it as the design heads toward a plan everyone then pitches in to build. Thus, one must conclude that risk analysis is a key and final prerequisite to the "planning process."

Notes

1. Do not ask!
2. All of us were far more devastated by the loss of life and property, but that is another story.
3. Even though insurance would eventually pay to reconstruct the lost site.

Chapter 6
Writing the Plan

Now that the project vision has been sketched out, it is time to complete the detailed blueprint. To be blunt about it, most people dislike formalized project plans and the activities associated with creating and managing them. As we move from project to project, we repeatedly find a lack of enthusiasm for this process. Reasons for this range from not wanting to commit to dates, to the fact that it just is not easy to build a fathomable plan for a complex, multideliverable project.

Although you need this plan well in advance of implementation time, you might feel that if you do not dummy up one yourself, you will receive little of value from team leads. You could be right about that, but there is much more to the story. This chapter addresses this vexing challenge.

6.1 PLANNING PROCESS OBJECTIVES

First, I want make sure we have a good understanding of the planning process before worrying about whose plan it is. As you go forward from whiteboard diagrams, e-mails, and other documentation, keep in mind that:

- A plan is more than a schedule or Gantt chart.
- What most people call "the plan" is really "the schedule."
- Do not start scheduling until implementation strategies and Plan Bs are done.
- Task owners must buy into their assigned tasks, dates, and dependencies.
- The plan focuses on the results the project team was engaged to achieve.

Exhibit 1 presents the three outcomes you are trying to achieve as a result of the planning process.

These are lofty goals. Unfortunately, all the academic training in the world will not make you a competent planner because building a great schedule is largely a function of two things:

1. How well you have followed the script outlined thus far in this book, particularly in terms of getting your teams to do the detailed analyses that complex projects require
2. How well you understand the project and what steps you are about to take as project manager

Exhibit 1. Planning Process Objectives

- You are confident that the plan covers all requirements.
- The plan has buy-in from the team and senior management.
- You can manage the project with the plan.

Exhibit 2. Project Planning Tasks

- Understand your requirements completely.
- Write an implementation strategy for each key requirement.
- Roll those strategies into your master plan.
- Integrate your Plan Bs as described at the end of Chapter 5.
- Ensure that the critical path is the backbone of your schedule.
- Be as detailed as required to effectively manage the project.

Most important, the right plan is one that ultimately comes from you. That great piece of work reflects your critical path accurately and truthfully, and is the roadmap you use to make sure you do not get lost, even if the team contends they know better than you where the project is going.

6.2 SIX STEPS TOWARD SUCCESSFUL PLANNING

Exhibit 2 documents the process. To be effective, it must be iterative, meaning you will cycle through it several times. This is because planning is done in parallel with the requirements and design phases, so to some degree you are trying to hit a moving target. Exhibit 2 lists the steps.

It is not uncommon for project managers and team leads to essentially rush straight to the work, no matter what managed to find its way onto paper. You must guard against this. It is a good idea to approach any planning gaps as a teacher, cheerleader, and mentor, however, instead of with disappointment or frustration because, as mentioned, people really are uncomfortable with the process. To do that, you need to be okay with the process yourself. Let us review what we have accomplished thus far in our project narrative, and then take the next steps that will result in a superior project calendar:

- We developed our requirements and specifications (Chapter 2).
- The technology solution was designed and validated (Chapter 3).
- We wrote an implementation strategy for each solution (Chapter 4).
- We accounted for all identifiable risk (Chapter 5).

All that remains on our plate is the scheduling of tasks required to get the work done. Obviously, the tasks have to be identified and owners assigned, but at the high level that is already done. Implementation strategies and Plan Bs provide all the high-level tasks. You have been working with team leads for months on these plan components, so ownership is pretty well settled. Your rolled up implementation strategy should have identified dependencies and project milestones as well.

So what is the next step? No, do not launch that project planning application on your desktop just yet, tempting though that might be. Those planning tools have their merits, but there is a downside to them as well. They are wonderful tools for documenting a well-thought-out schedule, but far too confusing to use as the key means of understanding what that schedule should be.

6.3 STARTING THE SCHEDULE BUILD

This is not to say that if you follow the process advanced in this book, scheduling is easy — it is not. In fact, let me warn you that if you wait until you are drafting a schedule to figure out how everything falls together both logically and from a calendar perspective, chances are the resulting plan will be a jumble of tasks that is practically indecipherable and essentially useless to anyone other than the plan's author.

Where you begin is with your rolled-up implementation strategy. The idea is to take its main components and lay them out with only one or two levels of detail. Critical dates are assigned to these plan segments, and any key relationships, such as dependencies or linked task dates, are identified at this time. At this point, you may only have a plan with a few dozen "tasks." That is most desirable in that the relative dearth of tasks makes it easier to maneuver major deliverables and dates without the encumbrance of all that detail.

This process should start out as a paper and pencil exercise, and will be illustrated with the Vendor Management project described in Chapter 4. That initiative's rolled-up implementation strategy had four components, three of which will be referenced throughout the rest of this chapter:

1. Facilities had a primary site build-out including a data center, a call center, and most of the operations support staff. A secondary, re-mote site was specified for the telecommunications supplier support staff. The backup disaster recovery (DR) data center was to be housed there, too.
2. The operations deliverable consisted of developing a staffing and operations model, hiring to that model, and implementing it.
3. The technology component consisted of a functional design to support the statement of work (SOW), including order processing, publishing specified data to an internal Web site, and automation of supplier communications. There was also an infrastructure component featuring requirements for networking, two data centers, a call center, and disaster recovery (DR).

At this point, I find it incumbent to draw up the project like a process flow. That way, you can really visualize and thus validate the logic behind your implementation strategy. What logic? Well, for instance, do dates work? Are you relying on a single resource or team to do too much, or be in too many places at once? Also, as you look at the project from a logistical perspective, you begin to think about key issues like lead times. That is why you start your actual scheduling on paper with only a few moving parts because it is best to validate the big picture before trying to fit in all the little pieces.

The first schedule looked like the one in Exhibit 3.[1]

Keep in mind that now we are discussing the main project schedule from the project manager's viewpoint. Presumably, team leads are developing detailed plans for specific requirements while we are looking at the big picture. This is mentioned to give perspective to the unsettling comments about to be made about this first attempt at scheduling this extravaganza. After I made this first pass in real life, I was quite unnerved. I immediately felt compelled to find out whether team leads were addressing some painfully obvious gaps.

My problem was that I could not see how all this was going to come together. When I cast my mind's eye on the call center component of target state, I saw a room full of help desk analysts and other support personnel logging into terminals, looking things up with the technology, and conversing with end users and service providers via telephone or e-mail. After all, scope calls for this. The troubling question is: where does the schedule show when this call center vision will be constructed? If you look back at the schedule, you will discover that it does not. What, in fact, we have just uncovered is a scheduling dependency between the technology build-out and call center target state, not to mention the fact that I failed to document that in the first cut.

Speaking of the operations staff, it seems reasonable to assume that they will need training on the technology, as well as the call center procedures they will be asked to perform. When you talk about training, you think of curriculum, an instructor, a classroom full of local area network (LAN)-attached personal computers (PCs), and possibly other teaching aids as well. When does the schedule indicate this will transpire? It does not.

Our solution dictates two data centers with a DR procedure. That means that either the two sites are connected to allow data refreshes to the back-up computer systems, or we overnight backup tapes from the primary site to the secondary one. When will that design be complete? What are the scheduling implications of buying a T1 circuit to connect the two sites versus mailing tapes as the DR strategy?

Exhibit 3. First Draft: Vendor Management Project Plan

Month	1	2	3	4	5	6	7	8	9
Facilities	Call center fit out				Incorporate technology as available				
		Main data center fit out		Complete data center installations, connectivity			DR test	Move into full production	Move into full production
		Backup data center fit out		Complete backup data center installations, connectivity				Move into full production	Move into full production
Operations	Staffing plan approved		HR hires against requisitions submitted by program manager						
Technology development		Complete design		Develop and/or integrate hardware and software			Testing		Production
			Hardware, software ordered and installed						
					Call detail reporting service bureau goes live				
		Procurement Web site requirements complete			Develop procurement Web site and review with customer		Complete development and UAT[a]		Production
					Reporting Web site developed and UAT[a]		Testing	Production	
		Develop EDI[b] requirements			Deliverables TBD:[c] assumed rollout in year 2 or 3				

[a]UAT = user acceptance testing
[b]EDI = electronic data interchange
[c]TBD = to be determined

Although one can deduce other issues from the first draft of the Vendor Management schedule, these three should be sufficient to support this section's main thrust. Once again we are reminded that our charge was not to build a handful of finite, stand-alone technologies. Instead, we were tasked with constructing an organization that would be able to perform a specific list of functions described in the contracted SOW. To recap those duties, the target-state business tasks were to:

- Process specific types of orders with clearly identified suppliers.
- Validate subsequent invoices.
- Process them for payment.
- Charge the user for the cost.
- Report on all these activities via a new Web site.
- Provide a second Web site for customer procurement activities.

Indeed, we decided we would need a call center, two data centers, and a technology platform with software and a backup process to execute these duties, but that is the "how" of the project, not the "what." In Chapter 1, requirements were defined as the conditions the project must create to successfully execute project scope. This is the preeminent reality of technical projects, a reality I believe does not adequately drive the "planning process" in most projects because people tend to focus on the "how" often to the exclusion of the "what." I highly recommend another way of looking at this, which is to consider the project "how" to be the technology enablers of target-state business processes, which, in turn, comprise the project "what." Our client often stated that he did not care if we used computers, or monkeys, as long as the business deliverables were turned up complete and on time.

6.4 THE PROJECT PYRAMID

From a planning perspective, you can visualize this in a couple of ways. I prefer the project pyramid. The vendor management pyramid would look like the one displayed in Exhibit 4.

The base represents both the starting point and the foundation of the project. In this case, these are the two locations dictated by the implementation strategy. The main site houses the call center, while the backup site has an operations site plus the backup or DR computing system. The pyramid's "point" represents both the schedule end point and the focal point of the project.

For this part of our project, the focal point is functionality performed by the end users at the call center. The lower layers are the enablers of end-user function. In this case, the enablers are the two applications that run on the supporting infrastucture, i.e., the data center equipment. This would be the LAN, platform, and wide area network (WAN). The term "com-

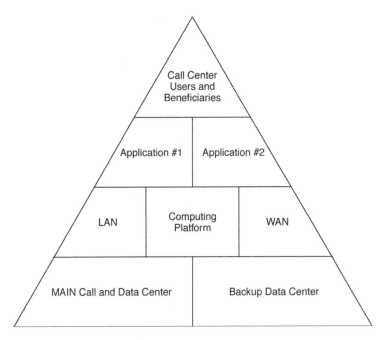

Exhibit 4. Vendor Management Implementation Pyramid

puting platform" indicates the systems, such as computers and tape backup libraries. In essence, the platform supports the applications that empower the end users to do their jobs.

This project had other pyramids separate and distinct from this one. These other pyramids are the two Web sites, where the "point" would be the customer logging in for reports or procurement activities. Two future pyramids, one for automated data transactions with suppliers, the other for the "customer-facing processes" would also have to be derived.

6.5 HOW TO USE THE PYRAMID

Use the pyramid to augment your implementation strategy from a scheduling perspective. Unless your target state is represented on the project calendar, I do not know how you can keep everyone's eye on the ball, including your own. Does that mean that from a scheduling perspective the project proceeds from the bottom of the pyramid to the top? Yes, it does.

The first step is to recognize that we have multiple pyramids that, in concert, cover the entire project. We just counted five pyramids for our vendor management initiative. Each pyramid should have its own independent schedule. It should be linked only to other pyramids for dependen-

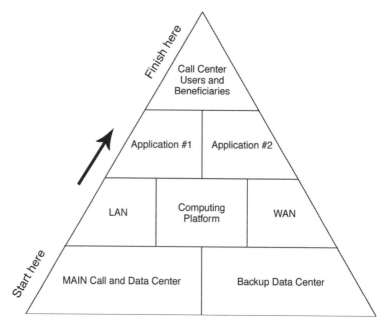

Exhibit 5. Vendor Management Implementation Pyramid Revisited

cies. Two of our pyramids were Web sites built for customers. It stands to reason that they will have to be installed in the data centers at some point, and thus have dependencies on the infrastructure that will include the LAN, WAN, and DR. We will not link them to the call center end user, however, because the "point" of the Web site pyramid is someone else (i.e., the customer/beneficiary). Having said all this, let us go back to the call center end user pyramid and revisit the schedule (see Exhibit 5).

The call center pyramid depicts the following scheduling strategy:

- The two facilities have to be prepped for the end user. This includes office construction, such as cubicles and conference rooms. Computer facilities will also be required. Deliverables include physical security, raised floors, conditioned power, racks, data cabling, and so forth.
- The infrastructure comes next. We need switches, routers, firewalls, and multiplexers for the local area network (LAN) and WAN. The physical computing system, such as servers and tape backups, must be installed in the racks. Then the operating systems, antivirus and monitoring agents, and other system utilities will be installed.
- Our third layer will be the applications used in the call center. This may be purchased and customized, or built from the ground up. Data-

bases, development or support tools, and Web servers may all be required, depending on system design.

- A team of call center and data center personnel will be hired, trained, and assigned to tasks and seats in the two facilities. After some period of orientation and practice, the sites will be open for business.

How do we know all this? The past few pages showed a transition from a technology-oriented schedule to an operations-oriented implementation plan. This change resulted from a variety of sources, including prior experience. Quite naturally, other team members provided significant input, including the client who drove the vision, the sales manager who in conjunction with the client crafted the SOW after winning the request for proposal (RFP) battle, and subject matter experts. Hopefully, the steps documented in previous chapters now make more sense than ever. One must truly understand the ins and outs of projects this complex before attempting to build the "real" schedule. As previously discussed, there is probably just one person on the project team who worries about everything coming together, and that is the project manager.

The next step is to revisit the schedule and change it in a way that better defines the direct path to target state (see Exhibit 6). We are still pushing a pencil around, and the computer is still turned off. For simplicity's sake, let us stay focused on just one site — the main call center/data center facility.

Not that we are finished scheduling the call center pyramid, but we have gotten on the right track compared with earlier in this chapter when practically all we saw was disconnects. Now, we can actually locate seminal events on the schedule, including sequences as well as significant points in time relative to other pyramid components. Although we have not drawn any arrows yet, the dependencies are becoming more obvious. For instance, when you look across the "staffing" line and go up one row, you can see that we have physical workspace available as new hires come on board. If you look at the "operations" row beneath "staffing," you can see that team building and training commences after the recruiting–hiring process is under way.

Also, the applications training component of operations begins as we are completing the installation and testing of the applications. In other words, users are trained in software modules as they come on line. With this project, we did not have the luxury of waiting until everything was done in one area before moving forward with the next steps. We were also aware that in today's workplace, you cannot identify new hires in January, and then tell them they cannot come to work (and get paid) until July. That may work for movie stars, but the rest of us do not live like that. Therefore, because we were bullied into an aggressive schedule, events were phased or staggered as their precursors began showing signs of life.

Exhibit 6. Second Draft Vendor Management Project Plan

Month	1	2	3	4	5	6	7	8	9
Data center	Prepare data center facility (power, raised floors, etc.)		Install WAN, data center LAN, platform		Install and test call center application software, data bases, etc.			Test call center applications	Operations dress rehearsal before production turn up
Call center		Design office space	Order, receive, and install cubicles, office fittings, and furniture		Install LAN, workstations, and phones in call center work space				
Staffing	Complete model			Recruit and hire to staffing model					
Operations		Complete SOW		Develop teams and train in operational requirements			Application training for users		

There is a lot more to be done with the pyramid. Before taking that path, it is important to go through the same exercise with the other pyramids. Again, we are looking for two things: first and foremost is the coherent organization of getting from each pyramid's base to its point, just as we did with the call center pyramid; second, we need to understand dependencies between pyramids as well. The quality, timing, and risk associated with these events need to be identified and scheduled as far in advance as possible.

It was previously mentioned that the two Web applications (reporting and procurement) would eventually have dependencies on the data center and the backup (DR) site. Certainly this is a requirement for final testing before going live. Initial development and testing need not wait for the facilities or the wide area network (WAN) to be available, however, assuming that alternate work facilities are available and convenient while the production environment remains under construction.

6.6 GETTING SERIOUS ABOUT YOUR SCHEDULE

Now that we have gotten a much better handle on the schedule, it is time to review it with team leads to ensure that everyone else agrees with the scheduling logic. These conversations may be difficult for a couple of reasons. Team leads may very well insist that their views of the schedule are better than your big picture, even though you are looking at all aspects of the project compared with their parochial views. You may be way ahead of them in terms of thinking this through. It is also possible that people push back because they do not understand what you are doing. Be patient. Understand that getting everyone on the same page is critical. If you are wrong or missed something, accept appropriate corrections with humility so long as you can be persuaded that you are in error. Again, it could be the critics that are mistaken, not you.

6.7 DRAFTING THE FIRST MASTER SCHEDULE

After these negotiating sessions are complete, it is time for you to go back to your cubicle and put together the first real schedule. You still should be working with a pencil or little pieces of paper with "events" written on them that you can shuffle around your desk or white board. What we are about to do is draft the master schedule, which could also be called "mapping the critical path." When all is said and done, critical path is:

- What you need to understand
- What you have to schedule
- What you want to manage

There may be thousands of tasks, but until you fashion the basic roadmap, your schedule will be twisted and gnarled, like a vine gone crazy on

Exhibit 7. Vendor Management Critical Path

March–April	May–June	July–Sept.	Oct.–Nov.	December
Complete SOW	Complete both facilities Data center infrastructures	Hire and train staff Install and test applications	Operational training and walk through	Open for business

your Gantt chart. I maintain that using such programs add to, instead of reduce, the confusion that is normal at this point in the schedule's evolution.

Our first cut at a critical path for the vendor management project is given in Exhibit 7. Once again, we restricted the view to the main call center and data center to keep this as simple as possible.

To borrow a concept from the data-networking lexicon, critical path is "logical," not "physical." This is the biggest cognitive challenge in scheduling — being able to recognize and handle the flow of a schedule as opposed to the literal, serial nature of tasks defined in a Gantt chart. This is another illustration of why you need to do all this preparatory work manually as opposed to using an automated planning tool. These automated planning tools are fine for documenting tasks and performing some calculations, but they do not lend themselves well to the process in which we are currently immersed.

Each block in Exhibit 7 is a project milestone. The critical path of a project is the journey from the first milestone to the last. Tasks that contribute to each milestone may have dates that are all over the place. For instance, the milestones for starting the call center and data center infrastructure actually begin at the same time the SOW milestone does. From a critical path perspective, however, the SOW must be completed before any other milestones are reached because the final details of the SOW will impact final headcount, for instance, or some data requirements for the applications.

Now that the critical path is identified, it is time to create the detailed project schedule. The first step is to reassemble the team leads and assign the "must start on" and "must complete by" dates. These "must" dates are driven by the milestones. Depending on the nature of each milestone, either or both of the "must" dates should be stipulated. In some cases, for example, either the "start by" or "complete by" date is compelling, while in other cases, both the beginning and ending dates are dictated by the critical path.

These sessions may turn into a negotiation. It definitely requires that everyone's cards get on the table, and timed deliverables are clearly defined and agreed upon. Until now, it is likely that team leads have been thinking along the lines of our first schedule that was driven by functional components as opposed to target state. Once we derived the critical path, however, it is now much more clear what has to be done, and when. It is now up to you to persuade each team lead to absorb these constraints and adjust their schedules accordingly.

You might be surprised by the position I am taking (i.e., suggesting that announcing critical path dates is a potentially controversial or contentious move). Remember, as project manager, it is your critical path, not theirs. Team leads may be working with constrained dates within their "sub-projects" that are milestones for them but not for you. The resulting discourse can be explained by as simple a fact as that they see the whole 9-month project time span as theirs within which they are free to do work as they see fit. That explains why it is up to you to do the analysis on the overall critical path, and then persuade them to dovetail their plans into your schedule. For instance, your analysis made it clear that the physical facilities and information technology (IT) infrastructure for the call center and data center must be complete by the end of Month Four, so that both staff hiring and training, and application installation and testing, can start at the beginning of Month Five.

This latter constraint has another implication as well. If the milestone is "Install and test applications," then the applications have to be ready for installation on Month Five, Day One, whether they are off the shelf, or developed in-house. That means that any procurement, custom coding, data migration, and test planning activities must be successfully completed by Day One, Month Five.

Therefore, the noise level may rise if the application team lead thought he or she had another few months, when user testing and training is set to begin, to get his or her house in order. Never for a moment assume that team leads do not think like that. They do, because they are:

- Busy with many projects
- Understaffed
- Not the best time managers

In any event, they will be quite content to take the extra time if you do not make your scheduling requirements well known and insist on them.

6.8 SELLING THE CRITICAL PATH

You are the project manager, so you need to drive this conversation with the goal that all scheduling conforms to critical path. Further, each team contributing to a critical path event must understand and acknowledge the exact terms and conditions of their milestone deliverables. You should approach this discussion with a negotiator's frame of mind. Up to this point, your conversations with each team lead have been about requirements, risk, and so on, but probably not too detailed about hard dates other than "production day." Now, you may well be saying that you expect some or all of their deliverables months sooner than they had anticipated. Push back should be expected regarding both the accelerated dates and quite possibly the completeness of the advanced deliverables as well.

Let us use the "applications ready for installation and testing" milestone as our model for exploration. You have just informed the applications team lead that his or her "must start by date" is the first day of Month Five. In the best of worlds, the response would be "no problem. All functional requirements will be ready for installation and testing on that date." The worse-case scenario, of course, would be saying, "huh?"

Assuming you find yourself somewhere in between, here is how to proceed. Once again, I leave the style to you but recommend the approach of asking, "Which requirements do you think you cannot deliver on Day One, Month Five?" When you have this conversation, you should be working at the level of detail described in the Integrated Services Digital Network (ISDN) project requirements in Chapter 2.

If he or she says 80 percent can be delivered, you should respond, "Great. Let us review the shortfall (the 'missing' 20 percent)." Use the detailed requirements document and note, line by line, which deliverables are in, and which will not be available on that day. Then you need to conduct two additional pieces of analysis:

1. Understand why each delayed requirement will be late. Many legitimate reasons exist for this. Typical examples include resource, management support, dependencies, and vendor performance. You might be able to mitigate some or all of these potential deficiencies, for instance, by rallying technical support or providing a technical writer to accelerate the documentation process. Other possible causes of delay may be more unseemly, such as internal strife, conflicting priorities, or poor management. These are often tougher obstacles to clear from your critical path, but they must be addressed just the same.

2. Assess with the team lead and relevant stakeholders the potential impact on critical path if you accept the delayed implementation of specified requirements. That can vary, depending on various factors. While delays are sometimes unavoidable, those with obvious negative impact must be revisited. In most cases, prioritizing deliverables is an adequate approach. For example, it is typical for an application to provide a finite set of user actions, which, in this case, are the tasks that the call center analyst performs to execute and

track customer orders. Obviously, bringing this functionality to life is on the critical path. Other application services, however, could be delayed if necessary, particularly if resource is the key dependency. Reporting modules would be the first place to look. Reports can take a lot of time to design, test, and modify, but from a critical path perspective, some of them may not be as compelling as making sure the sales order entry process is ready to fly when it is supposed to.

6.9 GETTING READY FOR THE DETAIL

The past dozen or so pages may have been tedious, but they summarize a process that can take weeks or perhaps months in real life. Although the benefits and risk-prevention value of documentation is stressed in this and most other project management books, the truth is that most of the work just described is verbal. If documented at all, it is most likely captured in meeting minutes and e-mail correspondence. Now, it is time to get the detailed planning on paper. Two issues need to be addressed before proceeding with the detailed project schedule.

Whose plan are you keeping? Although in practice one sees mixed views on this, I believe you should develop and maintain a "master plan" that is separate and distinct from project team schedules. This "master plan" should document the critical path, plus significant tasks or events leading up to the milestones. The temptation most project managers succumb to, however, is to create a plan containing every task every team lead should schedule and track. I have been down that road myself and definitely understand the comfort level one hopes to generate with such thoroughness. If you have done that, then possibly you discovered the downside to that approach. I have never found a way to track everyone's tasks and the critical path within a single, master schedule. This is because while various teams may contribute to events leading up to milestones, the end-to-end schedule for all their project assignments cannot be assumed to map to the critical path. Each team tends to have its own scheduling logic, making it impossible, in my opinion, to have all the details plus critical path in one schedule.

The other downside to this comprehensive, "capture all tasks" approach is your second decision point: determining the level of detail your plan should contain. Again, if your plan includes every task performed on the project, you will spend more time and energy creating and maintaining such a document than you will be using it as a tool to ensure success.

Remember our hypothetical airport project from an earlier chapter? Imagine being project manager on that job and tracking each of the 729 toilets that will be installed, plus the associated plumbing, tile work, privacy

Construction	Inspections passed	*** Milestone ***
Foundation done	Plumbing, electric,	
Building up	fire safety, building,	Certificate of
Roof on	heating, ventilation,	Occupancy for
Walls and windows in	and air conditioning	terminal awarded

Exhibit 8. Path to an Airport Milestone

stall installation, flush and fill testing, and inspections. Documenting to this level of detail would create thousands of tasks. Although this might seem like a silly example, the fact remains that large IT projects can easily generate this number of tasks, if you cared to track them this way.

Again, my preference is to drill down from the critical path to a level of detail that is actually useful for managing your project. Going back to the airport project, the milestone you would probably designate along your critical path would be getting a certificate of occupancy (CO) for the terminal building. The CO would be issued by the local government granting building permits and performing inspections that assure that all safety and building code requirements have been met. It is only after the CO is issued that airport employees and patrons can enter and use the facility, including the toilets.

Completion of toilet installs would contribute to passing a plumbing inspection that is a prerequisite to reaching that CO milestone and, as such, would be no more or less significant than getting the roof installed or passing the electrical or air conditioning inspections. Therefore, instead of your plan noting every toilet order, rough in, installation, test, and inspection, your airport construction master plan should look something like the plan in Exhibit 8.

6.10 FINALLY, YOUR PROJECT CALENDAR

I will not present a detailed Gantt chart to close this discussion, but do offer the following as the final schedule. I apologize, sort of, for its conceptual nature, but then again, that is your key interest as the project manager. Your final schedule should represent the critical path and the key contributing events that support each milestone. Therefore, Exhibit 9 indicates the major sequences along the critical path, with arrows denoting the dependencies. From this drawing, it is an accurate, if unpleasant, next step to document the details as required to complete your calendaring task as project manager.

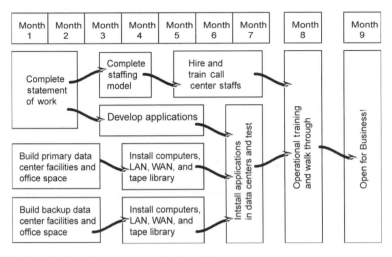

| Month 1 | Month 2 | Month 3 | Month 4 | Month 5 | Month 6 | Month 7 | Month 8 | Month 9 |

Exhibit 9. Vendor Management Project Plan

6.11 MANAGING TEAM LEAD PLAN DETAIL

So, although you are tasked with building a master schedule that documents the critical path and its milestones, you still should be concerned about the subteams' plans and schedules. They are responsible for the quality and timeliness of their work. Obviously, you need to have a level of comfort that their planning is adequate in terms of feasibility and coherence. How do you do that, especially if you are not all that familiar with how to construct a network, for instance, or build multiple Web sites?

First, let us define the mission of which two components are intended to determine whether:

- All bases are covered in the subteam plans
- Those plans are realistic

Never assume that either is true until you have undertaken some kind of inspection process. Let us start with completeness first. Virtually any technical project implementation has a generic, ritualistic quality about it. In other words, the elements listed in Exhibit 10 should be embedded in any project calendar. You can inspect for these elements and engage the team lead in conversations regarding the status of his or her scheduling for each of these "events."

This list should not be construed to precisely represent each subteam's project plan. Depending on the deliverables, some of the preceding items might be minimized, if not trivial, while others, once detailed, would make the Manhattan phone book look as simple as the bill of fare for a hot dog

Exhibit 10. Required Elements of Detailed Scheduling

1. Gather requirements.
2. Create design.
3. Get technical, business, and financial approvals.
4. Order equipment, licenses, tools, consultants, etc.
5. Build or install, and "unit" test.
6. User acceptance testing (UAT).
7. Train users and support staff.
8. Put into production.
9. Complete documentation.
10. Hand off to operations support.

stand. Be that as it may, each item requires exposition and validation. When reviewing a subteam plan for completeness, examining these ten areas is a relatively simple process. Because you do not want to come across like an Internal Revenue Service auditor, it is best to take a conversational approach. For example, when reviewing item four, procurement, consider asking questions such as:

• How long does it typically take this vendor to perform once they get our purchase order?
• Is this product constrained?

At some point, you should be comfortable enough with the process that you can get a good feeling about the schedule and move on, or move in with more pointed questions if a subteam plan component appears deficient to you.

Unfamiliarity with a technology can make you feel ill prepared to engage in this process. If this is the case, you might care to revisit the self-education process in Chapter 3, especially that section named "Understanding Implementation Requirements." In that discussion, IP Telephone was used as the technology straw man. I had never worked with it before, so I queried the IP Telephone team leads and skimmed the administrator's manual on the manufacturer's Web site. From an implementation perspective, I learned that, with the exception of the back office infrastructure, rolling out IP Telephone was pretty similar to installing more traditional telephony in a corporate site. That is a process with which I was familiar; it is fairly well documented in the trade press as well. As a result, I understood IP Telephone basics enough to at least have an intelligent conversation about their implementation plan.

The other thing you want to review subteam schedules for is feasibility. Not everyone who puts a plan together steps away from it far enough to see if it really makes sense. In fact, offering to lay your eyes on their plan, as a quick sanity test, is a good approach to getting access to their plans. To a large extent, that is what feasibility is all about — wondering aloud if the schedule hangs together, or whether there is possibly excessive wishful thinking over and above the optimism one would expect to find in any schedule. Here are five fertile grounds for exploration:

1. *Dependency.* When a schedule is linked to the output of some other process, two concerns arise:
   - *Timing.* Can any dependency reasonably be expected to occur at the date your project needs it to? An example is waiting for a global update to middleware that delivers mainframe data to Web servers, a process where you need to put up new Web sites as one of your project deliverables.
   - *Actual output.* Are we certain that the dependency will deliver as promised? If that middleware dependency is critical to our project from a data perspective, can we be certain that the middleware will deliver the data in a format, time cycle, and completeness that meets our specifications?

2. *Resource allocation.* For many IT processes, such as application development, estimating timeframes is notoriously difficult. Chapter 9 presents some specific ideas on this topic. From a scheduling standpoint, one should take heed that not every problem can be solved by throwing dollars at it. In this case, that would mean adding programmers after panic over deadlines sets in. There is always a learning curve associated with recruits. Toward the end of the schedule, the curve can be quite steep. This is doubly dangerous because incumbent staff productivity diminishes when tasked with bringing the rookies up to speed. Therefore, it is best to walk through resource assumptions with the team lead when reviewing this portion of his or her plan.

3. *Resource skill.* Superstars are in short supply, so overcommitting a key manager or subject matter expert can lead to the point of diminishing returns. If this key individual hits the wall before the work is complete, misfortune may soon follow.

4. *Scheduling logic.* You might feel hamstrung if the subteam's technology is not well known to you. There is no crime in reviewing a schedule and asking this very simple question: when does this thing come together? Ask team leads to walk you through their critical paths, and to highlight the key features of their milestones.

5. *Contingencies.* Engage the team lead in a discussion about where their schedule is tight and where slack might be found. You want to avoid the intimidating air of a military white glove inspection. Try to identify with your project partner where trouble may crop up and, conversely, where cushions may exist that could be borrowed from later.

I once had a very complex project for which I put together my first schedule 6 months before implementation was to start. After eyeballing it for a while, I went to the Networking team lead and said, "It looks to me like your team will have to wire up one floor a week for 37 consecutive weeks to meet the schedule. Am I right? And if so, is that doable?" He appeared a little taken aback at the question, perhaps because it was so early. Eventually, he came back and requested funding for additional resources. This is how you want it to work. Although I was fairly sure that he would have to knock off a floor a week, I had no clue whether he thought so too and, if so, whether he was adequately staffed for that workload. I did not know this manager well at the time, so I definitely wanted to avoid creating the impression I thought he was dumb or unprepared. It turned out he was neither, but one cannot expect to be that fortunate all the time. Remember, my job was to help him and all the other team leads to be successful with any means at my disposal, so that requires tact while not being too bashful about checking everything out as far in advance as possible.

6.12 PULLING IT ALL TOGETHER

Now you can turn on the computer and launch your project planning application. That seemingly innocuous move has been discouraged to this point because the preparatory work is critical and best done manually. Also, I have never been convinced that these automated tools are all that intuitive. Having said that, it is now time to talk about how to use the tool to get your plan documented and ready to use as a management aid as the project progresses. To summarize our scheduling accomplishments thus far:

- We have identified the master project's critical path, which consists of roughly 6 to 12 milestones.
- Each milestone has a fixed date and a finite number of contributing events that are important to us.
- We have become familiar with subteam key tasks that we choose to document and track, whether or not these events contribute directly to the master project critical path. Examples of these would be risk-sensitive events or key subteam dependencies.

Many excellent books are available regarding use of the popular scheduling applications, so the only value I can add is the following remarks. These tools are excellent for documenting tasks and tracking progress, as long as you do not make them too comprehensive or take the process too literally. This is not so much to disparage the excellent products out there as it is to say that it is virtually impossible to use all their powers in a complex project. Quite frankly, if you are adept at doing things such as "date math" in spreadsheets, those tools can be equally useful for plotting out the tasks once you have followed the process espoused in this chapter.

I personally find the Gantt tool most useful for validating assumptions about durations and dependencies, as long as I restrict the work to the milestones and down only two or three levels from there. In general, these programs work best when a project has a lot of sequenced, repetitive tasks not unlike the manufacturing environment where a "cookie cutter" process (i.e., repeated over and over) is used. Server upgrades, relocations, and large wiring or infrastructure upgrade projects are best suited for these types of programs. Projects that have a plethora of "one-off," seldom repeated, and largely unlinked deliverables are not so well suited, particularly if you choose to capture and track a lot of scheduling detail. In the final analysis, however, it is a matter of what works for you. As long as you follow the scheduling process outlined in this chapter and use any applications as documentation tools instead of planning tools, you will find that the focus on manual work can lead to superior results.

Note

1. Kindly note that the "customer-facing process" component was omitted for brevity's sake.

Chapter 7
How to Status Your Project

Equipped with a thorough plan and a logical schedule, we are finally ready to go to work. This is quite an exciting time. The team is bringing on consultants, sending off orders, and starting the process of turning those raw materials into a fine work of art. Common wisdom has it that it is also time for the project manager to pick up that clipboard and start checking things off like a foreman on a hectic loading dock. Further, we are taught that if by chance things go awry, recovery is simply a matter of fine-tuning dates, tweaking technologies, and in the worst-case scenario, invoking Plan B.

If it were that simple, project managers would not be needed. Instead, project management offices would only be staffed with:

- Project planners to build schedules
- Project administrators who issued status reports, transcribed meeting minutes, and processed purchase requisitions and timesheets

However, the job title includes the word "manager" for the same reason that captains are in the cockpits of commercial aircraft. Autopilot technology is wonderful, but there are times when only the presence of a skilled and experienced leader can avert disaster. Therefore, the focus of this chapter is the proper approach to project monitoring, including how to inspect for, and react to, pending exigencies.

7.1 RULES OF ENGAGEMENT

We have all seen political managers — those who take credit for project victories nearly as quickly as they assign blame elsewhere when the news is bad. Another profile worthy of mention in this regard is the "by the book" project manager who is well versed in our methodologies but, in truth, adds little more value than the political type. In the grand scheme of things, the project manager has enough power and skill to add tremendous value to the process.[1] Rule number one in this regard is that those project managers who fail to actively contribute to the daily struggle inculcating projects will likely be labeled irrelevant by stakeholders, including customers and beneficiaries. Once so designated, a project manager will be ignored, misled, or manipulated by agendas not necessarily aligned with the project.

If you are not seen as an effective manager, you will find yourself out of the loop. People will avoid you or say anything to keep you at arms length. Then, you will find it difficult, if not impossible, to really understand what is going on. In this very real and common scenario, control of the project has been wrested from you and, in most cases, the project will drift aimlessly, or even worse, start heading down the tubes. Guess who gets the credit for that state of affairs?

So, instead of worrying about how to manage your project by fiat, understand that you must be seen as a relevant and contributing team member. Once you have earned that level of respect, you will be able to enjoy open conversations with team leads that will help you understand the true project status. Those who provide status need to trust you. They may have reason not to, either because they have been burned by other project managers or they have not made up their minds about you just yet. If you earn their respect, trust will come along with it and the right information will flow to you when you need it.

With that comes a responsibility, too. If a team lead is struggling with his or her team, technology, or even management, there is a likely consequence that the timeliness or quality of his or her work is not in line with project expectations. As project manager, you have to be careful about how you publicize this information, and you undoubtedly need to help this poor soul in some way. Let us examine this leadership opportunity in more detail.

7.2 THE POLITICS OF BAD NEWS AND ESCALATION

This has two components: one is internal and the other is external to the project team. You have obligations to both sides of the project team fence. You want to keep the trust of the team lead who is mired in difficulty, so you do not want to brainlessly and perhaps cruelly announce to the world that Joe and his bunch, for instance, have fallen behind the eight ball. On the other hand, you are also responsible to your manager, the project sponsor, and potentially impacted customers or beneficiaries so you may need to alert them to brewing trouble. If you are really lucky, this issue will go away. If you are sort of lucky, the problem is one you anticipated as a potential risk, and you have a Plan B poised to kick in.

But if you are just not lucky at all, you have to step up to the plate because sticking your head in the sand just will not do. Elsewhere in the book, I mention that bad news has a way of getting out. You want to be the source, that is, the first to get the news out on the street. It must be packaged in such a way that people's reactions are: "That is too bad, but it

Exhibit 1. Preparing Information for Public Consumption

The ability of Project X to meet Deadline Y for Deliverable Z has come into question because of [event/condition] A that recently transpired, despite the expectation that [event/condition] B would have been the case. The potential impact to the project could be [missed date/incomplete deliverable/disrupted users/etc.]. Two approaches can be taken to alleviate this situation:

1. Approach E requires [hiring/buying/rescheduling/postponing] at an estimated [cost/impact] of F.
2. Alternatively, we could take Approach G. That would require the [hiring/buying/rescheduling/postponing] with an estimated [cost/impact] of H.

The project office recommends Approach E because it is [less/more] costly but does not require [schedule changes/hiring/recoding/etc.]. I have scheduled a meeting for tomorrow at 1:30 p.m. to review the situation and hopefully come to a decision regarding the best course of action to take so we can move forward ASAP.

---

sounds like you have it under control" as opposed to "How did you let this happen? Why did you not prevent this?"

Before you start sending out disingenuous e-mails that are little more than "CYA," think this problem through with your troubled partner. I follow a diagnostic process that is instinctive at this point because it is so simple. Also, I have had so much practice I can do it standing on my head. You simply need to ask, and understand, the following questions:

1. What went wrong?
2. What is the worst-case scenario in terms of project impact?
3. What is the best way to fix this?
4. What is the most realistic way of fixing this?

In other words, you need to understand the problem in terms of impact to the project and how best to effect repairs. Note the two "how to fix it" questions listed previously. The difference between the two is more obvious if:

• Question 3 is prefaced with "In a perfect world ..."
• Question 4 is restated as "What can we really do about this mess?"

One would be ecstatic if the answers are identical, but this circumstance, if serious enough, probably comes up during the project's "no luck at all" phase. The issue here is that the perfect fix may not be realistic in terms of timeframes, resource skills, headcount, funding, process conflicts, or technology issues. The other reason I ask the question both ways is to satisfy my packaging requirement for publicizing this negative information to the outside world. Once I understand the problem and possible remedies, I use the script from Exhibit 1 to prepare the information for public consumption.

Exhibit 2. Escalation Script

• Describe the issue being escalated in terms of project impact.
• Provide just enough detail to support any impact statements.
• The packaging is antiseptic (i.e., free of emotion and hyperbole).
• The issue is totally depersonalized; no names mentioned or blame assigned.
• Two options are presented even if one is highly preferable to the other.

The script works very well. Its most notable characteristics are listed in Exhibit 2.

Regarding the last point, never present a single option. This is particularly compelling if the preferred option is:

• Going to put stress on the organization
• A way out of the box
• Considerably more expensive than the alternate

You definitely want to have, and present, an alternative. This is the rationale behind asking the "How can we fix this?" question two different ways. I do this with the assumption that Question 4, the "What can we get away with?" question, yields the more politically correct answer than does Question 3, which asks what the best-case solution would be (i.e., solicits the perfect-world answer).

So as you present an option, you can play the preferred resolution against the one that, at first glance, is less onerous to senior management. In this scenario, you are probably asking senior management to cough up additional money or grant other concessions — something they are instinctually loath to do. If you anticipate this, offer a solution path that is in line with their comfort zones, and "yes but" them to death when they ask why you are pressing for the more complicated or expensive solution that, in fact, is the better approach. Keep in mind that effective communication starts with knowing your audience. Never forget to test their hearing because what they are apparently hearing is far more important than what you think you are saying.

Also remember that the team lead you are trying to help in this situation may have internal issues. His or her manager may not be willing or able to tackle the problem. If this is the case, then you must handle this with additional tact less you step on the wrong toes and possibly put your team lead in hot water with his or her boss, too. You just cannot be too careful with this one.

7.3 THE ANSWER MAN

Word gets around fast about your behavior in the scenario we just discussed. Whether you went out and uncovered this potential project jeopardy or it came to you, your reaction will be duly noted by project stake-holders. Let us assume you followed the advice presented in the last section and helped bail a team lead out. Other team leads and key stake-holders will somehow learn, almost instantly, that you "get things done." As a result, they all will come to you, not en masse, but every now and then, with their own issues. This is a good thing from the perspective that your relevancy quotient is on the uptick that I believe is desirable.

Still, this can be a bad thing from a personal standpoint because along with the reputation for effective problem solving comes the tag I call "The Answer Man." This is an admittedly fusty reference to a marketing campaign a few decades ago, wherein the Answer Man knew practically everything. The point is that not all issues belong to you or the project and, in fact, may be inappropriately brought to you.

Be that as it may, the reputation you gain from a problem-solving perspective is pretty binary. Either you are seen as a good way to solve problems, or you are not. Believe me, you want the former to be the perception, not the latter, even though they will come at you more than you like. It bears repeating that if they see you as not helpful, you get cut off in all matters, and that is definitely a very bad thing. If you have adolescent children, you definitely understand this situation. Unfortunately, that model holds for project managers, with the same jeopardies that parents face, at least in the professional sense.

Take heart by reminding yourself and your supplicants that you are not "The Answer Man," just a humble project manager. Still, you cannot stop there. Unless the issue at hand is an absolutely dead certain showstopper, you are a mentor and a traffic cop, not a priest or Web master. About 90 percent of the problems that hit your inbox can and should be solved by using one of the following tactics:

- "Let me make some calls. I think I know who can help but I have to check it out."
- "All right, I can fund two more consultants for 90 days each."
- "I will see if the customer is okay with that change and get back to you."
- "Call Maria. If she is not responsive, let me know, and I will call her boss."
- "I cannot make that decision, but will ask my boss to call yours, okay?"

The other 10 percent of the issues either require your special personalized handling, or you have to hand the problem back to them and say, "Sorry, I cannot help you." Before saying this, consider two things. The first is the impact on the project if the problem is not addressed and festers too long. The second, quite frankly, is a decision regarding the ability of the individual bringing the issue to your attention to solve the problem on his or her own. If the answer to both questions makes you queasy, then you should consider solving the problem yourself. In this case, you may want to check with your boss first or possibly get another team lead to handle it for you.

I recently had an experience of this nature, although the gory details are too lengthy to describe. The bottom line is that one of our project sub-teams was handed a serious problem that the previous owner failed to resolve. Leaving the issue open would definitely have exposed the project to incredibly bad publicity. The subteam lead who inherited the issue was not all that motivated to support one of his direct reports who was a key player on our project. I ended up running interference for this latter individual. Although the final results of our remediation efforts were satisfactory if not miraculous, it was a most unpleasant experience personally as well as professionally. I also had a real problem disengaging from the beneficiaries, who locked onto me as their personal "Answer Man." It took many months to obtain enough political cover to disengage from this group, even though the 3-month ordeal had thankfully turned into just another bad memory.

7.4 RAISING A PROJECT "JEOPARDY"

For some reason, when I think of project jeopardy, I am reminded of the kid who cried "wolf!" once too often. I am not sure why that is because, if anything, project jeopardy is called far too infrequently. Two possible reasons can be cited. First, some project managers may not actually recognize the need to cry for help. One of the reasons I wrote this book comes from having watched many project managers, myself included, struggle to understand our ever-changing projects. Big projects in particular can become overwhelming, confusing, or both. It is definitely possible that you are wandering around in a fog and do not know how close to the cliff's edge you have come; and, as a result, you fail to yell "watch out!" until you are on your way down.

The other interesting spin on this topic is the natural tendency of people to avoid the appearance of ineffectiveness or incompetence. To them, issuing a project jeopardy is tantamount to admitting failure, a tactic few project managers adopt as a career-advancing strategy. Project jeopardy, however, does occur, often through no fault of the project manager, or perhaps anyone else, for that matter. Putting aside self-promotion for a moment, let us examine this business of issuing a project jeopardy and then talk about how it should be done.

Section 7.2 laid the groundwork for jeopardy. The process is pretty much the same; however, in the nonjeopardy situations, I recommended keeping negative pronouncements low key and nonvolatile. Also implied was a reasoned approach that included a dialog during which you can steer consensus toward your preferred remedy.

The trick with jeopardies is recognizing that the issue before you is not something you can take a reasoned approach with and clear up with a few meetings pretty soon. It is also possible that the cause of the jeopardy is not all that dramatic, as the upcoming example will illustrate. What causes you to click on the hot end of the RAG (Red Amber Green statusing methodology) spectrum is the discovery of some event or condition that you and your team conclude:

- Will be a showstopper
- That someone important better be forewarned and engaged to push buttons you would not dare touch in your most brazen moments

Jeopardy arises from a variety of mostly mundane sources. Late shipments, nonperforming vendors, weather, faulty technology, and regulatory or financial issues can individually, or in sinister combination, puncture your life raft. Although you want to anticipate them and arm yourself with the right kind of Plan B insurance policies, when the truck is careening toward the ditch, those Plan Bs can seem childishly incapable of averting disaster.

The second of our four-problem diagnostic questions was: "What is the worst-case scenario in terms of impact on the project?" I once had a network engineer respond to this by saying, "We all die a slow and horrible death!" He was speaking professionally of course, but that was his way of saying "Pete, you better go do something fast!" Luckily, this warning surfaced a few days early. The problem had to do with a squabble between a supplier, the receiving department in the data center, and our purchasing department regarding the current location of several gigabytes of random-access memory (RAM). The memory had to be installed in the new firewalls before we could load the software that would allow us to reroute the network to the new demilitarized zone (DMZ) and triple throughput before the year-end freeze. If we were prematurely halted by the freeze, the network cutover would be delayed by 2 months. Missing this milestone would have been politically devastating because we were dealing with an impatient, if not hostile, customer.

I was aware of the dispute regarding the missing RAM. I had previously given my manager a heads up on this weeks-long dispute, and I tried to resolve the problem through all means at my disposal short of making the 100-mile drive myself to hunt down those pesky little memory chips. In fact, I had requested the authority to buy replacement memory as a contingency but was shot down, twice, because year-end cost cutting was in full flower.

Exhibit 3. Extranet Project Jeopardy

There has been an ongoing problem regarding a mis-shipment of RAM memory required to complete the configuration of the nineteen firewall devices. The Project Office and Purchasing have been unable to resolve the dispute among the vendor, the shipper, and the data center receiving department. The signature on the receiving document is indecipherable, and there is no log indicating the items in question were received. Both the vendor and the carrier claim the product was definitely shipped and received 6 weeks ago.

A project jeopardy is being issued. If the correct amount and type of RAM memory is not installed by Friday, the cutover to the new extranet connection will have to be postponed until after the year-end network freeze (i.e., the next maintenance window available after January 15, 200x).

I have validated with the vendor that if they receive a purchase order (PO) by end of business day tomorrow to replace the disputed memory, they will deliver those items to the data center no later than noon on Thursday. That would give us adequate time to meet the schedule without undue rush. The vendor has agreed to sell the memory at cost, thereby saving the firm approximately $3,500. The PO would have to be in the amount of $21,041, tax included.

Unfortunately, no alternative solutions are available to us. The software will not function properly without the memory. Please advise whether to proceed with the reprocurement process or reschedule the network cutover for January. Thanks.

In other words, this was a mess that had been going on for a while. When the engineering manager called me, he said, "Mr. Boss Man, if I do not have the memory by Friday, I cannot load the software this weekend, which is my last chance this year." Honesty compels me to report that I had lost track of the drop-dead date because I was consumed with other project issues. Lucky for me, I had long since escalated the issue and could prove that all attempts at remedy had hit various bureaucratic roadblocks. So, at least I was not exposed from that perspective. It is important that you have laid the groundwork for a jeopardy situation with prior status notes and escalations, preferably well in advance of issuing that call to battle stations. Given the way my previous attempts at fixing this problem had been rebuffed, I almost enjoyed issuing the jeopardy displayed in Exhibit 3 — all the way up to the CIO as I recall.

Exhibit 4 outlines the few differences between this document and the escalation script in Exhibit 2.

In other words, the point of issuing a project jeopardy is to tell the senior-level managers:

- What the problem is
- How you propose to solve it
- The most probable consequences of inaction

Exhibit 4. Jeopardy Document Rules

• Clearly state the problem and the consequences of inaction.
• Give a highly sanitized version of prior efforts to forestall this disaster.
• Provide one solution and the appropriate "or else."
• Avoid drama or hyperbole, but do not sugarcoat the problem either.
• Make sure the choices and consequences are clear.
• Give reasonable lead time, but set a "need by" date and time for a decision.

Be sure to include dates, times, and a brief history in case they wonder what led to this demand for a quick decision on their part. Do not just say, "help me!" or "duck!" Be sure they understand what you are asking them to do. As long as you do this with a modicum of professionalism and literacy, you are likely to get what you need, particularly if you have credibility within the organization.

In case you are wondering how the firewall memory jeopardy turned out, about an hour after my friend in procurement faxed a purchase requisition for the replacement memory to the vendor, our engineering manager notified us from the data center that one of his guys found the missing memory in some boxes from a different vendor on a cart headed to the dumpster. The way I look at it, we made the deadline and saved the company $21,041 — too bad about those extra meetings, though.

7.5 CHECKING STATUS AGAINST THE PROJECT PLAN

Now that we have dispensed with most of the worst-case scenarios, it is time to look at the less challenging but important daily project management duties once implementation is under way. In reality, you should probably be tracking things before the actual build phase, particularly if the project is of the design–build nature or has other long, task-laden lead times.

Obviously, you reference the schedule as you monitor progress. Gantt chart programs have that nifty little "percent complete" feature that graphically depicts progress and can be used to automatically adjust completion dates. The question you need to ask yourself is whether this feature has value other than satisfying curiosity or providing hypothetical schedule changes. Just because dates start slipping does not mean that you can push everything back proportionately. If you use "must start by" or "must end by" constraints, you can control this. Also, you can view the implications of slippages on downstream activities, resource requirements, and the likelihood that final tasks have far less time to complete if you are having a tough time getting the show on the road.

The problem I have with this is that it is more like the dull sort of video game you would expect process-oriented project managers to play. The

Tasks	Begin	End	Days	% Compl.	0%	25%	50%	75%	100%
Router project	1-3	2/17	45	77%					
Design	1/03	1/17	14	100%					
Order	1/10	1/31	21	100%					
Rack and stack	2/01	2/02	1	100%					
Cable	2/01	2/02	1	100%					
Configure	2/02	2/04	2	100%					
Test	2/04	2/14	10	25%					
Change control	2/01	2/16	15	0%					
Production	2/17	2/17	0	0%					
Document	1/03	2/17	45	15%					

Exhibit 5. Using Percent Complete as a Status Monitoring Tool

fact of the matter is that you need to take more care of your precious time than managing it by blocks of time as represented in project plan software that uses percentage completion as a status establishment tool. I am never quite sure how that algorithm translates into effective project management, because very few information technology (IT) project tasks are repetitive such as installing windows in a skyscraper or attaching bumpers to new cars. In other words, our kind of progress does not necessarily translate effectively into arithmetic chunks. Exhibit 5 displays a common example; you can see where the holes may exist in the percent completion of status methodology.

This illustration suggests that the router project is 77 percent complete — a status shown to the left in chart form and to the right with graphics. If you run your finger down the table to the first incomplete task, it shows the test task as one-fourth done. That would be great if that task consisted of 12 subtasks of equal merit or value, meaning 3 of them have apparently been successfully concluded. The next task, change control, shows as 0 percent complete, even though the start date coincided with the project start date.

My concern with the approach revolves around the weight of completed and incomplete tasks. If the project is to move a pile of dirt, and if ten dump truck loads are assumed as the task, including three that have been moved, then it is probably okay to call that project 30 percent done. When it comes to testing routers or doing change controls on the network, I have experienced far too many nonquantifiable tasks and bureaucratic or technology hassles that defy quantification, or that necessarily track reliably against the calendar. Therefore, my review of the illustration is that the routers are installed and being tested with no known issues to date; however, I would go looking for that team lead and find out the status of the change control and documentation processes. If they really are at 0 percent, I smell big trouble coming.

It is not that I am opposed to asking someone if they are halfway done, other than to wonder how to define the midpoint of most IT project deliverables. To me, it is far more effective to get periodic word pictures from team leads and distill them into a few terse words that reference project impact in terms of status. Normally, these observations will be binary. That is to say, you want to report that progress toward Milestone Z is on track, or that progress is lagging behind schedule with the possible impact of delaying a downstream event, including project completion. This requires some intuition, but more important, having the kind of relationships with team leads that allows for the exchange of relevant information. In a perfect world, these folks are at least as motivated as you are to meet the schedule, and should be able to give you honest assessments as to their performance against all targets, including completeness, quality, compliance with standards and requirements, and, of course, the project calendar.

Your status should never be ambivalent. If you cannot make a positive or negative pronouncement, acknowledge that status of a certain component needs further investigation or evaluation. Provide a follow-up date along with this admission, and stick to it. This approach has many names, two of which are "truth telling" and "managing expectation." Hopefully, neither phrase requires further elucidation.

The next two sections illustrate what is being said here.

7.6 STATUS REPORT: SMOOTH SAILING

Notice that the writing in Exhibit 6 is clear and concise. As you know, status meetings are mostly talk, some of which is actually necessary and important. As previously discussed, you want to boil all that information down

Exhibit 6. Smooth Sailing

The following represents the SouthPointe project team weekly status report. The team met today as usual with no significant issues to report. The server equipment for the site file and print servers was ordered and is expected to arrive by month's end. Although that is a week later than desired, the server team manager reports that the prototype server build was completed and tested early, so she anticipates a more efficient build once the equipment arrives. This piece of the project appears to be in good shape.

The consultants requested by telecom began work yesterday on the router design as per last week's notes. They were hired at the recommendation of the router manufacturer, who stated the consultants did a good job with similar requirements at another client site. The telecom team lead reports that the requirements are being reviewed and expects the final configuration design to be completed and ready for testing by the middle of next month. This is also on schedule.

and put the results into one of two buckets. Either we are okay, or we are not okay. Throw in detail as appropriate to make the reading interesting and reassuring, but do not go down too many levels. For instance, it may have been quite a struggle to get approval to hire the router consultants, and then get the right ones on board. The real story may be awesome gossip, but the background is pointless. The status message is that we needed the help, we justified the expense, and we got the experts in when we needed them.

It may seem strange that I advocate this binary OK/not OK approach. In truth, that represents our reality as project managers. What I do wish to add, however, is the flip side of that approach that those of you with literary backgrounds may know as "foreshadowing." In other words, I believe in portraying status as OK/not OK, then laying the groundwork, possibly in caveat form, by foreshadowing potential future good or bad news. In the previous example, this was done with the sentences regarding the fact that although the server order will be delivered "a week later than desired, the server team manager reports that the prototype server build was completed and tested early, so she anticipates a more efficient build once the equipment arrives. This piece of the project appears to be in good shape."

Notice there is wiggle room on this either way. No one can say whether the late order will actually cause or not cause a problem. Should it turn out that the behind-schedule delivery leads to problems later because the server team manager's optimism was misguided, we have a way to discuss that in future communications without calling her a dunce. On the other hand, she finished the most recent deliverable early. That is a good thing, so I was able to touch both sides of the road while steering down the middle.

Exhibit 7. Rough Waters Ahead

The following represents the SouthPointe project team weekly status report. The team met today as usual and had to address two significant issues. Tomorrow is the deadline for ordering file servers for the file and print services at the new site. The decision on server model is mainly predicated on throughput and the number of users each server could effectively support. The server build team has been unable to complete its testing and is not yet prepared to make their recommendation. It was decided to give them one more week. We checked with the supplier and were informed that our delay of 1 week in placing the order for these 40 servers may cause an additional 2 weeks' delay in delivery due to current availability. The server build team said they could absorb this shortened timeframe by working an additional weekend. Final server model recommendation will be made no later then start of business this coming Monday November 28.

The other significant issue raised is that of engaging consultants to support the telecom team for the design of the router configurations. Although additional funding was secured, the consultants recommended by the router manufacturer are no longer available. Requisitions have been rushed to several other agencies, and the manufacturer's rep is checking with her peers to see if they can recommend any other consultants. It is too early to determine if the delay in bringing on consultants for this task will cause a problem. The current plan calls for the design to be complete and ready for testing by the middle of next month, so we will track this very carefully.

This approach also telegraphs a strong command of the project and its details. You definitely want to impart an aura of comfort and control with every pronouncement, whether it contains the best of news or not. This is simply good public relations.

7.7 STATUS REPORT: ROUGH WATERS AHEAD

Review Exhibit 7. Hopefully, you noticed that we reversed the fortune of the same two issues discussed in the previous example. Also notice that the issues are clearly spelled out and their impacts noted. Ambivalence is acknowledged in the router consultant issue. In this case, we are not sure whether or not the inability to hire the preferred consultants will become a problem (i.e., if we can find equally qualified individuals in a timely manner). Obviously, this could become problematic, so we used the status report to do a little expectation management. I used the foreshadowing technique to lay the groundwork for some serious escalating to take place real soon. If you read between the lines on this one, you might infer from the phrase "are no longer available" that perhaps there was a snag in the funding process. Perhaps there was. Although I would not advise you to shout from the rooftops that the request sat ignored on an important person's desk for 2 weeks, I would also not recommend that you allow the inference that the project office dithered on this one.

Exhibit 8 lists the key attributes of a good status report.

Exhibit 8. Status Report Guidelines

- Be clear and concise.
- Describe the project impact as positive or negative for each item mentioned.
- If impact is uncertain, say so, but include finite follow-up action items.
- If an explanation is required, keep it simple and depersonalized.
- Do not load up on minor victories to offset bad news or to look busy.
- Convey a positive attitude about the team and its enthusiasm for its duties.
- Do not repeat old news. If an issue lingers, escalate it. If it is over, forget it.

7.8 HANDLING CHALLENGES TO THE SCHEDULE

Suppose your schedule is heading toward a milestone, and you are tracking ten major tasks that lead up to that key project event. Each of these dates has varying significance and associated risk or pain, compared with its nine sibling tasks. If you have done your job, you understand this and, thus, know how to evaluate progress in a practical sense. Part of doing this well also requires that you develop a decent sense of anticipation. It was mentioned in Chapter 6 that there is a generic flow of project regardless of project type, technologies deployed, and so on. One can similarly anticipate characteristic opportunities for date slippage.

In assessing project status, you should approach it with a detailed understanding of the work underway and tasks remaining, while looking ahead for the most likely contributors to tardiness.[2] Exhibit 9 lists the most common schedule killers, many of which you are already painfully aware.

Because nearly all projects contain these elements, they are potential weak points you should locate and monitor on subteam schedules. As an example, a week before testing is due to commence, ask the team lead if he or she foresees any issues with starting and completing that task successfully and on time.

7.9 GENERIC REACTIONS

So far, I have offered an approach to having truthful exchanges with team leads regarding their progress, and I have identified likely trouble points. Earlier we discussed contingency planning. A good Plan B will have a "go/no go" date (i.e., a trigger date at which time it will be determined whether or not the risk mitigation strategy should be invoked). So, you add those items to your project surveillance as well. Most project issues will arise from these areas during implementation. In other words, most potential issues should be known in advance.

If that is the case, then what is the response? Plan Bs have responses already spelled out, so that should be a straightforward process, assuming you have done a good job preannouncing the potential for this and make

Exhibit 9. Factors Contributing to Date Slippage

Procurement issues	Purchase orders filled out wrong, or lost.
	Painfully slow approval process.
	Procurement office does not press supplier.
	Company on "credit hold" over a billing dispute.
	The lawyers are haggling over a contract.
Supplier issues	Mis-shipments, backorders, or installations.
Infrastructure	Incomplete cabling or element configurations.
Change control request	Signoffs or change windows missed.
Construction	Permits not issued.
	Contractor did not build to design.
	No certificate of occupancy.
Engineering	Hardware, software, or system not completed.
Operations	Documentation incomplete; training not performed.
	Monitoring tools not installed.
	Disaster recovery not implemented or tested.
Security	Account or password administration issues.
Testing	User will not participate or sign off.

people aware that a Plan B is going to be kicked off. As for the others, those generic opportunities for delay, it simply makes sense to anticipate them, test for their presence, and follow up. Never assume that people will remember to do certain things or are necessarily motivated. It never hurts to make those preemptive phone calls or send those confirming e-mails taking the approach of "Dear Laura. If there is any reason why you will not be able to execute that change control (No. 123445) that we discussed last week, feel free to respond, or call my cell phone (123) 456-7892. Thanks."

Remind yourself that you must always follow up. It is far better to be embarrassed about being a nuisance double checking everything than to be ashamed because someone else did not perform as expected, but you failed to stay on top of that.

7.10 ADJUSTING YOUR SCHEDULE

In many of these cases, midstream corrections are required in terms of changing dates. On a previous project, we had a new building of a few dozen floors that had to be wired for voice and data. The schedule called for doing two floors at a time as follows:

- Install two local area network (LAN) switches per floor.
- Install LAN and analog cards in each switch.
- Cross connect and patch data jacks to assigned switch ports.

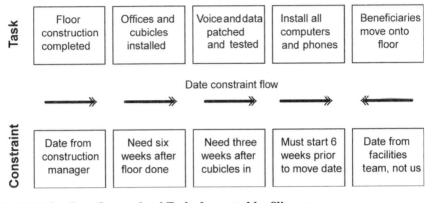

Exhibit 10. Date-Constrained Tasks Impacted by Slippage

- Cross connect and patch analog jacks to assigned switch ports.
- Test throughput at each connected jack.
- Document all connections, and turn these as-builts over to network operations.

The implementation schedule for this process was dictated by two dates. The first was the date at which time the construction company handed the floor over to our telecom department to perform the preceding tasks. The second date was the lead time required by the team that would come in after telecom to install computers and test them prior to the new users moving into the building. The move dates had been set a year before we started scheduling the technology implementation and could not be changed. Graphically, the implementation plan looked like the one in Exhibit 10.

The project team built an elegant schedule based on this logic and validated the furniture turnover dates with the general contractor's project manager. This was done 6 months in advance of the start of floor turnovers. Of course, as we got near the starting line, the construction manager advised us that his turnover dates for floors and furniture date would slip significantly. With our move-in dates intractable, however, this meant we would be squeezed on the telecom and technology installation time side of the schedule. We, in turn, forced a recommitment from the construction side, so that the following durations and dependencies were renegotiated. Both the original and adjusted durations are documented in Exhibit 11. It also shows the new scheduling strategy we negotiated for each of the dozens of floors with which we had to work.

All parties had to increase staff levels or resort to overtime to accommodate this more aggressive schedule. This example illustrates the process

Exhibit 11. Adjusted Completion Schedule by Floor and Major Task

Task	Original Duration	Adjusted Duration
Furniture installation	6 weeks	4 weeks
Telecom installation	3 weeks	2 weeks
Technology installation	6 weeks	3 weeks
Net change in total	15 weeks	9 weeks

Exhibit 12. Implementation Issues Log

Issue	Opened	Owner	Status	Status	Due Date
Need additional servers	9/16	Pete S.	9/27	Seeking funding approval	10/15
Vendor contract unsigned	8/21	Joan K.	9/27	In legal department	10/31

you must follow as you learn or presume that delays are pending. It is crucial that you understand your schedule, particularly the critical path and key dependencies, before entering any such negotiations. That way, you can protect your resources and deliverables as much as possible. Being late does not always matter, but reacting poorly to significant slippage can be disastrous.

7.11 ISSUES LIST

This chapter could have been titled "I Thought I Had Seen Everything When ... " Each project can invoke the bizarre, although the most prosaic mishaps can be just as disruptive. Once, I failed to receive a crucial overnight delivery because the courier's plane suffered a flat tire before takeoff — the courier chose to wait for the next available 737. This turned "next day" for them into "two day" for me; however, the fact that the cause of a delay defies imagination is not as important as how you react to these delays.

No matter how thorough and successful your preparations were, unanticipated problems will crop up in a frequency proportional to your project's size and complexity. There is only one way to deal with this: develop and maintain an issues log. Exhibit 12 depicts how each issue is assigned an owner and how the status of each issue is monitored until it is cleared.

If you do not faithfully observe the guidelines given in Exhibit 13, do not use this process because it becomes irrelevant and damages your credibility as a project manager.

You have to decide how directly involved you need to be in bringing each issue to closure. You do not want to "own" these one-offs unless the

Exhibit 13. Issues List Guidelines

1. Keep the list "net," as shown.
2. Do not belabor the issue on the chart other than to give it a descriptive title.
3. Do not track progress in a narrative form.
4. Review of this list at team meetings should be a recurring agenda item.
5. Restrict verbal updates to the degree that project impact can be assessed.
6. Discourage attendees from opining on issues they do not own.
7. If others should be involved, steer those conversations offline.
8. Solicit additions each week, and track these as well.
9. Publish this as part of the meeting minutes.
10. Delete but archive resolved issues in case the issue is revisited later.

logical owner is incapable of addressing a particular issue for some reason. The project office may also take ownership of any issues that cross team boundaries. The most compelling reason for you to assign an issue to yourself is, of course, that it is something so critical to project success or politically volatile, that you would be ill-advised to let anyone else handle it, no matter their level of competence or professionalism. In any case, as project manager, you own the process of identifying and facilitating the closure of all these unique or critical path issues. Let us take a look at the worst-case scenario: a major project milestone is threatened and you must personally see to its timely resolution.

I did a project where users were converted to a new operating environment whereby their desktop personal computers (PCs) were replaced with new laptops using an upgraded operating system. We changed the servers they logged into to access their applications and data. Services such as mainframe printing were also impacted. This project involved 400 users, 24 servers, 70 applications, and 3 data centers.

Several processes, applications, or services failed during the rollout. Some were easily fixed while others went through what I call the "bad car mechanic" scenario. You may be familiar with this; a mechanic replaces part after part, at your cost and inconvenience, in the hope that the malfunction will magically disappear sometime before you rebuild the whole thing. Some of the errors or problems confronting us were these:

- LAN access to network resources was not thoroughly granted.
- Applications were installed on the wrong new servers, or installed poorly.
- New production servers were undersized and required capacity upgrades.
- Printing services were improperly implemented for some users.
- New laptops were not consistently configured.
- Managing complaints was neither proactive nor customer-friendly.
- The new operating environment confused customers.

- The customer kept changing the deployment schedule.

There is a way of looking at this and alleging poor planning and management. Although there is some truth to that, the not-uncommon reality of this initiative was somewhat akin to childbirth. Although the results of this process are full of joy and gratification, the final hour is not all that picturesque or serene.

The previous listing documents the root causes of hundreds of complaints recorded during the rollout. Appropriate remediation was not always obvious. Closure rates were worsened because, as is often the case, end users are not the best partners in the fault management process. For instance, when they said they could not print, from a technical perspective there were a half dozen possible error messages, but the user rarely wrote it down so that our team would know where to start. As a result, each new service call was an adventure, at least until a technician realized that User 119's problem was the same as User 12's. Naturally, some technicians had not experienced User 12's problem and had to analyze the problem as though it had not previously been seen.

Needless to say, the team got bogged down in determining which of the three support groups (and their managers) owned the problems, thereby introducing additional frustration and delay. There was also an ugly political backdrop to this, as there was a chance that this would turn into an insoluble disaster and a real public disgrace. To some, avoiding the crown of thorns or trying to put it on someone else's head, therefore, became part of the exercise. Even I started managing individual problem resolution because the responsible parties were overwhelmed. I was not technically qualified to step in like this, but the milestone was beginning to look unreachable, and we were ready to invoke Plan B, which was a rollback to old technology as well as sending out our resumes.

You can expect dozens of e-mails to be generated as situations like these boil over. They become chain e-mails with more senior names being added with each click of the "send" button, and the situation is exacerbated. As this comedy turned into a tragedy, the customer went from a state of confusion, to alarm, to an irascibility bordering on hysteria. That is when the project manager needs to invoke the all-hands triage approach to get this thing back under his or her thumb. Exhibit 14 lists the steps one must take to defuse this type of situation.

In other words, be proactive, especially with the customer. Engage the customer if this could turn ugly, and keep them in the loop. Your being passive gives them the opportunity to drive you, which surely will make matters worse! Follow up methodically. Once people recognize you are on it until the smoke clears, two good things will happen:

Exhibit 14. Triaging Unanticipated Project Disasters

---

1. Blow the whistle and yell, "time out!"
2. Find out who needs to come to the table.
3. Get everyone together quickly — by phone if the team is dispersed.
4. Do not make face time a requirement if it introduces delay.
5. Ask for a summary of the issue(s).
6. Ask what the resolution should be.
7. Ask who owns the fix.
8. Ask what the owner needs to fix the problem or problems.
9. Ask when completion is likely.
10. Be supportive; volunteer to make calls or drag in more resources.

---

1. The "resolver" will clear the troubles, if for no other reason than to get you off his or her back.
2. The customer will settle down after observing your commitment to resolve everything ASAP.

In practice, this process is usually invoked just after the ship you are steering hits the iceberg. I am not a sociologist and therefore cannot explain why things get this bad before you have the good sense to blow the whistle and initiate the recommended triage procedure, or something akin to it. One wonders, however, if being slow to get into this mode actually helps because by the time you hit the panic button, everyone else is sufficiently concerned if not scared to guarantee focus and commitment to cleaning things up. Maybe the lesson is that adrenaline is a wonderful thing, and that hysteria cleanses the soul!

7.12 WHEN LATE MATTERS

In the Chapter 5 discussion of Plan Bs, risk analysis was approached largely from a technical perspective (i.e., by preparing for the eventuality that the technology does not pan out). From a timeline perspective, the question is a little different. As we monitor progress against the schedule, we may find ourselves wondering about the negative impact that could accrue if we deliver well but late. In other words, what are the consequences if the project team, or one of the vendors, overshoots a date?

Again, this exercise is not so much academic as it is about understanding your schedule, particularly the critical path and dependencies. Going back to the Big Thirteen interrogatory in Chapter 1, it is also important to leverage your understanding of the environment and business drivers that are an integral part of your project knowledge base. Let us examine a few scenarios to see what this is all about:

- *Circuits are delivered late.* If project scope is adding bandwidth out to the Internet or to other corporate sites, the impact may be modest. If the circuits add connectivity to a new site, however, this could impact move dates or system rollouts. In other words, late turnups could have serious implications. Because there may be no workaround, you must stay on top of the vendor mercilessly and, hopefully, have a time cushion built into your downstream schedule. For your information, this class of vendors can be preposterously late.

- *The servers hosting the new payroll application will not be ready for parallel testing during the next payroll processing period with the legacy system.* Although your wishful thinking suggests that the test can be postponed, you get chest pains after learning that the business staff assigned to the test will be tied up with other duties for the next seven payroll cycles, so rescheduling your test is not an option. In this situation, it looks like you have to find a way to meet the original schedule when testing is feasible.
- *Your new building will not be ready for occupancy per the move schedule.* Before addressing this, be sure you understand whether moving people out of their current location is actually more compelling than getting them into the new one. If that is the case, the right answer may be to find short term staging space for them. Do not overlook things like desks and chairs, filing cabinets, network connections, phones, and security access to the temporary site.

You may be familiar with the old canard that asks, "If it takes one woman 9 months to have a baby, how many months would it take nine women?" Although slippage can be mitigated with added resources, some tasks appear to be immune to the piling on of resources or additional funds. Understand how this might apply to your time line.

The bottom line is that some deliverables can slip and some cannot. Remedies are available for some missed deadlines, whereas others cannot be fixed or explained away either, unfortunately. One reason why deliverables often lack the quality or performance originally envisioned is because these quality assurance processes get turned down or shut off to meet hard target dates. Typical processes that get short-circuited are extensive testing (and repair), training, documentation, and the thorough turnover of new systems, facilities, and processes to trained and enthusiastic operations personnel.

7.13 QUALITY OF DELIVERABLES

So where are we? In this chapter, we have examined a variety of tools and techniques available to help keep you on top of the project and poised to take corrective action. Dozens more scenarios could be explored, but a gap would still exist between what has been discussed in this book and what might surface in your projects. Therein lies both the challenge and reward of project management work: its unpredictability and the opportunity to react with creativity and focused hard work.

"So where are we?" is a good question to ask yourself and the team. Start asking it early, and keep asking it because it is not always easy to tell where "we are." Nasty obstacles can pop up at very inconvenient times. On the other hand, as previously documented, some parts of the process can look very unseemly until completion, and there is no getting around the bad press you may be accumulating. Most problems are recoverable, but you may have to accept the fact that perfection is elusive in the IT world.

There is a beginning, middle, and end to every project. As project manager, you are charged with getting everything and everybody to the finish line in great shape. In theory, that should be pretty simple because you properly understood the requirements, you implemented them as best you could, you tested to validate success, and you documented everything.

Testing provides the final answer to the "so where are we?" question. The test plan, which we alluded to as success metrics in the Big Thirteen, should be designed to validate that requirements were met. In some cases, this can be restated as how well requirements were met. Too many technologies are out there to allow for a detailed discussion on test planning in this book. Suffice it to say that you were advised to champion this responsibility from Day One, and get the team thinking along these lines as well. Try to test things as early as possible. This gives the team adequate time to react to any issues raised by the test, proof of concept, or pilot process.

7.14 CONCLUSION

Some professional head football coaches are complimented as great game day coaches because they function with competency, creativity, and a joyful work ethic when the pressure is on during crisp, autumn Sunday afternoons. In my case, I am not so sure about the greatness, but I do love the action when a project is really kicking. Instead of abhorring problems, I attack them the moment I sense trouble, because I enjoy the challenge of properly identifying and then resolving them, preferably before others have taken note of them. Unlike the head coach of a sports team, however, project managers never possess unencumbered autonomy. You may be in charge of the project but probably little else. This is why having a strong set of interpersonal, political, and problem-solving skills, as well as a long list of allies and compatriots upon whom you can call for personal and organizational support, is extremely critical.[3] This is also why you need to understand the realities of your project, your environment, and your team so you can help everyone be successful without anyone, or everyone, going crazy.

Notes

1. Refer to subsequent chapters on team management and senior management for exceptions.
2. Similar to when you drive with an eye cast up the road in anticipation of signals and oncoming traffic.
3. These skills or attributes are covered in Chapter 16.

Chapter 8
Managing Project Information

Careful documentation is a critical element of successful project management. If assumptions, decisions, and significant detail are not formally recorded, socialized, and refreshed in a timely manner, you are left without an audit trail regarding decisions that have been made. Among the consequences of poor documentation is the increased probability that you will be attempting success in an environment of reduced accountability. This is because deniability and chaos are inversely proportional to the level of published detail. At the end of this chapter, you will find a discussion on meeting management. Although it is a fascinating topic, it does not warrant its own chapter. It makes sense to include it here because the most important output of any good meeting is useful documentation.

8.1 DOCUMENTATION GUIDELINES

Exhibit 1 outlines the recommended thought process for documentation.

8.2 WHAT YOU SHOULD DOCUMENT

Here is a listing of documentation your project will benefit from managing on a formal basis. Many of these document types are discussed in more detail elsewhere.

- *Scope.* This is your project's Ten Commandments. It should be limited to a few concise declarative sentences.
- *Issues log.* This lists each issue by name, owner/resolver, due date, and current status.
- *Assumptions, requirements, and specifications.* These are clearly worded descriptions of the project deliverables or "solutions."
- *Implementation strategy.* This tells the story of how each requirement will be fulfilled.
- *Plan Bs.* A description of any risks that require an alternate implementation strategy and the detail of that strategy.
- *Project schedule.* The project schedule outlining the critical path and key tasks contributing to project milestones.

Exhibit 1. Documentation Guidelines

- Large projects have far too much detail to be managed with a PDA or in your head.
- Good documentation combats faulty or selective memories, including your own.
- Do not use e-mail as your preeminent methodology because it is hard to keep organized.
- Whenever possible, update existing documents instead of issuing new ones.
- Always circulate documents, and solicit and incorporate legitimate feedback.
- Archive dated documents so they can be redistributed if required.
- Use a central repository, such as an internal Web site, to promote universal access.
- If possible, delegate a resource to manage this process.

- *Roles and responsibilities.* For groups with significant deliverables, including internal and external vendors, the "who, what, when, where, and how" should be committed to writing and published. For internal teams, including them in implementation strategies is generally adequate; but with vendors, a contractual, statement of work (SOW) format is far more desirable.

- *Purchasing documents.* Presumably, your company has systems and forms for this process. Keep copies of any submitted for tracking, validating shipments, and budget management.

- *Budgets.* Your firm may have an online budget tracking system. You should track expenditures from your own point of view, because internal tracking systems are often inaccurate and not user-friendly. They also lag weeks behind so can be frustratingly dated. Use a spreadsheet to track planned, committed, and project-to-date expenses, and a running tab of dollars remaining.

- *Status reports.* This should leverage schedules and issues logs. Status reports are best used to advertise success, indicate completion of tasks against the overall plan, and briefly describe the impact of any open issues or delays. You should also recognize upcoming events, and update them with subsequent releases of this document. Stick to the verbs on this one. Be honest and brief. Do not make this a puff piece, nor is it desirable to appear defensive or accusatory.

- *Meeting agendas and minutes.* I like to publish an agenda in advance of a meeting, and then use it as the basis for the minutes. Of course, I add items to the minutes if they come up in the meeting and are important enough to capture.

- *Inventory and other asset management.* You may be purchasing millions of dollars worth of hardware, software licenses, and services. You should account for everything on paper, even if your company has systems in place for this purpose. The mindset you should have is that in the event that there is a perceived or actual discrepancy, you want to be able to produce your own records, be they copies of packing slips or signed time sheets. Legibility and completeness count for more than fancy online forms as long as serial numbers, addresses, costs centers, and other tangible data are collected and can be presented as truthful and accurate.

- *Move schedules.* For projects where relocation of equipment or users is involved, establish target move dates early with as much detail as possible, and republish them as quickly as the information changes.
- *Transport logs.* Be sure and record equipment being moved between locations, including make, model, serial number, network names, etc. These moves can impact maintenance contracts, fault management system management information bases (MIBs), asset management systems, disaster recovery, etc.
- *User census and other detail.* Many hardware or software rollouts or upgrades, as well as other project types, require detailed surveys and analyses of end-user information such as home server, e-mail or network IDs, application access rights, and so on. Proper surveying and documentation has become a professional specialty. Automated tools are available for some components of this process.
- *Schedules.* These are used for circuit installs, power cutovers, and other service events.
- *Loaners.* You may elect to authorize the short-term deployment of equipment to accommodate workarounds, to be used as swing servers, or to curry favor. It is confoundingly easy to lose track of them. Put the terms of the loan in writing, particularly the length, as well as the optional purchase by the user if returning the item becomes unlikely or undesirable.
- *Job aids or user guides.* Some project output requires the production of cheat sheets, navigational aids, or training documentation to assist users trying to acclimate themselves to the new system, hardware, service, location, or phone system your project has put into their work experiences.

8.3 COMMUNICATIONS STRATEGY

Take a moment to think about how you want your project to be perceived by stakeholders, including beneficiaries and others not looped into your daily activities. This should be easy to do if you consider past experiences where you were a project beneficiary subjected to a personal computer (PC) replacement, being homed into a new server, or getting a new communications package for local area network (LAN) or Mainframe access. I will wager that experience was frustrating and possibly quite annoying. You may have had to rearrange your schedule to accommodate an installation. You may have suffered a service outage, or a temporary degradation in service, until everything got fine-tuned. You may have had to change the way you did things, such as learning how to enter hours worked in a new online timesheet system. You might even have been moved to a new floor or building and had to change your daily commute and find somewhere else to shop or get lunch. Under these circumstances, the biggest complaints you and your peers shared were probably:

- What are they doing?
- When are they doing it?
- Why are they doing it?
- How will it impact me?
- How long will it take to get used to these new attributes of my work experience?
- When will the supposed benefits be realized?
- Whose idea was this, anyway?

Do any of these questions sound familiar to you? Now, as project manager, you are on the other side. You should consider whether or not you want to address these issues should they arise as a result of your project. How would you do that? Would you set up a Web site? Would you send group e-mails, such as a newsletter? Would you hold regular status meeting with key members of the community impacted by your initiative? Would you say all these activities would take time, money, and resources that you do not have, so forget it?

Part of your communications strategy will be based on this conversation you have, particularly with your sponsor. The practicality of launching an information campaign should probably be evaluated against the risks associated with taking no action in this regard. Probably the best way to review this risk is to assess the degree of change your project will create in the beneficiary community. The greater the change, the more compelling it is to get something out there to the public. I have seen the whole gamut, up to and including a pretty impressive marketing campaign designed to familiarize people with the look and feel of the facilities and technologies being rolled out in a new location into which they would move.

Because we are looking at complex projects in this book, I think it is fair to assume that you need to do something. I would look to hand that problem to someone else, for instance, in Human Resources (HR), Facilities Management, Corporate Communications, or Corporate Training, depending on the type of project and the size and nature of the impacted constituencies. Meet with these people and articulate your concern that your team lacks the funding or skill sets to effectively educate beneficiaries as to the pending changes in their workplace, and let them handle it. Most corporations are sensitive to these matters.

Assuming that this tactic gets you off the hook as a public relations manager, you still are responsible for presenting your project via communications of some sort. Except for the most detailed and arcane design, imple-

Exhibit 2. Documentation Do's and Don'ts

- Publish documents in a timely manner, and keep them updated.
- Style and content must be net. Clarity, precision, and relevance are key.
- Avoid techno-babble, MBA-speak, and ambiguity.
- Focus on names, dates, and project impact or significance.
- Use strategic documentation (i.e., dealing with scope or design, and should be explicit).
- Touting technologies is irrelevant, if not misleading, from a project perspective.
- Explain technology with the "feature, function, benefit" approach (Chapter 13).
- Use it or lose it. Unrefreshed content goes stale.
- Aged or sloppy documentation creates a negative impression.

mentation, and operational support documentation, you should assume that anything else that escapes the gravitational pull of your core project team could end up on anybody's desktop. Not that I would censor each document as though it will be read by your CEO by the close of business tomorrow, but you never know.

What you do want to keep in mind is that you want to convey an image that instills confidence, respect, and cooperation to the degree possible in today's world. In other words, you want your project to look crisp and together, even if things are tangled and snarled like December's cross-town traffic in midtown Manhattan. To that effect, I created Exhibit 2 to outline the communication strategy you should tout and enforce to the best of your ability.

The credibility of your management and other aspects of the project can be tied to a successful documentation strategy. Documentation, or the lack thereof, can be used for or against you, so take heed.

8.4 MEETINGS

I debated where to put this topic. The final decision to place it in this chapter was based on the key point to be made about meetings. It is a common practice of mine to review assumptions that shape behavior, and I encourage you to do the same. On this topic, a most interesting dialog arises in that regard if you ask the very simple question: "Why do projects require meetings?" We could refine this issue by further asking, "What is so special about this next meeting that the same things cannot be accomplished by chat (i.e., e-mail), smaller gatherings, one-on-ones, or by whomever you choose to sit with at lunch?" And, of course, we can add another layer of interest by asking the corollary question "Why do people attend project meetings?" There must be some purpose other than the free continental breakfast, or the excuse to break from the drudgery of actually doing work, right?

Exhibit 3. How to Run Effective Meetings

- Publish the agenda in advance, distribute copies at meeting, and stay with it.
- If time permits, cover additional topics once all agenda items are cleared.
- Follow the same script with each item — introduce, discuss, resolve, close.
- Try to close the discussion on topics as quickly as possible — keep moving.
- Ten minutes before the scheduled end, close all discussion.
- Summarize all conclusions verbally just as they will appear in the minutes.
- Schedule any required follow-up meetings before adjourning this one.
- Publish minutes appended to the agenda document by the end of the day.

I can only think of one reason to have all these meetings: to make decisions with the right people around the table. Granted, team building and bonding are socially useful consequences of gathering together. Information exchange and developing empathy for the other person can all be positive results of meetings. Still, without decision making, meetings can be fun, entertaining, and even educational without adding one inch of progress toward project success.

The reasons are easy to infer, if you think back on the hundreds of meetings you have attended — not as leader, but invitee. Someone gathers the troops, possibly including customers or beneficiaries, in a room. He passes around reports or presentations and proceeds to talk at everyone, or he has someone do that for him. Then, the group discusses practically anything that comes to mind, with questions asked and issues raised in far greater quantity than answers seem to come forward. Before long, everyone's attention dissipates and a few begin taking calls on their cell phones.

The meeting is running long. Someone else needs the room, or a significant attendee has to rush off to the next appointment, so the meeting finally dies from lack of interest. At that point, the project manager looks down at his pitiful notes and wonders how to summarize what just transpired into published minutes that demonstrate how those in attendance earned their pay for that hour or two. As a result, minutes come out with as much substance as oatmeal, or are used to slip in decisions or opinions not formally agreed to by the group. Few of these results sound like the ball got moved down the field and, truth be told, it probably did not.

No one can deny they have been to a lot of these stinkers and presided over a few, as well. Exhibit 3 lists the effort I put forth to avoid perpetrating such injustice on my attendees. Although hosting business meetings is not the same as throwing a party at home, I hope you would not deliberately insult or antagonize either set of guests.

The best description I ever heard of managing big meetings is that it is like herding cats. Everyone has opinions. Most want to be heard, although some people's minds wander. Their pagers and cell phones go off, or their personal digital assistant (PDA) has a wireless connection that allows them to surf the net. I was in a meeting where an attendee muttered, "Cubs win!" while staring at his laptop.

Therefore, each meeting for which you are responsible should have firm objectives set by you. Hopefully, you will have positive input on this from conscientious team leads who lobby to get a topic put before the whole team. The second key point is that you want to condition the team and others who attend your meetings on a regular or semiregular basis to expect certain things and to adjust their behaviors accordingly. My premeeting mantra as I get ready to rev one up is: "tasks, dates, and owners." Sometimes, I literally recite this to myself as I wait for the elevator or stand at the copy machine putting the meeting package together. This is what I want to come from this meeting, or any other one I lead or attend.

- Things that need to get done
- Dates when they need to be completed
- Names of those willing to get these things done by those dates
- Any significant issues pertaining to these tasks

I am not particularly interested in the 19 permutations on the 47 options. Just tell me this: what course are we taking, when do we get there, and who is rowing the boat? I must confess that I probably have decided who should do what and by when, in advance of the meeting. I have found that it works far better if the meeting actually produces these results, instead of asking the team to vote my ideas up or down. I want the crowd buy-in, either because the particular item requires team effort, or I want the peer pressure of the other team leads to have a positive motivating effect on whoever gets tagged with a particular task.

Stylistically, different methods are used to pull this off, but if you set this tone and maintain it consistently, people will show up prepared with their issues looking for help, or for that brief moment of glory when they can report success with a previously assigned task. That is the real intent here: to get people to prepare for meetings where good things can and will get done. If you are going to improve your effectiveness as a project manager, it is because you understand that it is a leadership position. In this context, part of that responsibility is to provide the opportunity for problems to be solved. Use your meetings to do this. Also, good meetings help carry people emotionally from week to week. It is not that meetings should be run like a revival, but there is tremendous value in using the meeting as a tool in this manner.

As I said, meetings are about decisions, which, of course, are worthless without documentation, which is how we got here in the first place. Now that we have set the table for the climate or mood you hope to create and

Exhibit 4. Sample Meeting Agenda

SouthPointe Meeting Agenda/October 15, 9 a.m., Room 981, Building C
1. Status (voice, telecom, server, network monitoring, engineering).
2. Requirement for the legacy mainframe network at the new site.
3. Potential upgrade of desktop operating system.
4. Handling legacy LAN server protocols at the new site.

maintain for all your meetings, it is time to look at how documentation ties it all together. Exhibit 4 presents a typical agenda.

This example was taken from a weekly 2-hour meeting for an 18-month project that had as many as 30 people attending in person or via conference call. We always began with status, typically allocating ten minutes to each team lead, although sometimes they took more. Due to the size of the crowd and its makeup, it worked best to focus on one piece at a time, delaying issues with dependencies between or among sub teams until individual reviews were complete. Items 2, 3, and 4 in Exhibit 4 were issues that involved all the subteams except the voice team, which would be excused once it gave its status because their piece of the project was mostly, but not totally, stand-alone.

Minutes for this meeting will be appended to the preceding agenda document under each section, plus a section would be added for any new business that would find its way onto the group's radar screen.

8.5 CONCLUSION

In Chapter 7, I covered the preferred approach for documenting status, so I will refer you specifically back to the sections named "Status Report — Smooth Sailing," and "Status Report — Rough Sailing Ahead" for tips on appropriate style and approach. Just keep in mind that this process is something you want to lock into from the outset, and stay with on a regular and ongoing basis. As far as I am concerned, other than recording facts, the key to documentation is your understanding that it is:

- The project's official organ
- The means by which decisions and issues are clarified
- A recording of decision rationale
- An audit trail useful for many reasons down the road

The key to effective documentation is that its consistent brevity and clarity is such that people read it and respond in kind. If you find yourself juggling a controversial topic, get it out there in writing, and react to the flurry of responses it may generate by holding follow-up meetings. Do not attempt to resolve such matters via e-mail because you end up either with a chain letter or waging a war of words from which it is difficult to escape without many pointless or unfortunate avenues explored. If you understand how to use documentation as a tool, you will get that much further ahead of the game. In our business, that should be one of your biggest priorities.

Chapter 9
Manage Your Dollars

In this chapter, we will look at the critical elements of managing project dollars, which are:

- How budgets are derived
- What the budget should contain
- Seeking additional funding if required
- Understanding procurement and expense tracking
- How to manage the deltas, or budget versus actual

You may not have participated in the etiology of your project's budget. It pays for you to understand how the number was derived, however, because you will be held responsible for any overage, even if the original number was unrealistic. Project budgets typically have an inferred "must not exceed" characteristic, meaning that if the approved number is, for instance, $5 million, you cannot go back for another penny. Then, of course, there is the implication that failing to deliver the project at or below budget is proof positive of your incompetence. Perhaps, if budgets were in truth anything more than a projection, this career jeopardy might be fair. Because they typically are not, you are well advised to seek out any potential errors in your budget, and prepare to manage the budget as another kind of risk — that is to say, proactively, with a Plan B in place.

9.1 WHERE DID THE NUMBER COME FROM?

The following lists the most common budgetary processes:

- Some projects are driven by a need or goal mandated from the top, or by the environment itself. The family of Y2K projects comes quickly to mind as a good example of this class of initiatives. In such cases, budgets are "allocated" from a somewhat cursory estimate. With this process, in essence, the corporation is saying "we will not spend more than $X."
- There is the historical precedent model. On more than one occasion, when I have asked how the number was derived, the response was "the last time we did this, it cost $Y. Adjusting for inflation, less a 20 percent savings on cheaper technology, leads us to 118 percent times $Y." Of course, the historical value of Y may be no more valid than the adjustment factors applied against it, in this case 118 percent. Project accounting is suspect because of the way "scope creep," contingency,

beneficiary supplied funding, and other factors may, or may not, have been recorded as linked to the original project.

- A task force or consultancy may have done a bottom-up, piece-by-piece estimate, based on assumptions made about the design and the implementation strategy.
- Industry benchmarks can be used to approximate a budget. If a benchmark, for instance, suggests that the average cost to upgrade a network server to the latest version of your favorite operating system is $7,500 including labor, and you have to upgrade 250 servers, then the derived budget is $1.875 million.
- It is common practice to add a premium for contingency expenditures. I have seen the factor used range from 5 percent of total estimated cost on huge projects to an uplift of 10 or 15 percent on smaller initiatives.

9.2 BUDGETARY ASSUMPTIONS

As with nearly all other project facts, my advice is to validate the assumptions underlying the construction of your new "not to exceed" number, which is in the tens if not hundreds of millions of dollars on large and complex information technology (IT) projects.

- *Methodology.* Determine which of the five preceding options were used. Each has its obvious points of strengths and weaknesses. In the IT business, it is generally true that historical precedent has limited value, as IT projects tend to be rather unique, at least in the big leagues. Likewise, benchmarking has value to the degree that your project is not a one-off.
- *Labor.* Three methods are used get work done from a resource perspective:
  1. *Full-time employees (FTE).* Salaried employees can be assigned. Does your project get charged for their time in a real sense, or is that funny money that managers trade between cost centers to limit their "nonprofitability"? Most corporations have a standard, fully loaded rate of, for instance, $100 an hour for each FTE assigned to a project from a cost recovery perspective.
  2. *Consultants.* This is definitely real money. Do not forget the agency markup. You would pay $80 an hour for a $65-an-hour technician, if the agency gets a fairly common markup of 25 percent.
  3. *Outsourcing.* You may contract a firm to write code, move equipment, or configure servers. These charges are often fixed rates on a piecework basis, with overtime, expediting, and other potential costs spelled out in the contract.
- *Design assumptions.* No matter how the budget was crafted, it had to incorporate certain design assumptions. Some assumptions will con-

sider "solutions," in other words, how project scope would be implemented by building new systems, upgrading servers, retrofitting the network with larger bandwidth, and so on. From that point forward, one would expect unit costs to be used to create cost roll ups, so quite naturally unit assumptions exist upon which the final budget amount was derived. Likely candidates include:

- *Users.* This would apply to moves, new computers, software licenses, sizing servers, installing local area network (LAN) infrastructure, or fees for operations, help desk, or break–fix maintenance. In large corporations, these numbers have some precedence, perhaps contractually or based on internal charges long since established. For example, project costs are probably routinely charged within your organization for things such as moving a user to a different workspace, adding a server to the production network, and a myriad of upgrades to computing platforms. These known rates are often used to create cost projections for initiatives based on an assumed level of these activities. If it costs $5000 to certify a new server and connect it to the corporate network, and the project needs to add 17 servers to the network to support the rollout of the new payroll system, then the up charge for that piece of the project would be forecast as 17 servers × $5000/server, or $85,000.

- *Number of impacted sites.* This could be used for bandwidth or connectivity, licensing, operations, help desk and maintenance fees.

- *User functionality.* A software vendor may charge a fixed rate for each application deployed, such as payroll, general ledger, and sales order entry.

- *Standards.* Corporate standards may dictate the inclusion of virus or security scanning tools as well as server monitoring software.

- *Tools.* With or without standards, the build out of Web servers, middleware, databases, and other application infrastructure support should be based on the assumption that certain products are used.

• *Politics.* You would have to be pretty naïve to pose the question in these terms, but you should be mindful of the possibility that the final number had some political spin applied to it. Assuming that the executive in charge of presenting the final number for approval is relatively sane, he or she is faced with a dilemma. On the one hand, this person is astute enough to knowingly inflate the best-case number handed up to his or her to minimize the risk of showing a deficit at the end of the project. On the other hand, no one wants to price himself or herself out of the market either, knowing full well that some competing manager is likely to say, "Fifty million? Pshaw, I could do it for 35, tops."

I have witnessed or been impacted with several instances where deliverables were snuck beneath a large budgetary umbrella. In this scenario, a senior executive or program manager may take a few hundred thousand or even a million dollars from a big new project with ripe funding and divert those dollars to something else that has languished unfunded, possibly for a long time. I mention this because you might find, after your project is under way, that you suddenly have relatives you were heretofore not cognizant of, but are now responsible for, nonetheless.

Once you have cycled through this inquiry, it is time to vett the budget for yourself. Before that happens, however, it is important to have a clear understanding of the quality of data at your disposal to do that.

9.3 BUDGETARY SOURCE DATA

Inherent in any cost projection is a set of assumptions on unit data upon which the preponderance of estimates are based, as the previous section illustrated. I would like to zero in on this discussion by reflecting back on a project I served on as program manager for a vendor seeking a network migration project from a huge and geographically scattered customer. The proposed scope was to take a very mixed bag wide area network (WAN) connecting a few hundred sites to seven data centers and migrate it to a single transport type (Frame Relay) tying all sites to each other and to two data centers separate and distinct from the original seven. The current state was such that:

- Few sites were interconnected.
- The prevalent circuitry was 19.2 kbs leased lines.
- The communications protocols used were mixed.
- Nobody on the client or vendor side could stipulate with much precision what all these differences were, hence my previous use of the term "mixed bag."

My assignment was to generate a detailed design, with associated pricing, to effect these changes within several specific business, real estate, and technology constraints. The challenges we faced were:

- Identifying the legacy LAN and WAN infrastructure components at each site
- Identifying the applications and other IT processes required to support business as usual (BAU) processes plus the customer's intent to roll out centralized applications such as payroll and accounts receivable
- Understanding how to replace the centralized services currently housed at the data centers that would be disconnected from all users after the new network was in place and the new data centers were ready

- Creating a technology migration plan that met all requirements for current and future connectivity, performance, and access to centralized or standardized IT services

It soon became apparent that although the target state was reasonably well defined, the path leading to it was going to consist of:

- At least one plan for each of the hundreds of sites, due to the wide variance in application and infrastructure characteristics across all locations
- At least one plan for migrating and consolidating centralized processing services from the seven legacy data centers to the two new ones

For example, some sites would have to be rewired for newer LAN and WAN technologies. In most sites, the desktop personal computers (PCs) and servers would have to be replaced because they were incompatible with the proposed new technologies. There were protocol issues at some sites that did not lend themselves to the any-to-any network requirement. The risk associated with this latter requirement was quite high, given the nature of the business. Also, it was clear, at least to me, that multiple subcontracting firms would have to be engaged to ensure that an adequate quantity of specifically skilled technicians would be available to meet an incredibly aggressive, if not unrealistic, timeframe being tossed around a few layers above me.

Making matters worse was that the detailed site and user data the customer graciously shared with my team was woefully inadequate in terms of being able to quantify risk and develop a pricing mechanism that would be fair to both parties. The absence of centralized documentation in this regard was understandable, given that the client corporation was the result of a wave of recent multiple acquisitions within an industry in the midst of a consolidation frenzy. Before long, at my request, the customer-funded site surveys to determine the actual state of their IT environment.

This anecdote presents all the key challenges to effective budgeting of complex IT projects. It is quite difficult to devise a workable, priceable plan if you do not have an excellent understanding of the project starting line and all of its characteristics. In my simplistic way, I look at such a challenge on a "from–to" basis. This comes from the practical experience that you need to understand:

- Where you are coming from
- Where you are going
- What it is going to take to get there

The significance is that this view allows you to develop a fair unit cost for each site, application, or business unit to be converted from present to target state. Customers find this view much easier to understand and contemplate. Once you get the hang of it, you will find it is not all that difficult to produce.

The "what it is going to take to get there" piece can be divided into three parts:

1. Implementation strategy
2. Implementation costs
3. The success metrics that have a significant impact on the service levels and other telltale signs of the target state's quality and complexity[1]

In Chapter 6, I recommended that you understand and comprehend your critical path before you do any real scheduling. This approach is preferable to trying to make sense out of thousands of finite tasks. Budgeting complex projects is similar. Sure, at some point we want to count routers, servers, or users, and apply a number to that, but first we need to understand what we are doing before we start counting. So, as with designing and scheduling, budgeting is an iterative process intertwined with the other planning processes.

To see how this works, let us return to the current network migration example. As with risk, I prefer to take the worst-case scenario and educate myself back toward a simpler, less onerous, and cheaper solution than to build a best-case budget and add 5 or 10 percent to insure against the unknown. In practical terms, this means breaking the project down by its core implementation strategies and developing unit costs for each implementation strategy. That way, you or anyone else can:

- Review the resulting financial proposal
- Come to understand it
- Work to validate and eventually gain approval for it

Exhibit 1 provides a diluted version of the first pass we took at our budgeting scenario from an implementation perspective. As you review the detail, note that we broke down requirements into discrete tasks that we could derive average costs for, in other words, unit pricing.

Working with a team of two dozen engineers, I created this ala carte menu that showed pricing associated with each implementation element. Lest you think this sales scenario is inappropriate to a discussion of project management, let me bring this into sharper focus. From a budgetary perspective, the only difference in the pricing given to this external customer was the estimated cost marked up for the purpose of generating a profit. Otherwise, the number-crunching aspect of this is identical to the process you would undertake as a project manager validating costs for an internal customer, or a corporate cousin, if you will.[2]

Exhibit 1. Network Migration Budget Planning Worksheet

Requirement	Cost Elements
Create frame relay WAN with meshed topology and redundant access to two data centers.	Managed router network Specified bandwidth circuits (permanent virtual circuits [PVCs]) Data center routers and switches ($\times 2$) Network management hardware and software, including authentication
Connect each remote site to WAN.	Remote site routers, digital service units /channel service units (DSUs/CSUs)
Upgrade site LAN as required.	Hubs and data cabling Servers Retrofit PCs to meet new requirements Replace PCs that cannot be retrofitted
Migrating legacy applications to upgraded LANs (for local applications).	Flat rate per application, plus user tax
Roll out centralized human resources (HR) applications.	Data center server and infrastructure costs Disaster recovery infrastructure Site licenses Site installation and testing
Roll out other centralized applications.	Data center servers and infrastructure Disaster recovery infrastructure Site licenses Site installation and testing

What is even more relevant to your circumstance is this. Customers or beneficiaries, whether internal or external, tend to think of project costs in lump sum terms. Suppose the total project cost was originally pegged at $50 million. What subsequently emerges is this two-pronged expectation on the customer's part:

1. Everything they believe scope implies will be delivered in the timeframe, and to the extent that they originally envisioned.
2. The $50 million commitment they originally made is more than adequate to meet those expectations.

This mindset is so typical that you can count on it being held by your customer set. Unfortunately, in the case of complex projects, such thinking is generally a bit far-fetched, the nature of aggressive initiatives being what they are. The very important lesson to be learned from the sales environment is this. No sane salesperson would knowingly allow a customer to think that their expectation of getting everything they want for the price they are willing to pay is okay, if that expectation is ungrounded. To dramatize this scenario a little bit, from the salesperson's perspective, the cus-

167

tomer is looking for "champagne on a beer budget," whereas the salesperson wants to state, "Mr. Customer, you can only get what you pay for!"

Of course, this disconnect between customer expectations and a fair assessment of cost by the provider is handled more professionally than that. Still, the emerging delta between expectations and a realistic price tag based on a detailed analysis of the implementation strategy, risk, and other project realities must be managed. In the sales scenario, the sales person is obligated to reveal any gaps to the client. Unfortunately, this is far less likely to occur in the internally delivered project scenario, for two reasons:

1. Internal project managers are not often capable of uncovering these gaps through a detailed analysis as illustrated in this chapter.
2. A salesperson is far more motivated to find these gaps and address them than is the internal project team because the jeopardy associated with the relationship is far different. A salesperson lives in fear of losing the deal before it really gets started, so discovering and addressing this delta is a normal part of his or her professional workflow. An internal project manager does not have that fear and, thus, is less likely to worry about this delta because the assumption is that any budgetary or deliverables shortfalls will be absorbed through the normal give and take of corporate behavior.

I submit that as an internal project manager, you should feel compelled to demonstrate with reasonable certainty what the upper limits of your project output are going to be, based on committed funding. This should include a reasonable delineation of the features, functions, and benefits that you honesty believe can be produced with the resources granted to you.

At the beginning of this chapter, I presented a list of assumptions that typically drive budgetary estimates. There was one deliberate omission — the assumption that the business can afford to completely implement scope as originally conceived with that estimated dollar amount. The fact of the matter is that, with the exception of technical and logistical feasibility, nothing alters the scope of huge projects more than a rigorous budgetary analysis. Therefore, I see two benefits to this approach:

1. The budget is put together most accurately because it reflects the implementation strategy (i.e., what it is going to take to get from here to there).
2. It allows the customer to reflect on this and make hard choices about how best to spend whatever money they actually have. This is especially important if the budgetary "not to exceed number" is inadequate to accomplish everything stated or implied by scope. In the network example, the customer could plug the numbers into any deliverable and decide, for instance, if they really wanted to spend

$X per legacy application to enable it at every site on the new network. That might have been a desirable target state requirement, but if implementing it could break the bank, perhaps they are better served by rethinking their goals.

One decision made as a result of this presentation was to upgrade local PCs only for a few needing access to the new human resources (HR) application, instead of making it available to the tens of thousand of users we identified through our site surveys. The customer realized it was cheaper and in many ways more practical to hire an office administrator to run those applications for everyone else at each site, rather than upgrading dozens if not hundreds of PCs at all these sites so that everyone could complete their time sheets online.

In summary, once you get ready to finalize your budget or to validate it, it is best if your implementation strategy, or some reasonable approximation thereof, is already prepared such that you can have a realistic shot at generating appropriate numbers.

9.4 CREATING ESTIMATES

Unfortunately, there are no tricks to solid estimating other than covering the bases as thoroughly as possible. My personal expertise, if you want to call it that, is in the hardware and networking infrastructure arenas, which are simpler than some activities because the bulk of expenses are components with known costs. With this sort of estimating, you or your team can work closely with the manufacturer or qualified reseller to make sure that all:

- The right parts and pieces are considered in proper combinations and quantities.
- Extras such as cables, memory, software, engineering support, and maintenance are included.

In the area of labor estimating, making an educated guess and then doubling it is not a bad way to start. For example, if I were to recall that it takes 2 hours to upgrade an old personal computer (PC) with random access memory (RAM), a new hard drive, and a new operating system, from an estimating standpoint I would figure twice that, or 4 hours.

Why is that? Simply put, worker productivity is far short of 100 percent. Time is lost every day with meetings, vacations, tardiness, chatting, and shopping on the Internet. Because workdays are finite (i.e., people tend to go home at a regular time unless they are under the gun), you recognize that in your estimating by assuming longer work cycles than logic might suggest.

Exhibit 2. Resource Availability Rule of Thumb

	8-Hour Workday	7-Hour Workday
Total days in year	365 days	365 days
Less holidays	−10 days	−10 days
Less vacation	−10 days	−10 days
Less weekends	−104 days	−104 days
Less personal days	−5 days	−5 days
Net available days per year	236 days	236 days
Net available days per month	19.7 days	19.7 days
Gross hours per year	1888 hours	1652 hours
Less 1-hour lunch and break per day	-236 hours	−236 hours
Net available hours per year	1652 hours	1416 hours
Net available hours per month	138 hours	118 hours
Net available hours per week	31.8 hours	27.2 hours
Net available hours per day	6.4 hours	5.4 hours

Exhibit 3. Total Hours in a Real Workday

Line No.	Hours Needed	Hours per Week	Weeks Required	Days Required	Cost per Diem	Extended Cost
Line 1	1000	40	25	125	$750	$93,750
Line 2	1000	31.8	31.5	158	$750	$118,500
Delta	n/a	-8.2	6.5	32.4	n/a	$24,750

I do have a simple algorithm that is useful for sizing resource require-ments; in fact, it is also helpful for planning purposes. It is depicted in the following illustration as an unadorned arithmetical exercise of deducting weekends, holidays and so forth from the 365 days in a calendar year to show maximum hours available for work. It ignores overtime. I provided columns to distinguish between 7- and 8-hour workdays, because organiza-tions are not consistent in this way. You can make your own table if you have different work rules. Take a look at Exhibit 2, and then we will see how it can be used.

In an 8-hour workday environment, you can anticipate, for each resource, the following availability factors.

- Workdays: 236 per year or 19.7 per month
- Work hours: 1,888 work per year, 138 per month, 31.8 per week, or 6.4 per day

Now, I will provide the promised useful application of all this. Suppose a team lead requests that you fund a consultant for a deliverable estimated to take a thousand person hours. Most people would assume a 40-hour workweek, divide that into 1000 hours, and come up with a calendar time of 25 weeks to get the task done. That is represented by line 1 in Exhibit 3.

Line 2 documents how I calculate the resource requirement. It is based on the previous table, which, to repeat, says there are 31.8 work hours available per week over the long term, not the 40 hours that people generally assume. For dramatic effect, I have postulated that the consultant to be hired for this function is available at a rate of $750 per diem. The third line shows the delta resulting from the contrasting resource availability assumptions under consideration.

Compared with the traditional 40-hour workweek assumption made in calculating labor durations in line 1, my method in line 2 says you need 6.5 more weeks, or 32.4 more work days, at an added cost of nearly $25,000, to engage that resource to complete the 1000-hour task.

Remember the reality of engaging resources. These are not day laborers you send home due to inclement weather or some other condition that would render them temporarily unproductive. In the professional environment, they are on your payroll for the duration,[3] and your project coffers will bleed that money accordingly. Based on that workplace reality, it makes sense to have a realistic estimate of that cost. This is how I thumbnail the cost, assuming, of course, that the team lead's estimate of 1000 hours is credible.

While we have this tool in our hand, let us look at another way to use it, even though it is slightly off topic. Suppose we add a time constraint to the thousand-hour task scenario, specifically that the work has to be completed within a 7-month (i.e., 28-week) window because of some milestone or dependency. If you used the 40-hour workweek model given in line 1, you would say, "No problem, I only need 25 weeks, so I have 3 weeks to spare." Using my approach, you would say, "Oops, I need 31.5 weeks, so even if my 1000-hour estimate is dead on, I would be nearly 4 weeks late." If you buy into this model, you would then either work overtime with that consultant or add a second professional to make sure the work is done by your "must finish by" date.

You can shave this process any way you like. What I have recommended has worked fairly well, given the imperfections of the workplace and the occasional intrusion of misfortune. Intuitively, it would appear that the tardiness and cost overruns endemic in large IT projects are partly due to managers underestimating the time and dollars required to get work done well in a timely manner. Counting routers can be far simpler than guesstimating time. Hopefully, the thought process we have just discussed will minimize your exposure in this area going forward.

9.5 BUDGET LAUNDRY LIST

As you prepare or review your budget, it is a good idea to see if you have accounted for everything. Although Exhibit 4 may have gaps, it is an ade-

Exhibit 4. Budgetary Laundry List

Item	Description
PCs or laptops	Include mice, displays, network interface cards (NIC), memory, base OS, antivirus, wireless, USB ports.
Servers	Include RAM, disks or arrays, backup equipment and media, backup media multiple NICs, antivirus, monitoring, base OS, multiple CPUs, application toolsets (Web server, database, etc.), multiple power supplies, remote control hardware.
Software	Licenses, latest patches or upgrades, maintenance, companion tools.
Network infrastructure	Cabling, routers, switches with required components (dual power supplies, management cards, ports), monitoring tools.
Data center elements	Racks or cabinets for servers and routers; power; heating, ventilating, and air-conditioning (HVAC); security, fire protection; humidification; surveillance equipment.
WAN	Circuits, routers, multiplexers, DSU/CSUs, cabling from demarcs to racks, redundancy, monitoring tools.
Moving costs	For relocating servers or users. Includes labor, consulting and swing servers for relocating production applications.
Consultant fees	For staff augmentation, writing code, configuring hardware or software, project management, documentation, or testing.
Turnover costs	Fees, documentation, training, and tools.
Security	Physical or IT services or devices.
Miscellaneous project costs	Includes meals for off hours, extra PCs or laptops for remote work or consultants, test circuits, documentation, and hosting fees for off-site servers.

quate starting point for your next budgetary analysis exercise. Remember, you should be using this to check the work of others, not to do the work yourself. The benefit of arming yourself with this list is to allow you to ask semi-intelligent questions with the intent of ensuring quality and reminding others of things they forgot.

9.6 THINGS CAN LOOK ODD UNDER THE BUDGETARY MICROSCOPE

When you review budgets, take the time to investigate the detail. I once saw a line item for $2 million with a description I could not decipher. I ended up deciding it was probably either a very wild guess or a boondoggle. It turned out to be a little of both. Project dollars are used for many things, sometimes even for the project itself. Functional managers, who generally serve as project team leads as well, fight to grow and maintain head count because that is what they do for a living. Project dollars are very helpful in resource intensive environments and can be used to improve shortfalls in the (BAU) environment with varying impact on project activities.

Perhaps this should be put bluntly. On big projects, team leads deliberately pad some labor cost estimates, with the intent of addressing resource issues internal to their team that do not necessarily map to project activities. This happens with hardware, software, and training budget line items as well. No sane project manager would completely reject any such efforts at creative funding by key team leads; but there must be some sort of quid pro quo for the winking and head turning this sort of transaction requires on your part, or you end up getting little in return for your largess.

Another potential area for examination is hard to give a title to because the one I would like to use, "operational considerations," is somewhat misleading. Normally, a project is not based solely on postimplementation costs, but you cannot assume that the designers have acted in a financially responsible manner in this area. I had a situation where the engineers specified a pair of storage area network (SAN) devices. A SAN is a high-capacity disk storage device that multiple computing platforms can use to manage data. It is extremely expensive, or at least so it appeared to be in the context of this particular project. Quite frankly, it was difficult to understand the justification for that expense. Then again, I was not the final decision maker.

Anyway, during the process of trying to understand the proposed design, a heretofore-undisclosed design element came to light. It was a special network connection between two sites so that the data on one SAN could be automatically replicated to the SAN at the other location. It was further ascertained that the operational cost of this connection would be nearly $60,000 a month. Not even in my wildest moments could I justify such an expense, particularly given the intended use for the SAN, which as I said was somewhat dubious from the beginning. Although it is not a project consideration per se, it made no practical sense to do this, so we had the design changed. Intersite connectivity was achieved another way. That slightly increased project cost but leveraged the existing WAN infrastructure for free, resulting in a significant net savings to the corporation once monthly operational costs were included in the mix. The SANs remained in the design, but the questionable level of investment was diminished, from an operational standpoint, by $700,000 a year!

9.7 HANDLING PROSPECTIVE SHORTFALLS

If, upon a rigorous examination, you uncover a significant prospective shortfall, you must escalate this by taking the following steps:

1. Document the potential shortfall, providing detail as appropriate.
2. Describe the impact on your project if funding is not adjusted.

3. Back up your assertions using industry standards, previous experience, or a detailed analysis. This should be clear, concise, and as brief as possible.
4. Deliver it with a business-like tone that focuses on the facts. Avoid criticizing the original estimate because you may not know whose political blessing gave this budget its life. In other words, be respectful so as to avoid currying disfavor in unseen or unforeseen places. I like to use phrases such as:
   - "Based on a detailed analysis of costs after finalizing the design ..."
   - "After estimates were originally prepared, new information became available that indicates the original estimate of $X will have to be increased by Y percent because ..."
5. Have the team lead associated with the budget area under question participate in this escalation process because, in essence, you are going to bat for him or her.

If your project is quite large, chances are that you will find fluff from which you can divert funding for your shortfall, but I would leave that money untouched until you absolutely have to use it. The alleged tasks associated with that $2 million boondoggle I mentioned earlier were ultimately dropped from the project. Around 75 percent of the funds were given back to the corporation, but the project retained and spent that last half million on overtime, and justifiably so. The point is, we did not return the money prematurely and then have to go back to the well for it later when we needed it. No one ever questioned why the other funds were not spent, except, of course, those who had designs on it.

The best case in requesting additional funding is, naturally, that your request is cheerfully granted. The worst-case scenario is that your request is denied. Do not despair if that happens. You have put yourself on record as needing the money. If, or when, it turns out that you were right, management is less likely to hold it against you when reminded that the money you needed 6 months ago now blocks your critical path. This is how the game is played.

9.8 SERVICE DELIVERY AND COST RECOVERY

I have alluded to the potential of beneficiaries to be cranky if not disruptive, and I devote Chapter 13 to that interesting battleground. A word about them here is useful in terms of the budget. In most major corporations and governmental agencies, users (i.e., beneficiaries) pay for services received through various user-based taxes. In my experience, this generally includes desktop and laptop PCs, use of LAN and mainframe file and print services, e-mail, dial tone, voice mail, and so forth. Many, if not all, of your project deliverables cost the corporation an initial outlay for new equipment and licenses, services, salaries, and consulting fees. That is your budget. In the normal course of business, however, the end user receiving these new products or services as a result of your project will be charged, normally on a recurring charge basis per server, per site, or per user. So, as project manager, I may give the vendor $X million for laptops, but the beneficiary I install them for will pay the corporation back at a rate of a few hundred dollars per month, per laptop, over a 3-year period.[4]

What this boils down to is that beneficiaries see themselves as customers, and why not? With that title comes its privileges, which include fussing with you over such technology choices as vendor used, specifications, and whether or not they want to pay for the "cool stuff" too. Presumably, your technology team made such decisions based on merit or need, but that does not guarantee that the beneficiary community agrees on how you and your team propose to spend their money. In fact, in such a scenario, we had to ask the beneficiaries to provide additional money for certain features for which we were not funded but they demanded. Once that was hammered out, we had to enlist the beneficiaries' assistance with the "standards police," who took exception to the uplifted specs pushed on the project team by the user community.

9.9 WHEN IS AN APPROVED EXPENDITURE APPROVED?

In today's cost-conscious environment, even though a budget is approved, there may be additional steps to plan for and execute as part of the procurement process. There will always be a sign-off process for expenditures. Generally speaking, the total cost of each purchase will determine the management level required to approve that purchase. This individual may not be part of the project team or necessarily sympathetic to your objectives.

In some cases, you will need to escalate purchase requests to get products and services delivered in a timely manner. We have also been involved in purchase reviews where we had to present the requirement to an executive committee prior to the purchase order being cut, even though the items in question had long since been approved. To summarize, it is not really your money, even though it has that appearance.

9.10 WHERE DOES THE MONEY GO?

If cost overruns are typical, why is that so? You may select your favorite from the following list of potential explanations:

- If the initial budget was off target, you cannot win for losing.
- Even if you do a credible job of reforecasting the budget after a rigorous requirement development process and publicize the need for additional funding, the project number may remain locked in at the lower, inaccurate amount.

- Delays due to poor planning, performance, participation, and as the insurers say, "acts of God or terrorism," all cost money.
- IT projects have a way of being more labor intensive than originally thought. As the project begins to lag, it is common practice to throw more resources at the sticking points. That costs money.
- Requirements can change once the beneficiary gets involved. These changes are probably going to inflate actual cost beyond the original budget. We built out a new corporate campus and ran over budget on the network side by a significant sum. The main reason was that the customer wanted more LAN and telephone connections in conference rooms and other common areas than was originally planned. This required the purchase of additional telecom switch cards for dozens of floors. You can call this poor requirements gathering, or you can call it giving in to the customer (i.e., "scope creep"). The reality is that internally this additional cost will be recouped by the monthly service charge billed to the beneficiaries for those extra ports. Those funny money credits go to the service organization, however, while the overrun stays on the project books forever.
- There is a scenario I like to call "oh, you want it to work?" Sometimes, if you do not ask the right way, or the right person, you will fail to get the right answer. You may find yourself sitting in a meeting one day with technical staff or a vendor and have to bite your tongue when they tell you with a straight face that the "real cost" has just doubled because you never told them that conditions C, D, and E were in scope. Your distemper, of course, emanates from the fact that you thought that clearly stipulated conditions A and B quite naturally implied that C, D, and E would be required as well, and thus would have been covered by the original cost estimate.
- You do not watch carefully and get ripped off. Once a project code is published, all kinds of people may bill against it, some of who have no business doing so. Vendors cannot always be assumed to be on the up and up, either, although many such instances of internal or external fraud wind up being characterized as misunderstandings. Although it may be difficult to swallow, people are out there who, unfortunately, will take the opportunity of project chaos to literally steal equipment, for example.

9.11 TRACKING EXPENDITURES

Big-ticket projects tend to happen in big companies that have a rough time tracking costs. Purchasing and project management systems are rarely integrated. At least, I have yet to see one that does so with timeliness and accuracy. Timekeeping systems have no real controls, anyway. When we looked and ascertained that well over 200 people were charging their time against a particular project and we recognized less than half those names, all we could do was shrug our shoulders. We had enough trouble managing the important parts of the project without taking on the additional task of auditing hundreds of time sheets every week.

It behooves you to align yourself with the appropriate parties who can provide accurate purchasing numbers. This should include equipment, services, consultants, and so on. It can be hard to get that data in a reasonable timeframe and keep it updated, but it is worth a try. As the old joke goes: "A million here, 300,000 there, and pretty soon you are talking real money!" Someone is getting invoices from vendors and tracking them against the cost centers or project number near and dear to you. Find out who that is, and get on their distribution list. Assign your tech writer, if you are fortunate enough to have one, or someone else to build and maintain a simple spreadsheet. I have even tracked the data myself a time or two. No matter how it is done, I cannot tell you how wonderful it is to really know where you stand, particularly when unforeseen expenditures come up and you need to pay for them.

9.12 OVERRUNS

This is something you need to be monitoring in real time. Know your budget and track against it, or be in constant touch with the people in accounting or procurement who perform that service. On a large project, there will be plenty of give and take. For instance, we budgeted millions for a rollout component that cost 15 percent less a year later when we actually made the buy. In that same project, we abandoned a new technology after it was deemed unstable, but significant monies were spent before we pulled the plug. So, our savings in the first instance were essentially negated by the loss in the latter.

- *Cover yourself on overruns.* If you budget $X for a project deliverable and learn the procurement cost is significantly higher, get everyone to sign off on the delta prior to executing the purchase order. Document the reasons for the increased cost as part of the sign-off.
- *Socialize your savings.* Do not do this in a self-promoting way but simply to get a check mark on the debit side of the ledger. If your project is large enough, there will be offsetting losses soon enough, so any significant savings deserves visibility.
- *Challenge costs.* Vendors as well as internal service organizations want and need your project dollars. Some vendors will take you for a ride if you let them. As a general rule, treat project dollars like they are your own personal funds. More discrepancies come from honest mistakes than fraud, but either cause is more common in the workplace than most people care to acknowledge.

- *Spend wisely.* Throwing money at problems without adequate analysis and control is shortsighted and possibly dangerous. At the other extreme, being penny-wise and pound-foolish can be harmful as well.

9.13 CONCLUSION

What I have tried to do in this chapter is present valuable insight and guidelines regarding the budget process without getting overly didactic. As a consulting project manager who has worked in some of the biggest American corporations or governmental agencies, I can honestly state that the way money is handled, speaking both culturally as well as procedurally, is one of the most significant differences I see among clients. My personal experience ranges from being in total control of every penny, to having little responsibility other than for negative variances that eventually show up in the old "budget versus actual" column. So, although some of my advice and comments may not hold true in your circumstances, I urge you at the very least to understand how much money you have and how things are going in that regard. It is like eyeballing the gas gauge as your car approaches that long stretch of highway where no gas stations are likely to be found. If you ever ran out of gas, or project money, I am quite certain you understand what I am saying.

Here is one last statement about budgets. Sometimes, a few layers above you, a decision is made to extract dollars from your budget to supplement a shortfall elsewhere in that executive's realm. This has happened to me a couple of times, and without warning, of course. Therefore, it pays to comprehend where you stand because in the project world, money, as they say, is everything.

Notes

1. This is another rationale for including success metrics in the Big Thirteen interrogatory.
2. This is why, in addition to maintaining confidentiality, costs are not listed in Exhibit 1.
3. Most would walk out on you if you tried micromanaging their time sheets in this manner.
4. Or whatever the current depreciation schedule is.

Chapter 10
Understanding and Managing Vendors

Vendors can be significant partners in your information technology (IT) project. They may create, deliver, install, maintain, or support critical components of your target state. That being the case, implicit in your reliance on the vendors are one or more of the following:

- High-performance hardware, software, resources, or support
- On-time delivery
- Technical expertise
- Fast and thorough fault resolution
- Training
- Professional relations with your team, customers, and beneficiaries

This chapter has been written to address these expectations. As great as they are, they may be unrealistic. Having served on both sides of the fence in these relationships, it is my observation that vendor management from a project perspective is generally clumsy and haphazard. If true, that tends to make these relationships less beneficial and rewarding to both parties. Working on the assumption that we, as customers, cannot fix any vendor problems, we can still be aware of them and leverage that knowledge to our advantage. We can also acknowledge that large corporations generally make for lousy customers, whether through arrogance, incompetence, carelessness, or sheer size. The same faults can be attributed to many of our vendors, by the way.

10.1 ABOUT VENDORS

Once you plug a vendor's name into the plan against a major deliverable, you are assigning responsibility to them and designating them as a critical facilitator of success. Whether they are writing code, delivering systems, or cobbling technology together in your computer rooms, you expect them to perform on time and up to your specifications. Unless you manage them properly, however, there is plenty of history that suggests their success in this regard is not a sure thing.

179

Exhibit 1. Customer–Vendor Relationship Disconnects

• The vendor may lack the logistical infrastructure or resource that can meet your needs precisely while servicing other, equally demanding customers.
• How many superstars in their employ can be dedicated to your project.[a]
• Does your view of their deliverables, roles, and responsibilities match theirs?
• Vendors generally see the customer squeezing relentlessly on price, while demanding scope creep for free.
• Customers generally see vendors cherry picking (i.e., performing easy, profitable work while avoiding the tough, low-margin work that you really need them to produce).

[a]While you are at it, take the same look at your own team.

Why is that? Your company may already have paid this particular vendor millions, based on a longstanding partnership. Or, you have selected a vendor new to your firm — a vendor who now has the opportunity to get wonderful references from you after this project is done, and thus achieve greater penetration within your company with future opportunities.

You would think either scenario would provide the vendor with enough sensitivity to your requirements that the vendor marching with you in lock step to the finish line is assured, right? It would probably not happen that way. Honestly, though, one wonders why these relationships cause so much hand wringing and gnashing of teeth — on both sides, incidentally. Customers grouse about vendors, who, in turn, mutter among themselves about the unreasonableness of the customer set. Exhibit 1 offers a dispassionate look at client–vendor relationships in this manner.

Now that we have set the table for the discussion of managing vendors, let us look at the key areas.

10.2 EXISTING VENDORS

Many projects require the participation of vendors that your corporation or agency already has under contract. Vendors whose behavior is generally proscribed by this process typically provide "commoditized" products or services such as:

- *Network transport* — voice or data circuits and services
- *Hardware* — routers, switches, computers, and servers
- *"Shrink-wrapped" software* — spreadsheets, accounts payable
- *Operating systems* — desktop and network
- *Support* — help desk, fault management, "break–fix"
- *Procurement* — resellers who deliver equipment and software
- *Staff augmentation* — short-term help or technical consultants

A formalized relationship management team tasked with managing vendor relationships is probably in place in your shop. Vendor, product set, or service type may align the team. The focal point may be in a product man-

Exhibit 2. Rules of Engagement for Your Vendor Management Team

- Make them aware of your project and your interest in leveraging an existing relationship.
- Provide detailed requirements you look for the vendor to provide.
- Determine if any requirements are provided, or precluded, by existing contracts between your organization and the vendor.
- Ask what specific benefits may accrue to the project (e.g., discounts, free services, etc.) by using this incumbent vendor.
- Understand how you can, and cannot, communicate with the vendor.

agement group, or within the purchasing department. The degree of control they exercise over the relationship may be quite strong. Likewise, such mechanisms can be extremely political, particularly if you approach the vendor without understanding your vendor management's mission and process. In other words, circumventing their process, either willfully or through unfamiliarity, can be hazardous to your project calendar's health.

Therefore, if you intend to leverage existing relationships to buy products or services, make it your business to hook up with your internal vendor or product management team before you get too far into the process of engaging that vendor. This includes requesting budgetary pricing or initiating exploratory conversations regarding services they offer that appeal to you from a project perspective.

Exhibit 2 highlights preferred behavior when engaged with the people in your organization who are charged with overseeing vendor contracts.

I have seen cases where it is okay to go directly to the vendor without vendor management tagging along. I have also seen the opposite, where I could talk to a vendor about approved products or services (i.e., technical things), but was definitely prohibited from discussing pricing or other business-related topics. The bottom line is that you need to gauge, as early on as possible, how your company does business with this vendor and whether or not that meets your needs. I have had as many pleasant surprises in this area as disappointments. For instance, I learned that existing contracts with two big vendors provided certain project services at prices far lower than an internal group I was told to use would charge, with the same or better service levels.

On the other hand, I have been told that Vendor X could not provide a product or service I felt quite certain they could, or that their pricing, service levels, or availability was disadvantageous to our initiative. Equally distressing is the discovery that vendor management can exercise veto power over certain kinds of purchases, particularly based on technology standards. Please refer back to Chapter 2, where additional detail on this topic was provided under the tag of "standards police." You may find that vendor management appears to have more input about how you can implement your requirements than you do. Not that this happens all the time, but when it does, technology and calendar issues are usually too pressing to allow you the luxury of working your way through this without intense escalation and negotiation.

Not only can the process not necessarily be tailored to meet your needs, but there is a chance that the vendor is unaware of you and your project. I once had to escalate a technical issue with a vendor with whom we were soon planning to place a multimillion-dollar order based on corporate standards. I chose to go to the senior account manager to get our problem resolved. Fortunately, he knew about our project. Unfortunately, my name was unknown to him. As a result, his initial response back to me was a tad more lackadaisical and pompous than I was comfortable with. We worked our way past that glitch and resolved the real issue to my complete and total satisfaction — and rather quickly at that.

This is lesson one in vendor management for project managers. We may have been forced to buy through this person. He, in turn, may have felt I was just another yippy customer not in his cell phone speed dialer, at least until I took it upon myself to impress him with my importance! Some folks shy away from this scenario, while others enjoy thumping the table. The approach I prefer is to inform the vendor that I am responsible for making this project fly right, and I need his or her help to ensure that no one is embarrassed by the results. It turns out that this vendor rep was adequately conscientious once I pushed the right button.

That button is likely to be that these individuals have strategic goals within your organization — goals upon which their commissions are based, perhaps as much as those quotas related to sales volume. Knowing this, I asked the salesman what his strategic goals were. One of them happened to involve a technology we were considering using, so I offered to push his goal if he would move heaven and earth to solve my original problem. We both honored out commitments, and the project was definitely helped by this.

10.3 NEW VENDORS

Some project requirements may dictate that you seek out a new vendor for those deliverables. This would likely be driven by one of two conditions:

1. An incumbent vendor may be unable to meet your dates or certain product or service specifications, including price and availability.
2. Incumbent vendors may not be technically qualified or experienced with a particular deliverable.

Before getting involved in a detailed look at bringing a new vendor into the fold, I must surface a very old IT axiom, which alleges, "No one ever got fired going with IBM." I do not interpret this as disrespectful toward Big Blue, by the way. Instead, the message is that reaching out to new vendors or products can introduce a series of challenges that may:

- Require long lead times
- Introduce risk not previously experienced
- Take lots of patience to resolve

First, let us put a fence around this conversation by stipulating a few conditions:

1. You need to go to a new vendor because incumbent vendors cannot satisfy one or more of your project requirements.
2. The service you are trying to locate is more than a procurement scenario.
3. The potential deliverables are complex and largely customized.
4. Your company probably lacks the training and experience with the product one normally looks for in the aftermath of testing and implementation.
5. Let us also put aside the procurement process itself for the moment.

The level of risk associated with selecting a new vendor is directly proportional to the complexity of the goods or services you intend to procure from them. The uniqueness of the product or service should be considered as well. As an example, a few years ago, our engineers wanted to connect two storage area networks (SAN) located in sites that were ninety miles apart. These SANs are big disk arrays normally attached to servers using the Fibre Channel (FC) Protocol, which at the time could not span those 90 miles. The engineers came up with a product that converted the protocol from FC to Internet Protocol (IP), so the data packets could safely traverse the distance. At the other site, the IP datagrams were then converted back to Fibre Channel and stored on the alternate site SAN.

The somewhat frightening news was that only one vendor supplied such a product, and it was still in "beta" (i.e., preproduction) state. This, in essence, raises the risk to the next power, by sole sourcing a new technology not even in production and installing it in a huge wide area network (WAN) to provide site-to-site data mirroring for disaster recovery (DR). We insisted on pretty rigorous testing and kept a very close eye on the implementation before turning it into production.

10.4 VENDOR SELECTION PROCESS

In my experience, the disconnect between customer expectation and vendor performance comes from a breakdown in communications between the two parties, whether the vendor is new or entrenched. The difference, if there is any, in recuperation from this common experience is that the incumbent vendor probably has a long-term relationship that can be used to escalate and resolve unforeseen issues or misapprehended requirements. I have sadly learned more than once that new vendors may not know how to do this with you and your company, or anyone else.

From the point at which a vendor is selected, whether that turns out to be a new one or an incumbent, you need to treat the vendor as new to you, and be very careful how you proceed. Before that is covered, let us take a look at the vendor selection process, where the challenge often begins.

At a previous engagement, a fellow project manager was tasked with a project where the scope was to replace the electronic badging system used at a few sites. There would be one server at each site, plus a disaster recovery server elsewhere. The system would manage one hundred thousand badges and thousands of access points. The server platform and software had already been selected, so my colleague's project tasks were to:

- Write a request for proposal (RFP) to identify the right vendor.
- Select the vendor per internal procurement standards.
- Replace existing card readers with a new, specified reader.
- Replace the existing "last mile" cabling from hubs to individual readers.
- Test the system in conjunction with the application support team.
- Remove old wiring and readers after successful testing.
- Obtain maintenance on the new wiring and card readers, with specified service levels.

If you had to guess how many pages the RFP was when it went out, what would your number be? If your guess is under 100 pages, your commitment to brevity, although commendable, has knocked you out of the competition. Even with relatively detailed drawings or descriptions of the legacy system and the requisite terms and conditions, the RFP should have been approximately 50 to 75 pages, not the 300 or so it turned out to be. Although the intent leading to this overkill was clearly to make sure everything that could possibly be included was, the opposite results were obtained, including:

- Lack of clarity
- Disorganization
- Contradictory verbiage

Although I mean no disrespect with any part of this story, it is instructive in many ways. RFPs are often the strategic component in the vendor selection process. I think we all can acknowledge that obtaining satisfactory results for both customers and vendors through this process is statis-

Exhibit 3. RFP Process Disconnects

- The customer struggles to paint an accurate picture of target state.
- Precise customer data is rarely available (census, asset counts, site information).
- The vendor struggles to understand how much work (i.e., cost) is required to achieve target state.
- Service levels, training, testing, and staffing requirements are too open ended.
- Vendors strongly dislike being asked to state their "preferred" solution.
- Respondents' proposals are difficult to compare as "apples to apples."

tically dubious. I have personally written and responded to dozens of these documents, some of them having presumptive price tags upward of $100 million. I can recall numerous occasions, as a vendor, when I would read one of these huge documents and wonder what in the world the customer was requesting.

I can also assure you that if, as a vendor, you receive an RFP from a customer with which you have done little or no business, you are tempted to chuck it in the dustbin. This is because you figure you are being used to pad the bid list so the customer can claim that a lot of vendors had a shot at the business, even though the deal was wired from the start with an incumbent provider.

On the flip side, as a customer I have read responses and accompanying questions from vendors that made me wonder if some of these companies or their employees had read our RFP, or had experience in the disciplines or activities that were the RFP's focus. Exhibit 3 summarizes the inherent, or at least probable, sticking points associated with the RFP process.

These conditions are not always true, but they generally are. What usually happens is this; because the customer cannot fully describe the current environment, target state, and his or her preferred path to get there, that ball gets tossed into the vendor's court. In essence, the customer says, "Give me your recommendations on what target state should really look like, and the best way to get there." Vendors are not stupid, and they are somewhat paranoid about losing business over pricing. So, they perceive RFPs as if the customer is really asking, "What is your best price for giving us the world?" In fairness, the customer wants value at a controllable cost, whereas the vendor wants a happy customer at a decent margin, but you can see from these disconnects how impossible those goals often turn out to be.

What tends to happen, then, is vendors respond with unit or tier pricing. Because the demographics (i.e., census or asset data) is generally pretty lame, and everyone knows it, the vendor offers basic products or services at a unit price. The vendor is protecting margin by saying "We will charge you $2 a widget. You tell me how many widgets are in scope, and we will do the math together." There is usually an accompanying floor and a ceiling, meaning there is:

- A minimal billing assumption of, for instance, 10,000 widgets
- A "not to exceed" billing level of a million widgets

Tier pricing is the other workaround. It typically reflects a laddered service level proposition. It is similar to going to the car wash, where the soap and water is $5, the wax job another $3.50, and the vacuuming is free if you pay for the wash and the wax. In IT projects, tiers focus on things such as recovery times, hours of support, and other matters of convenience. "The more service you get," they tell the customer, "the more you pay." A 24/7 call center, for instance, requires a headcount of five to provide one agent taking calls around the clock, once vacation, shifts, and supervision are taken into consideration. Someone has to pay for that. There is this myth of economies of scale, but having done some of that work, I can tell you that leveraging such economies generally translates into generic, depersonalized, and frequently ineffective service to the end users. I am not too sure about the savings, either.

Vendors tend to shy away from precise responses from a solution perspective for two reasons:

1. They fear that any good ideas revealed in the response will be shared by the customer with the selected vendor, who would likely be someone else.
2. Some vendor reticence to indulge in RFP response specificity is based on the fear that their proposed solution will be perceived as culturally or operationally incompatible with the customer's environment. Although this is one condition the RFP process is designed to ferret out, no salesperson worth his or her salt is going to create the impression that his or her team is strictly left-handed, especially when claims of ambidexterity appear far more likely to carry the day.

The final consideration is this. Several chapters and thousands of words have been dedicated in this book to tracking down requirements, vetting the design, crafting the right implementation strategies, and indemnifying the project, the environment, and beneficiaries against risk. To do this well, you needed liberal access to all kinds of resources, and you presumably held countless meetings. Put yourself in the shoes of a vendor's project manager who reads through your RFP and wonders how to protect his employer while doing a great job for you without the same advance, unlimited access to everything the insiders have. As a consequence, vendors quite naturally feel compelled to jack up their prices to cover risk that may, or may not, be lurking out there in customer land.

You may not be shocked to learn that vendors tend not to trust customers. Still, it is interesting to take a moment with the worst-case scenario in this regard, one that seasoned vendor representatives and project managers have experienced on numerous occasions. In it, a vendor agrees to perform certain project services for a fixed price, with agreed-to drop-dead dates. Sadly, it turns out that the customer had misrepresented the work or the risk associated with it. Even though this miscommunication may have been unintentional, the vendor tries to negotiate a different price or gain time to overcome this emerging trouble. The customer does not want to look incompetent, or more broadly, does not want it to appear that the problem is internal. Whether brazenly or not, the customer starts pointing the accusatory finger at the vendor. Now the vendor, who to this point has operated in relatively good faith, has three choices:

1. Call the customer a liar.
2. Eat the cost and take the blame to keep the customer happy.
3. Escalate on the client side, taking the chance that the seniors will be reasonable.

Frankly, this is all part of the vendor–customer taffy pull, but it is in the mind of every vendor representative responding to your RFP. Because I am taking the customer's side on the topic for this book, I want to end this section by summarizing what has been said here. Using RFPs to select vendors is a minefield because many issues surround whether or not an outsider should commit wholeheartedly to a possibly ill-conceived or, at least, poorly presented initiative. The vendor is being asked to offer a best price for a potentially high-risk venture. Add to this the potential for either side trying to use the other, and you can see why this process is often frustrating and can lead to unsatisfactory results. It also shows why, so often, an incumbent vendor wins the business in the end because they truly have an inside track, and they find the potential risks less onerous than vendors who are asked to fly blind on this one.

10.5 DOING RFPs RIGHT

The purpose of the last section is to sensitize you to the vendor mindset so that when you manage your next RFP process, you can better understand why responses do not come back exactly as you expected. Keep in mind that the vendor really wants to know:

- What exactly is the customer asking for in terms of design, implementation, documentation, and support?
- How much work will the customer perform (i.e., what are the roles and responsibilities of each party)?

- How will risks and exceptions be handled? In other words, how is potential scope creep defined and addressed both managerially and financially?
- What is the preferred pricing methodology?
- What is the targeted price?
- What desired vendor services are "baseline," and which are considered optional and can be presented and priced as such?
- What future opportunities can result from a job well done this time around?

This last question may appear to be out of place, but it is not. Vendors quite naturally desire long-term relationships. From your RFP perspective, the opportunity for future business may give them cause to shave your potential costs up front, with the expectation of gaining future opportunities. This is, of course, a big carrot, but one you must use carefully. The vendor does not expect any promises, but is in actuality trying to gauge your willingness to negotiate and be open minded during this courtship. This is particularly true if the RFP deliverables represent a new technology or process for the customer.

If you do not do a good job of projecting your open mindedness, most vendors will respond somewhat cynically, unless the sales manager for a particular vendor is desperate to make quota or is new to the role and thus somewhat naïve. If you are not open minded because you prefer, or are directed to prefer, a specific vendor, understand that most vendors anticipate this. They may be disinclined to respond to you with value, either now or in the future. I see a lot of people disregard this, but in the business world as it appears to be shaping up at the start of the new millennium, I would remind you that your own personal credibility is all you have, given the disappearing corporate loyalty and tenure characterizing the workplace.

Exhibit 4 is dedicated to the RFP process and the steps through which you should manage, in case this is the vehicle selected for meeting one or more project deliverables.

It is important that you fully understand the project before launching into the RFP process. If the RFP is not clear, then you cannot expect the responses to add much value either. A rough RFP can generate a lot of chaos as potential bidders flood you with questions. You can expect a lot anyway, but you want to avoid spending any more time on that than you have to. In any case, it is important that you capture all questions, and distribute answers to all vendors on the bid list. Do not identify the source of any question. This may require paraphrasing some questions if the bidder uses language or product names that might reveal his or her identity. Pro-

Exhibit 4. RFP Process

1. Verify that existing vendor contracts do not meet project requirements.
2. Understand corporate RFP requirements (e.g., legal, procurement).
3. Clearly define scope, requirements, and implementation strategy.
4. Develop supporting data, drawings, and workflows.
5. Clearly define key milestones, including dates and attributes.
6. Clearly define risk.
7. Identify key tasks and deliverables desired from the vendor.
8. Identify any optional tasks that could be assigned to the vendor.
9. Gain stakeholder agreement on items 1 through 8 before writing your RFP.
10. Include project background, scope, and anticipated vendor deliverables.
11. Include all information that will help the bidders understand your project.
12. Include "boilerplate" terms and conditions your contract will incorporate.
13. Include a schedule for the process, with deadlines and decision dates.
14. Include vendor selection criteria.
15. Issue the RFP.
16. Solicit questions.
17. Distribute answers to all questions to all respondents.
18. Hold a bidders' conference to allow one final round of clarification.
19. Perform a thorough analysis of all responses.
20. Make your vendor selection as per your predefined process.

tecting anonymity helps maintain probity, which you should feel obligated to do.

It is also a good idea to schedule a bidders' conference. This should occur sometime between publishing answers to the initial bidder questions and the due date of the final responses. Be sure everyone has a chance to participate. These meetings are generally quite awkward because you are hosting a room full of competitors. I like to review the project one more time, go over the published questions and answers, and allow some time, but not too much, for questioning. It is important to try to control this session because you can expect one or more individuals to try capturing your attention as though this meeting were a sales opportunity.

During this process, you must avoid communicating with individual vendor reps about the RFP from the time its existence becomes public knowledge through the award date. I once protested an award to a different vendor when it was quite obvious that the customer was cozying up to that vendor at everyone else's expense. I actually got an audience with the firm's senior procurement officer as a consequence. Although he denied my supposition of favoritism, the bid went to the suspected favorite. Oddly enough, however, I began receiving business from this customer who had previously ignored yours truly and my company. In some instances, the repercussions for being disingenuous with this process can be far worse than getting a cranky letter from a disappointed salesperson, so be circumspect in this regard.

Many RFP issuers predetermine a selection criterion and, in fact, may include it in the RFP itself because most bidders are going to ask on what basis the award will be made. This process often is a scorecard system, where the first level of analysis is based on the percent to which each bidder professes compliance against individual RFP requirements. Pricing is generally, but not always, given as a key but not sole determinant of the award. Be sure and leave yourself wiggle room on this. Unless your procurement rules stipulate that the lowest bid must win, you want to reserve the right to make your final decision on the overall quality of a particular response in conjunction with other factors that you do not necessarily have to share with the vendors.

Vendor relationships created in this manner end up going through the contract process. During this phase, people in purchasing and legal will become your best friends. This is rarely a quick or pleasant experience. This document will end up with a statement of work (SOW) detailing what is required of the vendor. Of course, a pricing section is included, where the actual costs are embedded, along with payment and penalty schedules. Organizational commitments may be included, too, whereby the two companies formalize the interactions from a management and escalation perspective. And finally, there will be terms and conditions regarding exit strategies, indemnifications, protection of intellectual property, and so on.

It is difficult to generalize regarding the proper level of your involvement in this process, other than to mention that it is not unusual for it to drag on for so long that work is started and dollars are expended by both sides before all the paperwork gets hammered out. The other issue to anticipate is that once the lawyers get involved, the process tends to turn into a risk-avoidance exercise. Each side will be looking to protect itself from any evil the other side could knowingly or unwittingly visit upon the other. Besides being the root cause of interminable delays in getting the final document executed, it gives project managers reason to worry that the contractual definition of deliverables, roles, and responsibilities might be diluted beyond recognition. There is no magic bullet for this other than staying involved and trying to keep things moving along.

10.6 THIRTEEN STEPS OF VENDOR MANAGEMENT

Whether you add a vendor through the RFP process or choose to leverage an existing relationship, from a project perspective, you and the vendor need to find a comfortable middle ground from which you can work together effectively. Although you cannot treat them exactly as you would internal subteams, neither can you hold them at arm's length like a mute

Exhibit 5. Thirteen Steps of Vendor Management

1. Maintain a detailed, written audit trail of all discussions and agreements.
2. When documenting vendor tasks, the operative phrase is "the vendor shall."
3. Get a written commitment on vendor team members, escalation, etc.
4. Roles and responsibilities are clearly written and agreed to.
5. Rules of engagement should include onsite attendance requirements.
6. Implementation strategies are mutually agreed upon.
7. Reserve the right to review vendor designs and request changes.
8. Project plans are submitted in advance for your approval.
9. Test plans are submitted in advance for your approval.
10. Specify documentation required from the vendor, including media and format.
11. Specify support and maintenance to be provided.
12. Prearrange change control processes and pricing to address scope creep.
13. Any training provided by the vendor must be preapproved by you.

porter in a five-star hotel. In the end, your expectations are the same with a vendor as they are with subteams, so you are going to walk through all the processes already documented in this book, as appropriate. This may include requirements and specifications, risk, implementation planning, and scheduling. Exhibit 5 is presented as a checklist to guide you through this vendor management process.

As early as possible, you need to facilitate a target state walk-through wherein both sides agree on project objectives. Then, you can engage them in discussions regarding implementation strategy and risk analysis. These conversations can start as a white board exercise, but the emerging results must be formally documented, preferably before that first shovel full of dirt gets moved. If you need 12 things done or 7 specific functions provided by the new software, spell them out. You should dialog with the vendor and any customers or beneficiaries during this exchange to gain confidence that the project will be a success and that everyone will remain on speaking terms from start to finish. Any scope, performance, or timeline issues should be identified and resolved at this point, when you have the best opportunity to fix things.[1]

Understand your vendor's processes. By taking the time to understand how he or she does business, you can more readily adapt to, and resolve, issues that are bound to arise. If your vendor is having people or supplier problems, you need to understand this sooner rather than later and escalate or resolve as necessary. Vendors are loathe to blow the whistle on themselves if they are experiencing backorders or performance slippage, but you need to know this as soon as they do so you can keep your project on track. Sometimes this requires managing them more than you would like, but that is life in the big city.

Exhibit 6. General Vendor Guidelines

- Understand any existing vendor terms and, if necessary, change them.
- Do not assume an incumbent vendor will do what you need.
- Always spell things out, leaving nothing to chance.
- Extract confirmations in writing.
- Do not turn checking status into a witch-hunt, but do stay on top of things.
- Be ever vigilant and proactive.
- Make a point of understanding how to trust and manage each vendor.

Build relationships with key vendor personnel. Although you want them to respect your internal protocols and you should do the same for them, it is important that you are comfortable picking up the phone and speaking with more than one person in their organization. To do this effectively, you need to understand the role of each of their key players, and leverage them accordingly. For example, the technical lead is a wonderful person to discuss all the "bits and bytes" with, but do not lean on him or her if you have business issues with the vendor. The salesperson is best for that, but not for griping about delivery schedules if the vendor has assigned you a project manager. Going to the wrong person on the vendor team with an issue can be frustratingly unproductive. If the vendor team is new to you, it is best to ask them who handles which issues along the lines of the descriptions in this paragraph.

Do not forget that somewhere in the background lurks a senior executive or company owner, if the outfit is small enough. Make it a point to check in with that person from time to time. Establish a relationship and provide feedback, being sociable even if you have issues or concerns with vendor behavior. Vendors are not very proactive in this regard and generally do not engage at the executive level until after something untoward has occurred. I have found it helpful to build such relationships before the wheels fall off. Then, when you do need senior management involvement from the vendor side, they already know you. The benefit is that if misfortune puts the professional relationship under duress, they are less likely to feel ambushed at the personal level, which of course would only make them less responsive in ways you would find timely or expeditious. This might appear to be somewhat backward. In fact, I have been known to chide vendors for making me work so hard at being a customer. Still, this is another typical case where, if you understand how things are, right or not, and compensate for them, you will end up far better than if you wait for the world to behave as you would believe it should.

Exhibit 6 summarizes the key principles to follow when you resort to a vendor solution for part or all of your project.

10.7 CONCLUSION

Dealing with vendors can be frustrating. Your vendor representatives do not always have the full weight of their organization behind them. If they are small companies to begin with, or extremely busy or disorganized, the staff assigned to you may be stretched. You may find they have inadequate back end support. Instead of getting angry with that, understand how any such dysfunction is impacting your project and try to work with your management and theirs to resolve that. As was stated earlier, senior management on the vendor side is typically reactive, so no news is good news to them. If you disagree, make them aware of your concerns and lobby for joint, successful resolution.

I have had many positive vendor experiences and been proud of the work done by my colleagues when I was on the vendor side of the IT world. Quality people are the key to successful projects, no matter what logo appears on their paychecks.

Note

1. This is also the time to clearly identify which side (you or the vendor) is going to pay for or provide specific equipment, software, facilities, and other potential logistical costs.

Chapter 11
Manage Your Turnover

Your project should have a beginning, a middle, and an end. The first two phases should occur naturally, but it may take an act of the Creator to close it down. Obviously this is particularly true for poorly defined deliverables that never quite work, or if you have been infected with that nasty scope creep virus. Traditional project management methodology teaches us that the handoff of deliverables to "maintenance and operations" is your last task before typing up your lessons learned and moving on. The inability to do so deftly can also delay closure, sometimes forever, or so it seems. In this chapter, I review what it is going to take to get there.

11.1 THE HANDOFFS

Depending on your project's deliverables, you can expect one or more of the following groups to be looking for handoffs from you.

- Desktop support
- Local area network (LAN) server support
- Mainframe and midrange services
- Data center operations
- Help desks (voice, data, applications, e-mail administration)
- Telecom (routers, switches and hubs, cable management)
- Network address administration
- Facilities (building management)
- Risk management
- Security
- Disaster recovery (DR) and business continuity
- Tape backup and archiving

Ideally, each of the impacted groups will play an aggressive, proactive role in your initiative, starting at the project kickoff meeting. Based on my experience, I would be looking to them for the following results:

- They will educate your team on current operations practices, tools, and direction. This would possibly have an impact on technologies you will have to use, documentation requirements, and implementation strategies.

- They should provide support for change control, specifically explaining how modifications can be made to the production environment for servers, connectivity, applications, and login IDs. Of particular interest in this area are maintenence windows, lead times, and possible blackout periods,[1] all of which can introduce dependencies into your scheduling.
- They will make sure that tape backups, disaster recovery, password administration, application access rights, virus scans, security applications, and "heartbeat" monitoring tools are properly planned for and implemented.

Perhaps I have worked for too many clients, but I find these processes, which are driven as much by bureaucracy and logistics as they are by technology or common sense, quite difficult to understand. This has other benefits, however, beyond the guide dog role I ask operations managers to play on the project team. In today's environment, many requirements will be placed on your technology rollouts from the support side of the house — requirements you will have to meet before your rollout will be taken under the corporate support umbrella.

For example, servers connected to the production network probably have to be built a certain way, possibly using specified makes and models. Software for virus and security scans, heartbeat monitoring, and remote access are commonly specified and required, too. At the very least, you can assume that operations-driven requirements will add tasks and costs to your implementation. It is best to know this up front, so you can plan the tasks, budget the costs, and identify resources you may need to ensure compliance with these operations standards.

By the way, if you think about it, the ongoing participation of the operations staff should be of value to them too. If, as is likely, you are rolling out new products, their early involvement should help prepare them to assume production ownership of your target state. At the very least, logic tells us that they should learn a lot by looking over your shoulder while you build out a new world. You may further reason that these people should enjoy learning new technologies, which would spice up what appears to be prosaic daily routines.

That is our theory, anyway. Experience, unfortunately, teaches us that such thinking is in reality a lame sales pitch project managers make to operations people in the hopes of luring them into the project early on. The reality is that asking them to line up shoulder to shoulder during your planning and implementations phases is somewhat akin to inviting the building maintenance staff to lend a hand when you are pouring the foundations.

11.2 PRODUCTION SUPPORT MODELS

At least, that is what operations people think, because their reality is different from ours. Project managers like to slam-dunk everything, but the operations group will slow you down to a crawl because of the way they work. In my view, two flavors of production support exist in corporate America.

11.2.1 Historic Model

A very finite size staff labors, sometimes heroically, to fix things after they break. They have little time for planning. Most of their forward thinking is speculation on their next disaster. Many fixes applied on an emergency basis are Band-Aids™, so nothing is ever really finished or completely documented. This is not a criticism, by the way, but an observation regarding the fragility of technology and the stop and go nature of supporting it. A good analogy in the mundane world is the busiest road you can think of, probably the one on which you commute each day. We all grumble about potholes, lousy signage, and too few lanes, but when is there time, assuming there is money, to maintain or upgrade the beast? Do you want them to shut down 80 percent of the lanes during the day when you are using them? Or do you want to pay prohibitive tolls or taxes to subsidize costly night work so you won't be inconvenienced? You probably do not want either option.

The information technology (IT) maintenance and support organization faces similar challenges. As you might expect, these people have somewhat harried and defensive temperaments to go along with their jobs. From a project manager's perspective, it takes special social skills to earn their trust before getting much value added from them. The good news is that you can sometimes get things done through negotiation and quid pro quos, and you do it in stealth mode (letting your conscience be your guide, of course).

11.2.2 Emerging Model

The other operations model is the direct opposite of the first. This one is a heavily process-oriented way of doing business, something you may have experienced in the mainframe world. The way this model works is by the book. You have to fill out umpteen forms to move or install new servers, make changes to existing equipment, get a new router port configured, or be granted a firewall exception. This process can be extremely lengthy and rather abstruse to the average project manager. The waiting part of the cycle may be weeks for a task that literally takes moments.

If you think about it, this approach is extremely logical to the operations manager who wishes to avoid being bullied into reacting to everyone else's emergencies. Therefore, to some degree, the convoluted paper chase is like quills on a porcupine (i.e., intended to repel the hunter, not make the carnivore's job easier).

The other troubling aspect of this model is the operations paradigm that has increased in popularity to the point of domination in today's environment. Because IT operations are tricky and expensive, someone has sold executive leadership on the idea that support should be automated and generic. The strategy states that call center machines can be programmed to automatically generate alerts based on predetermined, self-diagnosing actions by the possibly "troubled" network elements, servers and applications. Further, a technically unskilled "analyst" can react to those alerts with choreographed actions, which basically boil down to dispatching specified personnel. One of IT's dirty little secrets is that the same harried technician we just said has little time is the person generally dispatched by the multimillion dollar support center! This individual cannot be assumed to be an expert on everything, so he or she may only be the first step in a long list of phone calls, customer complaints, and meetings to calm everyone down before the problem eventually goes away.

11.3 UNDERSTANDING THE MODEL

So there you have it, a very complex support culture and process you need to finagle your project into, taking care not to be too disruptive while doing so. Once you understand this, you can appreciate that the only valid approach is to be somewhat educated as to the particulars of your environment's operation and support culture before you attempt to negotiate your handoffs. Do not wait for operations to "belly up" to the bar. At least in my 20-year-plus IT career, of the hundreds of operations managers I have known, with few exceptions they are definitely not the proactive sorts. Further, I believe it is up to you to understand what challenges your project presents to them. I recommend that you:

- Understand what postimplementation support will be required by your project.
- Discover which organization(s) will provide that support.
- Analyze to what degree that organization is capable of meeting those support requirements and what "customization" may be required.
- Work with operations to close any gaps between your requirements and their capabilities.
- Be prepared for a response from operations that includes funding requests for training, equipment, and head count expansion or backfill.

11.4 SUPPORT REQUIREMENTS

From a project management perspective, three classes of support requirements are used: business as usual (BAU), customized BAU, and totally customized support. BAU requirements are, of course, the most desirable class because they are a known quantity and probably the least painful to leverage on your project's behalf. The most common example is network infrastructure. Let us say you build out a new office building into which you are moving thousands of users. From a network perspective you are going to build a LAN inside the building to give users access to file and print services. The LAN will then attach to the corporate network, normally through dedicated bandwidth connected to the corporate backbone. This link will provide users with access to corporate computing services, such as applications and data resident on servers or mainframes located elsewhere and e-mail, of course. The support requirements for your building are going to be:

- Managing the routers that connect the building to the Internet or corporate backbone (the wide area network [WAN])
- Managing the hubs or switches that connect local users, servers, and printers to the LAN
- Monitoring these components for outages and throughput degradation
- Supporting moves, adds, or changes within the building that involve network-attached devices
- Coordinating network carrier activities (i.e., the phone company providing the leased lines from the building out to the "cloud")
- Some involvement in protocol or address management that controls user access to local or global computing resources

11.4.1 BAU Support Requirements

For these BAU support requirements, there is a 100 percent probability that infrastructure and process are already in place. Your telecom or networking department has standard monitoring tools, change control processes, and a field team that must accommodate your new site in the example being followed. That may require expansion because this is a new site, but basically they will inform you of specific requirements your project needs to fund and manage through implementation. This will include their specifying the design of the LAN and WAN devices, protocols, and speeds (e.g., gigabit Ethernet). For this type of project, support customization is rare.

11.4.2 Customized BAU Support

The second class of support requirements is BAU plus some customization. An excellent example of this type of project is a firm-wide upgrade of LAN servers network operating system (NOS) to a more current version. Although a support infrastructure is in place in the legacy version, pending

199

upgrades to the more current NOS version may be new to your company. If that is the case, your support requirements will include:

- A certification process to validate that all new servers are hardened per corporate standards for security, virus protection, and so on; this will also probably include a directive on how the new NOS is to be implemented on the actual servers. These requirements, in my experience, are quite specific, so you cannot simply hire outsiders to gin up these servers for you.
- Training for local LAN administrators
- Training for help desk personnel and technicians, plus specialized troubleshooting processes, need to be implemented if the change to the NOS environment introduces operational support risk, as would be the case if communication, resource management, or authentication protocols change.
- Some application issues can arise from server upgrades to any network operating system, including gateways, terminal emulation, and browsers.
- Customized help desk notification and training may be required in anticipation of increased user complaints. Your pilot testing should be designed to assess this potential support requirement.

11.4.3 Totally Customized Support

The third class of support requirements is total customization. This would be the result of a new technology being rolled out. One common example is the introduction of a self-service payroll reporting system. Let us say that your new system allows employees to log in through the corporate intranet and enter their hours worked and time taken off for sick days or vacation. Supervisors will approve employee submissions and forward them to payroll or human resources (HR) for processing. Because this is a whole new way for your company to do business, a customized support process is required, with the following deliverables:

- A special help line number will be required specifically for this system. It must be staffed around the clock if your firm is global, or at least extended beyond business hours to accommodate telecommuters and road warriors.
- User training is required at rollout time and must be available for future new employees or when features are added to the original system. Common training options are "leader led," a document e-mailed to everyone, or a Web site offering interactive training and help screens.
- If the system is not intuitively easy to use and flexible, manual edit or correction processes may be required. This usually means staffing a Tier II group at the main help desk.

- If a Web site is used as described previously, provisions must be made to maintain that site, keep the content current, and so forth. This may not sound like support, but what else would you call it?

11.5 RUNBOOKS

You may know this documentation by some other name. I have come across it at enough different client sites to assume you know that before a centralized support operation such as a data center or network control center will take over the day-to-day monitoring and fault management of your project deliverables, they expect you to produce specific documentation. The purpose of this documentation is to provide the nitty-gritty that someone who gets called in during off-hours can review and get a feel for how to go about troubleshooting the down server or intermittently crashing application, database, or network element.

Perhaps this is a trifle beneath your lot in life, but I can assure you that on every large project in which I have been involved, I have spent more time than I care to recount participating in the generation of this documentation. Requiring that the project create runbooks makes sense, but I know of few project managers who feel compiling a runbook themselves is a good use of their time. Here is the issue. At some point, the nonexistence of a runbook is going to give operations the chance to inform you that you cannot play in their sandbox until their runbook process, whatever that might be, is completed to their liking. This might sound a little bit like the arbitrariness of an income tax audit, and it very well may be, but it is something that has to get done.

Exhibit 1 lists the elements commonly found in these runbooks. However, the contents, format, and process may vary from company to company. Besides, chances are the average project manager has little idea what is involved, so Exhibit 1 is a great place to start.

Chances are, your operation team will have a very specific runbook process. In most places I have worked, it is basically a word processor template with sections or chapters divided up along the lines of Exhibit 1, although at one site I had to enter the data into an online database. It is generally a requirement that the runbook process is complete and accepted by the support team before your applications can be brought into production. It is generally not the case that operations will assist very much in the creation of this documentation.

11.6 NEGOTIATING SUPPORT

In the complex corporate environment, most support is rendered through centralized operations that have specific capabilities or lack thereof. The support profile can vary from data center to data center should you work

Exhibit 1. Runbook Contents

* *Hardware information* — including server make and model, network interface cards (NICs), memory, internal or attached storage, tape backup units, serial numbers.
* *Software information* — including specific version levels for operating system (OS), tools, database or Web server brand, monitoring tools, and homegrown applications.
* *Application overview* — a basic description of the application's business functionality; this should include user demographics or profiles (i.e., United States only).
* *Application architecture* — how data is gathered, how it moves through the system and interacts with users and possibly other systems or platforms.
* *Hardware architecture* — how the servers are cabled to the data center LAN, as well as to each other or peripheral devices, if applicable.
* *Addressing information* — such as IP addresses and Domain Name System (DNS) names.
* *Start-up processes* — when a server is powered up, the sequence of software loads leading to its production ready state.
* *Shutdown processes* — what is the preferred method for downing the server?
* *Monitoring points* — what systems or processes should be monitored automatically or manually to ascertain the current health of the system?
* *Escalation* — detailed list of individuals to be called, based on the problem's severity, or the volume of end-user calls into the help desk.
* *Backup* — if backups are required, schedule and type (e.g., incremental versus full), how to rotate tapes, offsite tape storage requirements, etc.
* *Disaster recovery (DR)* — if this is a requirement, how it is implemented must be documented.

in a big organization. Differences can be found in technologies supported, service levels, and ease of physical access for project engineers. Regarding this last point, keep in mind that the operations team is rarely looking for new customers. So your arriving on their doorstep at the last minute with no paperwork, and worse, no prior consultation or schmoozing with the appropriate individuals, is a good way to delay your production turnups.

Just as project managers are often seen as free-spirited and arrogant, data center supervisors can be pretty inflexible unless you are willing to play by their rules. Not that this is always possible, but it is worth making the effort. I have found the best way to handle this is to reach out and identify the key individuals, well in advance of your critical dates. Introduce yourself, describe your project briefly, tell them what you are looking to do, and ask how that gets done. I have had varying degrees of success with the following data center support management types:

* *Implementation manager.* Most facilities have an intake team to transition equipment into the environment, similar to an internal project manager. They are possibly technology specific (i.e., mainframe, midrange, etc.).
* *Network/telecom.* This team is responsible for the management of the LAN and WAN devices and connections, as well as the assignment and configuration of Internet Protocol (IP) addresses and switch ports.

- *Voice/telecom.* Some data centers support voice applications that use interactive voice response (IVR) or computer telephony integration (CTI) technologies. These applications integrate voice and computer functions.
- *Hardware implementation.* This team manages the real estate in which computing platforms are installed (i.e., floor space, racks, and cabinets).
- *Hardware repair.* This is the break–fix team that is also responsible for hardware upgrades such as adding storage, dedicated tape units, or network interface cards.
- *OS.* Baseline support is provided for the various operating systems you will find in a full service data center. This team probably also handles things such as security or antivirus software.
- *Monitoring.* Monitoring tools that trap Simple Network Management Protocol (SNMP)-type alerts regarding basic hardware health are increasingly common in all computing platforms these days.
- *Web masters.* A lot of shops have teams dedicated to supporting the various "canned" Web server systems and tools.
- *Database administrators (DBAs).* DBAs are commonly deployed to support these repositories of corporate intellectual property and operating data for the name brand database management software.
- *Change control.* Most data centers allow changes to applications or systems during specific maintenence windows, and may in fact be the only personnel allowed to initiate upgrades to application executables or database table structures. Details on this vary. Normally, some sort of online process is in place whereby you request changes weeks in advance of your targeted date.
- *Storage management.* Long a mainframe specialty, this technology has proliferated with devices such as storage area networks (SANs) and network attached storage (NAS) into the distributed processing world. This team sometimes has disaster recovery responsibilities as well.
- *Tape and archive.* This team manages the backing up of data and systems as well as the physical management of media for offsite storage, rotations, and transport to disaster recovery (DR) processing centers.
- *Security/demilitarized zone (DMZ).* Some applications support users outside the corporate network, be they a mobile workforce, customers, or trading partners. If your project is in this area, you will undoubtedly have concerns regarding firewalls and proxy or reverse proxy servers, as well as authentication, encryption, and other related technologies.
- *Disaster recovery.* This team is responsible for coordination and testing of DR requirements of business critical applications.
- *Call center.* Most troubles, whether detected via monitoring or user-reported, are managed through a call center that opens trouble tickets,

assigns resolvers, and follows up with support, development, or user personnel as required or as dictated by corporate IT policy.

When I compiled this list, I had no idea that the final team count would be as high as 15. Depending on the nature and complexity of the project, you may have to deal with many, if not all, of them. Keep in mind that these people are process-oriented. Precision and completeness in documentation is heavily enforced, and lead times are long, even after intense escalations. They may not appreciate your misapprehending the word "No." Sometimes, it appears that project managers do not understand the word "No," even though that appears to be support personnel's favorite word.

That statement may not seem fair to either side, but it points you in the right direction when reacting to the processes that will be thrown at you when you attempt to invade their inner sanctums. Hopefully, a few well-placed phone calls will smooth the way. You are always better off establishing relationships with the appropriate players in these teams as required. With any luck at all you will be working with them in the future, so you want to make sure you get and remain on a friendly basis with them. Chances are they have more leverage than you because it is unlikely you can wander into a data center with a pair of pliers and a couple of CDs and make anything you wish happen. This is not the old LAN room model.

11.7 CONCLUSION

In summary, it is critical to your success that you hand your implementation off to a support organization that will step up to whatever user discomfort is induced by your implementation. Project managers tend to dislike and therefore avoid this, but a sloppy job here will come back to you in a painful and embarrassing manner. Trust me on this one.

Note

1. Times when network changes are prohibited, most notably around fiscal year-end.

Chapter 12
Handling Your Team

Throughout the book, there has been a commingling of task-oriented project management work with advice regarding the human commerce associated with these professional duties. The remainder of the book focuses on this latter aspect of the project management experience. The topic of this chapter is working with your team. Subsequent chapters will examine your relationship with the customer and beneficiary set, your management, and finally, with yourself.

12.1 WORKING WITH PEOPLE AS A MANAGER

I have believed for a long time that effective project management requires many of the same skills and attitudes that good parents possess. As in the home, workplace supervisors are focused on success and thus attempt to control everything to ensure those results. The problem is that no human being is truly controllable. If you try to micromanage a child or a team member, you are more likely to create rebellion than compliance. Some children or project team members will fight you openly, whereas others will take the passive–aggressive approach, in which case you just might find yourself doing their work for them.[1]

Although the labyrinth of human behavior is beyond the scope of this book, I do strongly urge you to leverage your understanding of it. Always keep in mind any insights you may have into the personalities of team members, including your own. We all have weaknesses that can dilute our ability to remain rational, alert, and motivated each day. It is as important that you know your own hot buttons as you know those of the people surrounding you. A lot of business problems stem from people not getting along. You do not want to exacerbate any preexisting chaos with your own arrogance, impatience, or procrastination.[2]

People can overreact, particularly when under the influence of stress. Sometimes, we meddle in the affairs of others trying to fix things that, in truth, would go away if we kept our hands in our pockets, or that do not matter as much as we think. If, as some parents do, you manage every second of every day, you end up exhausting yourself and alienating the targets of your relentless scrutiny.

Please do not infer from these words that I am advocating a hands-off approach. The success of your project, or lack thereof, can and probably will reflect on your career in powerful ways. So, you had better develop a style with which you feel comfortable for dealing with the people problems you will find over and over again in this business. To that end, let us take a peek at the biggest of these challenges.

12.2 LEADERSHIP

Once in a while, you may need to get up on your hind legs like you really are running the show. Pick your spots carefully because if you constantly act like you "own" the project, you may find yourself alone in a lifeboat from which the oars have mysteriously disappeared. I believe that effective management is largely a function of the effort you put forth to facilitate the success of those you lead. This is a selfless orientation. Although we all want to see our name in lights, working toward team goals should be your primary focus. If you are perceived as hardworking, diligent, and a problem solver, you are seen as a real leader. This is a good thing because, despite the cynicism endemic in the workplace, people are still looking for this kind of leadership. Assuming you can provide it, that would be a wonderful thing, and it would certainly boost your ego. Self-promotion may be the way to go in show business, but it is a real wet blanket in the project world. This may sound crazy to you career slaves out there. Give it a shot, and let me know if I am wrong about this.

12.3 YOUR ROLE VERSUS THEIRS

I was inspired to write this book for many reasons, one of which is that so many project managers do not understand the job that they subsequently underperform with predictably discouraging results. This is not a finger-pointing exercise, by the way, but simply an observation, similar to the kind a baseball hitting coach would make after noticing that an otherwise talented hitter takes too much of a back swing before driving the bat through the strike zone.

Generally speaking, when a project manager misses the mark like this, the misperception of roles and responsibilities falls into one of two categories:

1. The project manager is the clipboard and whistle type, who is standing on the sidelines with a somewhat worried but detached air.
2. The project manager is down in the trenches with team leads, but doing their jobs for them.

The downside to the aloof manager was covered in Chapter 7, but a few more words are in order for the "down in the trenches" type. If I had to describe the job in one sentence, it would be this:

The primary duty of a project manager is to see that the value expected and paid for, as defined by project scope, is delivered on the customer's behalf in a civilized manner.

Does that mean that the project manager is therefore responsible for:

- Developing requirements?
- Designing solutions?
- Ordering equipment?
- Chasing people around for updates on tasks they are paid to perform?
- Harassing vendors to deliver or perform according to contracted terms?
- Finding out why George or Mary did not come in today?
- Writing code, installing routers, pulling cable, or building servers?

The answer to each question should be "Never." Your team should have technical experts, technicians, and engineers who do the work, and since it is such a large project, team leads who manage these groups. If I were restricted to a single sentence to describe how most project managers fail, it would read like this.

Most project managers who fail do so because they assume responsibility for performing other people's tasks, including the assumption of a team lead's responsibilities because that individual is unproductive so far as the project is concerned.

That being the case, there is not enough time or energy left to do the project manager's job effectively. This happens for two reasons:

1. Team leads and other players dump on project managers who let them.
2. If a project manager is uncertain about his or her duties, he or she is far more likely to look for things that "need doing," and then go do them.

It is really that simple. So what is the key to success, then? The simplest answer I can offer is the model of the head coach on a football team (see Exhibit 1). That person manages two teams, including the assistant coaches and the support staff, which includes the trainers and equipment managers. The assistant coaches, in turn, coach specific player types such as linebackers or receivers.

Can the head coach reach down and interact directly with a running back, thereby bypassing the coach of that squad? Sure. Can the head coach reach down to all 58 players every day to see whether they learned their plays, did their push-ups, and passed their drug tests? Can the head coach keep his job (and his sanity) over the long run? That appears unlikely, if not impossible.

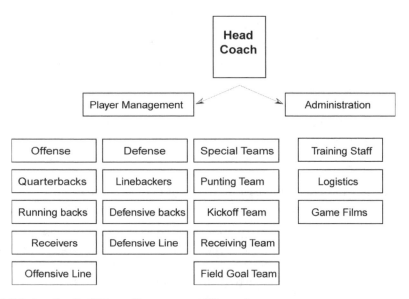

Exhibit 1. Football Team Management Hierarchy

The reason for the hierarchy is simple enough. Let us step two layers down from the head coach to, for instance, the assistant coach in charge of the defensive linebackers. He teaches those players the techniques of the position and instructs them on their customized duties for the team's next game. Does the head coach do all the thinking and coaching that goes into this work for each of the dozen or so squads that comprise his team? That would be impossible, considering all the game films they review, new plays they draw up, subteam meetings they plan and run, and on-field training and coaching they are responsible for. What about on game day? Does the head coach throw the pass, tackle the other team's fullback, kick the field goal, or recover a fumble in the end zone for the winning touchdown? This could happen only in his dreams. What the head coach does is:

- Decide what type of players and strategy he needs to win the Super Bowl.
- Work with the general manager to build that team.
- Hire and manage the assistant coaches to implement that winning strategy.
- With the assistant coaches, formulate a winning game plan each week.
- Get the team fired up.
- Keep the owner out of the locker room.
- Protect team members from media criticism of last Sunday's debacle.

If you go back through the previous chapters, it should not be hard to see the strong parallels between the head football coach and the project manager. For me, the key similarities are:

- Facilitating a sound plan that ensures team goals
- Mentoring the experts managing pieces of the big picture
- Tying all those pieces together into a cohesive, successful team effort
- Keeping the team on task with enthusiasm and purpose
- Being the public face that graciously accepts blame while delegating glory

This is a job that requires public determination, mentoring, patience, and never letting them see you sweat. The quarterback may be a dunce, but if he can hit that receiver in the end zone when it counts, let him get the big bucks and the adulation, even if you have to stay up all night explaining the playbook to him. It is all part of the job.

12.4 DECISION MAKING

Sometimes, on large projects, your team leads will get caught up in some controversy that from your perspective is trivial, if not manufactured. It might be technical, logistical, or far more social in nature, something we used to call "clashing egos." In a group setting, practically any minor issue can turn into a big one in which team leads get at each other's throats, and you feel compelled to intervene.

Throughout this book, the idea of consensus has been stressed with regard to teamwork. Unlike more traditional business units, project teams work best under the principles of democracy as opposed to alternative forms of governance. The vision of the American founding fathers asserted that:

- The majority rules.
- That majority is based on sensible discourse, not gamesmanship.
- The minority graciously accepts the will of the majority.
- The majority does not lord over the minority.

Adopting these principles is very important, because you want buy-in from the whole team once an issue has been debated and its potential outcomes weighed with honesty and fairness. Without buy-in, people's future cooperation cannot be assumed, and you wind up fighting more battles than you have the time, energy, or guile to win. Schisms in the team will appear. If you have made enemies, they will lobby against you, possibly at every turn, just because that is how the real world works. This may be done behind your back while they smile in your face. "Et tu, Brutus?" could be the final words of a bleeding project manager about to share Caesar's ignominious fate.

With buy-in, however, you have cooperation. Those opposed to a particular decision are more likely to take on the air of the loyal opposition than guerrilla warriors. This is because they feel they have an equal chance of being on the winning side the next time around. This is definitely the mood you want to pervade your team. The sharp, high energy level that healthy competition creates is okay, too, and is far more desirable than having a team of saboteurs or apathetic "yes men" for that matter.

There is also the practical matter that the democratic environment encourages team members to work together, possibly without your occasional knowledge or participation. Control freaks who pose as managers will shudder at this vision, of course; however, five will get you ten that if you insist on being looped into every project conversation or decision, you will become an anathema to the team and burn yourself out to boot.

This is not to say, however, that the majority is always right or that your project is immune to power plays that corrupt the decision-making process. I have seen instances where team leads articulate bogus arguments to advance personal agendas. Perhaps the worst I ever saw was a consultant looking to increase billable hours by creating confusion regarding "technical issues" — a tactic to which he felt the project manager was vulnerable. Vendors are also notorious for muddying the waters in this manner, although their agendas are usually pretty transparent unless you are incredibly gullible. I have also seen my share of the "we would tell you but then we would have to shoot you" approach by a clique within a project team when their rationale was challenged. Quite frankly, calling their bluff is not a bad response, but that depends one's personal sense of adventure.

Anyhow, at some point you are likely to find yourself suspending democracy long enough to mandate a decision. Your heart may be pure when you do this, but the team or portions thereof may react to your momentary lapse into dictatorship with rebellion. Parents often resort to saying, "because I said so" when their managerial prerogative is questioned by their offspring. You will be lucky to pull that off more than once in your project management career.

The trick is to have previously established yourself as an even-handed player and one who is willing to make that occasional deal. Fairness is important in that you want to be seen as a manager who does not let the same people lose all the time. I have seen cabals take over projects to the detriment of team unity and the project manager's reputation. These undesirable consequences can taint the project and linger on well past the here and now. Here are a few ways to tread lightly on this one:

- Be sure that the loser does not feel that way for too long.
- Give a team lead a discrete heads up that you will be throwing your weight behind an opposing point of view or player.

- If you proffer an olive branch, make it count. Sincerity of intent counts for naught. If you tell someone you will make it up to them, do so in a meaningful and timely manner.
- If you are a person of integrity, people will give you the benefit of the doubt even when you rule against them. They will understand that you are doing so with the project's interest in mind, not to throw a bone to some other project posse. The loser may take time off for a good sulk, but, as a rule, they will return to the fold.
- Do not socialize with one part of the group to the exclusion of the others. Breaking this rule is the best way to ruin your reputation, with the possible exception of getting caught in a bold-faced lie or some other duplicitous act.

I decided not to plumb my experience for instructive examples for this topic out of respect for previous and current relationships. Suffice it so say that if you take this section to heart, sooner or later you will find yourself in one of these scenarios and the appropriate remedy will reveal itself to you.

12.5 INFIGHTING

When the inevitable friction arises between team players, it is natural to make judgments, take sides, mete out punishment, lecture or hector, and so forth. Ask yourself what purpose it serves when you act out your frustration. Although it is not a bad idea that stakeholders recognize you have a bite to go along with that bark, it is a hand you do not want to overplay, either. Remind yourself that taking sides or playing favorites is quite dangerous. It may be true in the business world that we do not worry too much about the self-esteem of those with whom we interact. Still, do you really want to make enemies, or get too cozy with a particular player at the expense of others, similar to spoiling one child while holding a sibling to higher standards? The individual you ignore or demean today, whether that person is a senior vice president or a shipping clerk, can practically be guaranteed to show up on your critical path tomorrow.

12.6 COACHING AND MENTORING

One of the benefits of parenting is watching your child's ability to interact with the world grow under your tutelage. You understand that the youngster needs to be taught most things because the world is not an intuitively obvious place for children.[3] As a project manager, you will feel frustrated at times by team members who do not seem to produce. Or perhaps they hide problems that you have to ferret out,[4] and then fix for them. I am quite confident that if you reflect on past struggles, you will recognize this behavior.

Exhibit 2. Performance Issue Root Causes

- People procrastinate with tasks they do not know how to tackle.
- Inaction may be related to a previous failure with a similar responsibility.
- Their organization may not support the required course of action.
- They are overwhelmed with other duties.
- They lack time management and prioritization skills.
- They erred grievously and a cover-up, instead of remediation, has ensued.
- Their energy level will not allow them to keep pace.
- Discontent over job security or recognition leads to diminished performance.

You, on the other hand, have been elevated to the role of project manager because you have pulled a rabbit out of the hat at least once in your career, and that got you noticed. You are probably a doer and a practical, "stick to the verbs" kind of thinker. It is naïve to assume, however, that all your team leads are accomplished in this way, or that they can imagine knocking down tasks in a time and resource-constrained environment like you probably can.

It is in your best interest to recognize team member performance issues right away. Exhibit 2 suggests the most likely causes.

Those readers old enough to recall the 1980s remember that, as managers, we were asked to recognize these characteristics in our charges, and help them grow past any such deficiencies. We expected the same from our bosses as well. Not that the workplace was a never-ending group therapy session, but coaching and mentoring were part of the employer–employee relationship.

In today's world, that relationship can more accurately be described as "lead, follow, or get out of the way." We are no longer incentivized to provide a handhold for the less efficient among us, even when we need productivity from their slots. So, you ask, if it is highly unlikely that I will have the opportunity to replace underachievers or miscreants on my team and doing the work for them is undesirable, what recourse does a project manager have under these circumstances?

Obviously, the preferred remedy is to set up a tutoring session with the troubled soul, exchange high fives when he or she connects with your teaching, and move on to your next challenge. This approach is most effective in the areas where your team lead's weaknesses align with your strengths and responsibilities (e.g., planning or vendor management). You cannot, however, take ownership for training someone on his or her technical deliverables. Back in my youth, I could do a credible job of network design. I had the experience, and the technology was far simpler than it is today. Now, my previous expertise is useless. If I would not hire myself as the network team lead, why would I then pinch-hit myself for a player who does not perform as required?

Therefore, this business of tutoring, coaching, or mentoring may not be the most practical way to address performance issues. Still, you have to do something. The right approach will depend on many things, most notably the personalities involved, including your own. Remember, in today's world, this is not a conversation about training, motivation, or career development. It is about getting tasks done with the understanding that failure is not an option. If a key team key player disavows task ownership, you must reassign those orphaned deliverables to someone else because denying responsibility is one project disease for which there is no known cure. Your options are:

- Do the work yourself. (Avoid this at all costs.)
- Get the nonperforming individual replaced. (Good luck!)
- Assign it to one of your own project office staffers.
- Get funding for consultants or a vendor to do the work.
- Get an alternate project team member to assume responsibility.

This situation calls for common sense, tact, and quick action once you recognize what is going on. I believe in following my instincts instead of waiting for the disaster that my inaction practically ensures. In other words, "you snooze, you lose."

12.7 OWNERSHIP

Work ethic varies from person to person. As a committed project manager, one of your biggest frustrations is that without your intervention, a lot of the grinding, annoying work will not get done because it lacks glamour. Even after 20 years in the business, I sometimes find myself playing clerk, courier, meeting scheduler, and caterer. Getting people to pitch in can be difficult. Although you are in the middle of the scrum, it may appear as though the others are having fun watching from the sideline while you run around like an overstimulated gerbil.

What particularly annoys me is that most tasks take less energy to complete than people spend avoiding them. As the old saying goes, "If you want something done, give it to a busy person." Tasks that often fall into this bucket include:

- *Meeting tasks.* These tasks include scheduling rooms, coordinating everyone's schedules, catering, taking and publishing minutes, and following up on action items.
- *Procurement tasks.* These tasks include chasing down missing documents or shipments.

- *Customer or beneficiary tasks.* These tasks include creating effective presentations extolling the financial, logistical, or technical benefits of your project.
- *Picking up dropped balls.* These unwelcome loose ends usually center on documentation for training and operations.

12.8 FOLLOW THE BOUNCING BALL

Confusion in the project world is hardly a rare condition. In fact, you might discover that team members cause this for their own nefarious purposes. Regardless, large projects present those moments when something is broken and a quick fix is not readily apparent. If you take a step back and compare the cacophony of your present initiative with former ones, you can find a pattern that should give you hope that all is not lost — at least not yet.

I have given this phenomenon other names too, such as "Curing World Hunger." I recently got involved in a data center remediation project tasked with cleaning up operational and staffing snafus. I became involved to help implement "fixes" documented by a SWAT team audit. At the first meeting I held to begin formulating an implementation strategy for these requirements, the subject matter experts began stampeding toward rebuilding the whole data center. Not that the requirements on the agenda were trivial, but the team went off to try and cure world hunger when making a few cheese sandwiches was all that was needed.

I have seen this happen so many times that I use the confusion to gain some insight into the technology and technologists who were previously unknown to me. Within hours after this particular meeting, however, I sent out a note that clearly put a fence around implementing the requirements given to us and excluding all the other "nice to have" ideas from project scope. Although this process can be troublesome, it happens all the time, so if you have not learned how to watch out for and avoid it yet, take the time to do so now.

12.9 PROJECT TEAM TABLE MANNERS

Like a good parent, an effective project manager sets goals. He or she also lays down the gauntlet in terms of how things shall be. Some of this is a matter of taste, although other choices are imperative. For instance, as a parent you might prefer the civil and orderly dinner table where the kids are fairly quiet, the best manners are displayed, and everyone eats the peas. Other parents prefer the occasion to be more freewheeling, where chatter and camaraderie are encouraged. This is okay, too.

Exhibit 3 lists what I believe are the rules of the road for you and your core project team.

Exhibit 3. Project Team Table Manners

- *Be prepared.* Team members must know their jobs and participate accordingly.
- *Be respectful.* Kidding around is fine, but be supportive of one another, not critical.
- *Be helpful.* Hiding information or otherwise being uncooperative is unacceptable.
- *Be proactive.* If you see storm clouds brewing, pass out umbrellas.
- *Be generous.* Lend Joe a hand if he needs it. Would you not expect the same?
- *Be a team player.* As a former boss often said, "There is no 'I' in 'team'."
- *Be humble.* A losing team has no winners.
- *Be focused.* In the project world, the bottom line is tasks, owners, and dates.
- *Be positive.* No one likes a wet blanket.

You establish these attributes in your project by acting this way yourself — firmly but with grace. Do it consistently, and all but the most dense or dysfunctional people will catch on. Do not be surprised if some are reticent to behave this way publicly even though they will work this way with you beyond the glare of the public lights. That is a good thing, and it is something you can encourage as well. I was on a huge project where the chaos was unrelenting in the early months. It made me recall a similar circumstance years before in an equally sized and complex endeavor that I supported as a vendor. At lunch, the project manager acted like a comedian, but when the bell rang, he was most organized and detail-oriented leader I have ever encountered — before or since.

I eventually understood the effectiveness of his "game face." He commanded respect by being more together than anyone else on the team. He made you feel like your respect was needed for him to do his job, and he was very clearly committed to that accomplishment. His theory was that if stakeholders respect the leader, they rally around the cause far better and their own behavior becomes more mature and professional. This does not eliminate the noise of human interaction, but it does create an environment where the unavoidable flare-ups pass more quickly and things roll along more like one would hope.

12.10 CONCLUSION

As project manager, you want to set the tone of professionalism and respect for one another. This may require deliberate action on your part, because conflict, fighting for recognition, and finger pointing are natural consequences of being human. There is no reason to expect the citizens of the information technology (IT) world to be any different. Team members, customers, beneficiaries, corporate staff, and vendors can make you crazy; they also threaten team serenity. It should be your mission to minimize that by your own behavior, and the types of behavior you encourage actively or tacitly by the choices you make in the areas covered by this chapter — whether you agree with my views on them or not.

Notes

1. And do not think they do not know that!
2. Just to name a few common "dysfunctions."
3. Not to mention adolescents and most adults!
4. If you are not blindsided by them first!

Chapter 13
Managing Customers and Beneficiaries

Without a doubt, the most troubling aspect of any complex project is having success with your customers and beneficiaries. Numerous references to this project management challenge have been made throughout the book. Now, it is time to give this subject our full attention, starting out with a little self-disclosure. Prior to becoming a project manager, my information technology (IT) background was spent selling, delivering, and managing the sales and delivery of highly technical IT services. Among other things, this was excellent preparation for project management. Despite what a lot of people think, the sales profession is tough. It takes hard work to be effective, and it is more about hard work than golf. I know very few people who spend a lifetime in sales. Everyone I know who spent significant time in that profession neither regretted the lessons learned nor leaving that line of work for a more emotionally stable career opportunity. What I am going to do in this chapter is apply some of the tricks of the sales trade to the quixotic world of customer and beneficiary management for project managers.

13.1 HOW IT IS SUPPOSED TO WORK

When walking through the requirements gathering process earlier in this book, I spoke of the need to articulate assumptions as the first step toward defining project deliverables. Working with assumptions is fine as an early step, but they must be closely examined to be sure that they are based in reality and can garner a reasonable level of universal acceptance. Let us take a moment to examine the assumptions most project managers make about customers and beneficiaries. We will start by revisiting the distinction made between these two classes:

1. The customer funds the project.
2. The beneficiary reaps the rewards of the project deliverables.

Sometimes, the customer and beneficiary are one and the same. The larger the project is, however, the less likely this is to be true. This is because large projects are generally "top down," that is, driven by signifi-

by Customers   **by Beneficiaries**

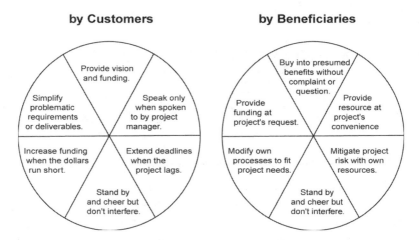

Exhibit 1. Expected Behavior

cant corporate objectives that tend to cross the parochial boundaries of individual departments or business units. Therefore, with most complex IT projects, the customer will be the corporation funded through the IT department, whereas the beneficiaries would vary depending on project goals, for instance:

- Everyone
- Anyone with an office in the Pacific Rim
- All users still on unswitched, 10-megabit Ethernet local area networks (LANs)

Now, let us look at Exhibit 1, which includes the basic assumptions made about these two subsets of the corporate citizenry.

If these assumptions were actually true, it would be because you stumbled across the perfect customer and beneficiary. I have yet to do that. Especially with complex projects with millions of dollars on the table, no customer in their right mind is going to sit idly by and trust you to deliver exactly what they believe they are paying for without their ongoing advice and consent. Similarly, no beneficiary is going to resist the temptation to leverage those millions to his own benefit, regardless of scope or anything else that constrains your behavior.

Please take a moment to reflect on this issue vis-à-vis your own experience. This chapter is based on the idea that these assumptions are naïve if not unfortunate and, if believed, can introduce as much risk into a project as anything I can imagine. If I am not communicating this concept well, ask yourself how many times you have been angry with a customer or beneficiary because they were making your job harder! Salespeople joke all the time that if it were not for customers, the job would be easy. Right. Without customers, there would be no sales jobs or, in our case, project management positions.

13.2 THE CUSTOMER MAY NOT ALWAYS BE RIGHT

But the customer is always the customer. Call them necessary evils, call them a nuisance, but call them. Here are a few more strategies or tactics used by good sales people that you should consider adopting:

- Engage your customer in your processes.
- Solicit their opinions.
- Create an open relationship based on honesty and professionalism.
- Do more listening to them than speaking at them.
- Push back politely if you feel your boundaries are being challenged.
- Be sure they get bad news from you before someone else tells them.

In other words, treat them the way you expect to be treated at home, in the workplace, or at the mall. I have seen many problems created by managers reluctant to deal with customers, so they end up avoiding them, shaving the truth, or even lying. The trouble is, people resent being treated shabbily and usually find out if they are. That is a really difficult perception to correct, and it generally leads to a lot more scrutiny or micromanagement than you need. In my view, having these good customer management skills is a far more accurate gauge of project management competency than the ability to create an awesome-looking Gantt chart or being a guru in the technologies you have been engaged to deploy.

13.3 LEAD, FOLLOW, OR GET OUT OF THE WAY

As mentioned, the common assumption is that beneficiaries will welcome you and your team as conquering heroes. Based on my experience, however, I look for beneficiaries to have two burning questions once they get wind of a pending initiative. From their point of view, these are:

1. What is this project going to do for me?
2. What is this project going to do to me?

These are legitimate questions, particularly the latter. Similar to Pavlov's dog, I am conditioned to react to this second question as the foreshadowing of pushback. I recommend that you be on the lookout for it, too. If beneficiary resistance arises, you need to avoid the mistake so many project managers make, which is to dismiss this condition as simpleminded whining or resistance to change. Although beneficiaries do sometimes complain needlessly or hate change, they are not children you can patronize or bully. It is far more intelligent to treat them as highly skilled professionals who can play you many ways. They may:

- Cooperate with you
- Resist you overtly
- Demand additional or modified benefits from you (also known as "scope creep")
- Sandbag you (i.e., let you fail by not making you aware of risk)
- Go over your head to the point of getting you relieved of command
- Sabotage your project

The bottom line with beneficiaries is to treat them as partners. Doing so makes the lifeboat a little more tipsy and harder to steer through rough waters. But, as the previous list suggests, more harm than good can come from holding beneficiaries at arm's length.

Perhaps the best way to look at it is that beneficiaries see projects as potentially disruptive activities being funded with their own money. This attitude about money is similar to that found in some families, wherein some family members feel entitled to a significant share of family assets, regardless of fairness, previous participation, and so on. In other words, beneficiaries may feel they have as great a say in how your project money is spent as you and your team do because beneficiaries are part of the same dysfunctional corporate family![1]

13.4 SPEEDS AND FEEDS

Part of a project manager's job is proselytizing your project's benefits, as was described in the Big Thirteen interrogatory introduced in Chapter 1. With many stakeholder audiences, such as operations, networking, and so forth, the pedantic facts of your project are generally adequate for this purpose. With customers and beneficiaries, however, it is crucial that you have a sales pitch that is truthful and thorough regarding the intended value of your project. Even customers need a pretty complete briefing because, although they probably suggested the original project scope, they cannot be expected to:

- Infer the same deliverables that you and your team came up with as a result of the requirements gathering you sweated your way through
- Agree with your implementation strategy and proposed risk management Plan Bs

The best way I know to do this sort of thing is through the use of a sales presentation strategy known as "features, functions, and benefits." I was introduced to this approach at a sales training boot camp in the 1980s. Do not be alarmed by the date because, even in business, things other than wine age well. We dubbed this approach as "speeds and feeds" in a some-

Exhibit 2. Target State Sample

Deliverable	Description
Telephony	IP Telephone
IP mainframe printing	Print jobs rerouted to IP-LAN printers
Wireless LAN	Conference rooms and other public spaces

what sarcastic characterization of the nature of IT sales. In those days, the sizzle was all about automating the paper chase, compared with today's obsession with "Webifying" everything. Exhibit 2 is an abbreviated version of the target state document presented in Chapter 3 for the purpose of illustrating the value of the speeds and feeds approach.

As we go through this concept, remember the key messages that the customer and the beneficiary are seeking:

• The customer wants to feel comfortable about the return on his project investment.
• The beneficiary wonders what the fuss is all about.[2]

I have seen many project managers flounder in this area because they cannot effectively communicate, in clear business terms, how each proposed project deliverable adds value. That is one reason why I included the second of Big Thirteen questions presented in Chapter 1 (i.e., the benefits, or "why are we doing all this?" question). When you are preparing your sales pitch to reassure customers and engage beneficiaries, keep in mind that it is not your mission to justify project scope. It is your job to:

• Present the solutions or project deliverables.
• Explain what they do.
• Illustrate why those results will serve beneficiaries well.

In fact, it is a wonderful idea to start thinking about these presentations when you are working with the team on requirements and specifications. As each potential deliverable pops up, ask yourself and the team how you would justify that particular solution to a customer or beneficiary. It is possible that you find you cannot. Chances are, if that is true, that the real driver for that suspect requirement could be the dreaded "if you build it, they will come" approach. This condition evolves when a project team gets so enamored with a technology that they want to spread it all over the world whether or not it is truly needed (and cost justifiable).

Let us walk through the feature, function, and benefit analysis with these three target state elements (see Exhibit 3).

There is nothing revolutionary about this approach. The beauty of it is that it helps you be net and crisp, and thus command your audience's

Exhibit 3. Target State Feature/Function/Benefit Sell

Feature	Function	Benefit
IP Telephone	Traditional telephony services, plus interactive handset screen gives access to directories, other features.	Uses same cabling as LAN. Lower switching upgrade costs. Less costly to install and support. Longer product life cycle. More user features.
IP mainframe printing	BAU mainframe reports now available across IP-based LAN system.	Standard reports available on ubiquitous LAN printers. Costly printers only required for high speed or forms. Costly legacy mainframe network retired.
Wireless LAN	Users can access LAN services with wireless laptop when unplugged from wall or floor data jack.	Laptops can be moved to common or shared workspace to enhance collaborative work and productivity at meetings or in the cafeteria.

attention. Notice the dearth of technical information in the example. The setting we are discussing is not well suited for "tech talk." You can also be certain that the audience is not the crowd who would take much interest in all the "gee whiz" features you might want to boast about. They may drag their technologists along with them, but you do not want to go there. Technical discussions in mixed crowds, that is to say group settings where attendees are both technical and nontechnical, tend to lapse into argumentative one-upmanship that, in turn, bores, annoys, or frightens the senior beneficiaries you are looking to engage. Trust me on this one!

13.5 THE DYNAMICS OF PUBLIC PRESENTATIONS

So a lot of work has gone into fashioning a beautiful set of overheads, a meeting has been scheduled, continental breakfast has been served, and you run through the presentation. I have been on the "giving" side of this dozens of times, and have been the receiver hundreds more. Experience teaches us several key points, as listed in Exhibit 4, that are worth examining before you make your next presentation.

Regarding the last bullet in Exhibit 4, there is an old saying in the sales profession: "He who speaks first loses." Think about it.

13.6 MANAGING OBJECTIONS

Objections to deliverables, schedules, costs, and other project attributes are bound to surface during your initial presentation and subsequent dialogue. Salespeople are trained to anticipate and manage objections as a natural part of the process. Project managers are not, and they, quite naturally, respond poorly. We tend to react negatively to objections and those

Exhibit 4. Public Presentation Do's and Don'ts

- Be as casual as possible.
- Look everyone in the eye at least once during your pitch.
- Be yourself.
- This is not a bully pulpit, but the opening of a dialog with valued project partners.
- Guard against appearing like a "know it all" (i.e., arrogant).
- Do not "blow off" questions. Try to table as many as possible for future follow-ups.
- Avoid detailed technical conversations. These tend to generate noise and frustration instead of meaningful results. It is also a perfectly fertile ground for your potential enemies to sow the seeds of misperception.
- Keep this meeting to an hour or less (i.e., brief). It is likely that you cannot personally answer all the questions. You do not want your team shouting out too many answers from the back of the room. That introduces chaos into the meeting and tends to open up those dreaded technical discussions.
- Do not assume anything about anyone in the audience you do not know. You may find yourself zeroing in on a smiling face when, in fact, that person is not worthy of the attention, possibly to the degree that you look politically inept.
- Do not be surprised at any hostile questioning, even from those you thought were friendly or sympathetic to your cause. Some people have a meeting persona that is far different from their casual behavior.
- Do not get defensive or argumentative.
- Thank each questioner, even if he or she is hostile or negative, and defer further discussion to "a more appropriate forum."
- Be especially wary if a very senior person is in the audience. That tends to silence the more thoughtful in the crowd, while those desperate to catch the executive's attention prattle on without adding much value.
- Treat the audience with grace.
- Use self-deprecating humor to diffuse tension.
- It is better to leave things hanging by tabling them for future examination than to belabor issues to the point that unfortunate or misleading comments slip out. I have seen this very thing turn relatively benign issues into controversies that can take months to resolve. Someone on your staff, for instance, may talk so much that he or she ends up increasing anxiety, when the intent was to be reassuring.

who raise them, sometimes taking offence at the negativity both professionally and personally.

Some objections will be unfair. Personal attacks are not all that rare. Take heart, for there is a tried and true method for dealing with this sort of thing. The goal in sales is to remove objections as an obstacle to closing the deal. Yours should be the same. Do not, however, misconstrue the goal of eliminating objections as a green light to dismiss them as poppycock or allow yourself to be drawn into a debate either. The correct approach is to interpret any expressed objection as an indication of a level of discomfort that needs to be diminished to the degree that you get buy-in and, thus, move forward with common purpose.

You want these customers and beneficiaries to be friends and allies, not enemies. To that end, salespeople are trained to:

- Be receptive to objections instead of dismissing them out of hand.
- Fully understand the objection from the customer's perspective.

After hearing the customer out and repeating the objections, ask, "If we can minimize or eliminate your concern, do we then have the basis for doing business?" This question may sound odd if not presumptuous. Its purpose is to gauge the potential customer's willingness to negotiate and, more important, close the deal. On the other hand, fighting objections tends to:

- Make the dialog contentious
- Increase the likelihood of nitpicking
- Generally muck up the relationship

Good sales people and project managers react to objections in a positive way, thereby generating good will and facilitating team building. You also need to consider that the first objection raised may not be the real show-stopper, so asking if solving the articulated objection closes the deal opens a dialog wherein the customer can say, "yes," "no," or "yes, but … ". Sales-people are further trained how to react to each of these. "Yes" is easy, whereas the other two obviously require more questioning with a casual air and, more important, a seemingly open mind. In many sales scenarios and practically all project settings, the customer is likely, if not compelled, to do business with you. Even if their objections will ultimately be rejected, you must go through this to allow them to save face by articulating their concerns. As we shall see, the beneficiary may wish to save face or may wish to drive you ruthlessly, but, in any case, you must remain gracious and be able to backpedal without stumbling. Keep in mind that politics might eventually dictate that deliverables, schedules, or funding issues will be revisited based on this pushback, so you want to leave yourself room to save face as well.

When you think about it, reacting negatively to objections (i.e., with hostility or disdain) probably delivers a message to that customer or beneficiary that they are ignorant and uncooperative, and that you are arrogant and it is hard to do business with you. How you navigate around these perceptions once they set in is beyond me, so let us see how we can avoid getting there in the first place. Let us play this scenario out with the IP Telephone deliverable mentioned earlier.

Suppose some "doubting Thomas" interrupts your presentation by asking, "Isn't IP Telephone new and unproven technology? I read somewhere that it is not reliable and that the per user cost is a third higher than private branch exchange (PBX) or central office switching. Why do we have to pay

Exhibit 5. Empathetic Response to Objections

I understand your concern regarding the reliability of IP Telephone. When we started going down that road, the project team was a little skeptical about the technology's maturity, too; however, we evaluated the top three manufacturers' products, and visited sites where these products were installed. They were similar in size to our new site and had pretty comparable business requirements. Anyway, as a result of our research, we made three decisions. The first was obviously the product selection. I would be happy to send you the document covering our analysis of the three products we initially thought were equally capable.

Second, we hired the integration firm that did the installation and support at the site we felt best matched our requirements to do the heavy lifting for us because we are in a learning mode ourselves.

And third, quite frankly, we anticipated some concern about product maturity in the user community in addition to our own, so we are installing the base infrastructure from a cabling and power perspective that would allow us to bring in a PBX switching system, practically at the last moment. We do not think we will need to resort to that strategy, but we have about 6 months to go before the first batch of users start moving into the site. So, there is still plenty of time to revert to legacy technology, if becomes necessary.

Finally, let me address the cost issue. The company decided it was time to roll out this technology, to prove it for future voice deployments. That is why we are here today. I honestly cannot comment on any cost issues because I am not an expert on the comparative pricing of IP Telephone versus PBX or more traditional telephony. What I can do is check with the Voice Product Management group who sets pricing of voice technologies for end users, and see what I can find out about what they intend to charge users for IP Telephone. The project team has no say in that, but I will be happy to find out what I can for you.

that much more for something we can get with a technology we understand and trust?"

I have seen presenters respond to this kind of objection by scoffing or launching into a sermon on the irrefutable wisdom of the design intent. Any such reaction essentially says to the objector, "It is going to happen. Get over yourself!" Ouch. Suppose, instead, we followed the course of action recommended in this section. If we did, we would start out with an expression of empathy and then address the objection itself in a manner similar to that displayed in Exhibit 5.

The backside of handling objections properly can be seen in this example as well. You should have a good story to tell, and you should be able to tell it with clarity and respect for your audience because that is what professionals do. It is also why I keep circling back to the Big Thirteen interrogatory in the first chapter; going through that process is how you learn that good story.

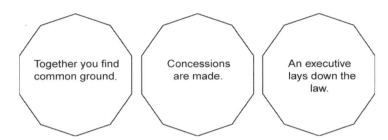

Exhibit 6. How Objections Get Resolved

13.7 YOU CAN RUN, BUT YOU CANNOT HIDE

Remember where we are in the project cycle. Probably, there is a proposed set of deliverables and a tentative schedule, but nothing is set in concrete. Perhaps I am a little naïve, but the things beneficiaries squawk about still surprises me, and what does not appear to bother them at all during this process. In other words, if I bet on their objections beforehand, I would lose most of the time.

So be it. Let us regroup. We have previewed the project and discovered that the beneficiaries have issues with our plans. Truth be told, they had probably already heard rumors about the project prior to your presentation and took the time to brew a few objections beforehand. If you managed these objections satisfactorily, you have, at least for now, snuck the ball over the net to their side. Because their participation in your project is undoubtedly mandatory, however, at some point these objections must be resolved. Only a few outcomes are possible (see Exhibit 6), whether the issues are technological, logistical, or financial.

It is incumbent upon you to understand the beneficiary's point of view. Earlier, we recommended the application of empathy in response to beneficiary concerns. Empathy, even in the workplace, is more than the simple application of tact. To understand what this means, it is useful to understand the two common types of beneficiary objections.

1. *Reluctance to participate.* I have personally experienced many versions of this, ranging from a mistrust of proposed new technologies, to resistance to a major corporate relocation based on issues of geography and culture.
2. *Risk avoidance.* At the start of this chapter, one of the key beneficiary issues I always look for was expressed, in their voice, as "What will this project do to me?" If beneficiaries believe that risks outweigh benefits, objections will be elevated in direct proportion to the damage they fear.

It is my belief that one must categorize major objections as being in either of these two classes because that will, in turn, dictate your strategic response. How so?

Reluctance to participate generally leads to a myriad of seemingly unrealistic objections. Depending on the political weight behind the resistance, this type of objection is likely to lead to concessions being made by the corporation to make the objectors more malleable, if not cooperative. The form that concession takes depends on many factors. The most extreme case I can cite involves the corporation providing millions of dollars in subsidies to the complaining business unit to provide budgetary relief for beneficiary costs accruing from the project that it was originally assumed the beneficiary would willingly pay.

If risk avoidance is driving objections, a different strategy will likely emerge. This is where empathy really comes into play. Basically, you put yourself in the beneficiary's shoes. Your goal is to understand what risks they feel are appropriate to elevate in the form of objections. The way to start is to ask yourself what changes your project will introduce into the beneficiary environment that could disrupt their workflow. Here are the likely suspects:

- *Business as usual (BAU) work processes.* A beneficiary's environment can be assumed to have a cyclical nature that is based on their work. There would be associated deadlines, and possibly blackout periods or maintenance windows that you need to understand as potential scheduling dependencies.
- *Resource issues.* Your project may demand time from key beneficiary personnel that creates inconvenience for the beneficiary organization. Although they may present their world as running more smoothly than the best Swiss watch, the converse to this is far more probable.
- *Legacy systems stability.* Operating system or browser upgrades can wreak havoc with applications, particularly those written in-house that are more than 3 years old. One wrinkle on this is the enforcement of corporate standards. Project-driven server builds, for instance, may require the installation of specified revision levels as the project adheres to corporate standards. Older servers may be back-revved and thus incompatible with the new standards. This kind of problem is difficult to anticipate and even harder to fix.
- *Access to systems, applications, and data.* The Domain Name System (DNS) is a wonderful thing, but many programmers and integrators use hard-coded Internet Protocol (IP) addresses that may cause applications to no longer be accessible under certain project conditions. We had a beneficiary lose access to an external application site when we reengineered the security devices protecting the network. This is another difficult risk to forecast, because far more renegade (i.e., un-

227

documented, noncompliant) network connections, servers, and applications are deployed in the environment than you might think. In this example, even though the connection was in violation of corporate security standards, the project caused the outage, so we were on the hook for its resolution.

- *Operational considerations.* The care and feeding of applications can involve processes that projects compromise. This potential set of risks includes change control for application updates, tape backups and restores, disaster recovery (DR), and regularly scheduled database refreshes such as mainframe downloads. These risks can emanate from server relocations, network changes, resource moves, and network or operating system upgrades.

- *Financial considerations.* Examples of this have been referenced throughout the book. Your beneficiaries may have to expend real money to accommodate your project. Or, they may be saddled with depreciation or usage fees when they "accept" project deliverables, such as hardware, software licenses, or network access fees. This can mean millions of dollars to them. You may be enamored of the project, but they may wonder what benefits are obtained for such a sizeable expenditure. That is why you must do such a great job of understanding and evangelizing on that very topic.

Other potential risk issues must be considered as well, but this list highlights the most common ones. Depending on the nature of your project, it is highly probable that beneficiary risk avoidance objections can be traced back to this list. Also keep in mind that the risk may be technically possible, though unlikely. Or, if it does come to pass, the actual impact would be far more negligible than beneficiaries are now claiming.

On one of my largest projects, a slew of such concerns came at us from the beneficiary community. I offered them access to our test environment well in advance of production dates, even though we were pretty certain that the perceived risk far exceeded the likely outcome. You should always take this approach, even though the customer may throw the ball back in your court. In this case, the beneficiaries countered that, due to other tasks at hand, they would be unable to assign adequate resource for testing until the last minute. Naturally, we could not force them into such a short window, given the time of year and nature of their data processing responsibilities. As a result, we had to back off from some of the technology upgrades we had been planning to perform on their behalf.

Notice the wording of the last sentence, which said "perform on their behalf," not "perform at their request." From their point of view, these upgrades were being imposed on them in a way that made the risk too burdensome for their BAU processes. They did not care to fund additional resources to mitigate these risks up front. In this case, appropriate testing was not something we could do in proxy for them.

13.8 EVALUATING BENEFICIARY RISK

Chapter 5 is dedicated to risk, so there is no need to revisit the nuts and bolts of the subject here; however, caution must be taken with this process when discussing beneficiary risk. In Chapter 5, the basic assumption was that most risk is identifiable well in advance of implementation, meaning there is adequate time to come up with effective workarounds. When risk arises in the beneficiary environment, the project may not have adequate lead time, knowledge, or funding such that risk can be properly addressed. It is extremely important that any issues that arise in this context are quickly and meticulously documented for appropriate analysis and escalation. The latter act may be required because truly onerous beneficiary risk might require a major overhaul to your design, schedule, or budget, as I have experienced more than once. That is definitely not something you want to do without the support and cover of senior management.

Although it is not fair to assert that all beneficiary claims of risk lack credibility, they are definitely problematic and not always easy to evaluate. There is a tendency of the beneficiary set to overstate their concerns in an attempt to leverage project dollars to ameliorate long-standing problems the project exposes but did not create. This is perhaps the most likely way for "scope creep" to invade your project. In an attempt to be a nice person, you find yourself getting deeper and deeper into issues that are clearly beyond your scope.

13.9 RECOGNIZING SCOPE CREEP

Speaking of which, scope creep usually begins innocently enough. You barrelled into discussions with beneficiaries. You gave them a reasonably in-depth look at your project by:

- Taking them through the "features, functions, and benefits spiel"
- Highlighting key dates
- Soliciting their support

Perhaps at that time, or soon thereafter, an emissary, who expresses concerns about the project, approaches you. This conversation is neither rancorous nor difficult, but some issues are elevated to you, most likely in the "heads up" format. As a consequence, you agree to a series of meetings with beneficiaries and appropriate members of your team. Your expectation is that your team will provide clarification that will reassure beneficiaries that everything has been well thought out. By way of response, the beneficiaries ratchet it up a bit, making you aware of certain technology or date-driven facts that give you pause to wonder what else might have been missed. Before you know it, these discussions have turned into joint planning sessions. Polite inquiries from beneficiaries have now turned into demands or at least discussions of new requirements for your project.

That, of course, should immediately set off bells in your head warning you that the scope creep virus has infected the project. Chances are, however, that you remain on cruise control, doing what project managers do best, which is to arrange and referee meetings with the right people at the table. Discussions become very complicated and the pressure starts to mount. Soon you find yourself backpedalling and explaining why the project was not planning on doing so and so by such and such a date. Again, this is another warning sign of scope creep, but like most project managers, myself included, your focus remains on relationship building and looking for real risk that requires this level of detail and concern.

You should definitely keep in mind a few warning signs, however, to become aware that scope creep is lurking at your door. Here are my favorites:

- *Schedule changes.* If you find yourself going back to the project calendar and trying to squeeze start and end dates, or move milestones around by more than a week, you are flirting with scope creep.
- *Design changes.* After meetings with beneficiaries, your engineers start talking to you about additional hardware or software tools. When you ask why these items were not on their original wish list, they tell you about customer or beneficiary-driven requirements that surprise you. This is definite evidence of scope creep.
- *Staffing changes.* In a similar manner, if team leads come to you requesting additional consulting or vendor dollars to beef up the programming, networking, or support teams, this could be shoddy planning or their knee jerk reaction to scope creep.

13.10 REACTING TO SCOPE CREEP

Whether you use these tips from the experienced project manager or Tarot cards, once scope creep is detected, you must react quickly. Those planning sessions I described earlier, which emerged from an initial beneficiary objection, are like planning your own execution. The further you get into those discussions, the harder it is to extricate yourself from them without incurring beneficiary wrath. The psychology of scope creep is pretty interesting. Once you cross the line of information exchange between the project office and beneficiaries to discussions regarding how to change the project to mitigate their risk, beneficiaries generally infer from this your acquiescence to accept their problems as yours to fix. It is admittedly hard to say no, but you must do something once you recognize you are getting stampeded into changing your plans significantly to suit your beneficiaries.

What to do? As previously discussed, these discussions should be carefully documented. As a salesperson, I was taught, from the moment an objection is raised, to echo it back to the beneficiary in my own words and haggle, if necessary, over the words until both sides are comfortable that the issue has been properly articulated. In the project context, you would likely engage operations or technologists on both teams to further explore the issue, possibly even to the degree of crafting a solution.

During this process, you must make it clear that these conversations are provisional. You must specifically state your concern that although their risk is genuine or these new requirements make sense in a general way, you are quite sure that the project is neither tasked nor funded to address them. Do not create the impression that this process is bogus, but disavow the alternate perception that executing the emerging plan is a no-brainer and that you are empowered to address their requests in a manner that will please them.

In other words, you are not the scope police. You are the project manager. The issue driving potential scope creep should be thoroughly documented, with potential solutions written up as well. Make your beneficiary contact aware that you will present the findings to your management, and encourage your counterparts to do so as well. Let management fight it out once the issue is properly framed. Try to sublimate your own feelings when you send the package up your management chain. If you are asked your opinion, render it, but do not get emotionally invested in it because it may come back to you as a new requirement. Scope creep will generally be allowed if the beneficiary has any political skill or organizational clout and the issue is genuine enough. If this happens, you do not want to be on the record as fighting it. If you lose, your credibility and perceived level of power is publicly diminished. I can think of few scenarios where this would be desirable.

Should this scope creep be blessed, be sure and put together the right plan. It should include a new schedule and design, as well as requisitions for additional funding and resources as appropriate. Just because senior management approved this project change does not guarantee that you automatically get the relief you need to add this new set of requirements to your already full plate. It is up to you to be sure that happens. Exhibit 7 summarizes the right steps to take, and how to take them, when the diagnosis is "lurking scope creep."

Keep in mind that scope creep poses two challenges to you and your team:

231

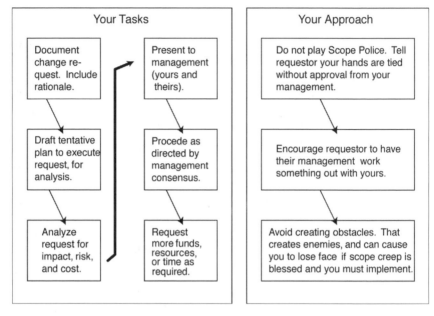

Exhibit 7. Managing Scope Creep

1. You face a funding challenge if you believe that adding requirements, or making existing ones more complex, adds to your cost.
2. You face management and resource challenges if modified scope raises concerns about your team's ability to absorb these new or more complex requirements and to deliver them with the skill, headcount, and timeframes at hand.

If either condition is true, it is time for you to ask management to consider whether the company should step up to the plate and fund the additional expenditures for hardware, software, consultants, or overtime. That is not your call. So, instead of wasting time and creating enmity by serving as scope police, let senior management duke it out. They should resolve these discrepancies, with your advice and consent, of course.

13.11 JOINT PLANNING WITH BENEFICIARIES

Whether dealing with original project requirements or those added or modified by sanctioned scope creep, it is paramount that you engage the beneficiary in very carefully managed and documented planning sessions. Exhibit 8 is offered as a script worth following in this regard.

At the start of the chapter, I mentioned the common view that beneficiaries are expected to stand on the sidelines applauding your effort and the

Exhibit 8. Planning Steps with Beneficiaries

1. Define the requirements to be planned.
2. Agree on contacts, escalation points, and rules of engagement.
3. Establish roles and responsibilities.
4. Assign tasks and dates to requirements.
5. Incorporate risk planning as appropriate.
6. Develop detailed test plan.
7. Negotiate service levels.
8. Make sure appropriate members of your team concur.
9. Make sure that senior management, on your side and theirs, agree.
10. Proceed with the plan, managing according to the rules of engagement.

naïveté or shortsightedness associated with this expectation. Although you do not want customers or beneficiaries peering over your shoulder or backseat driving if you will, you do want them to have skin in the game. To the degree that you can get their management to commit resources, dollars, and organizational support to your project, your chances of success are enhanced considerably. To the degree that you are unable to leverage their commitment, you are likely to get mired in confusion, obstruction, and a lot of discourse that is counterproductive, to say the least.

To justify this last paragraph, I must resort to the "skin in the game" paradigm which basically states that beneficiaries place value on that which they receive to the degree that they participate in the accomplishment. As an extreme example of this, I recently saw a newspaper story of an heiress suing the trustees of her multibillion-dollar inheritance for unfairly diminishing the value of the trust fund before she was given access upon turning 18 years old. Apparently, the diluted billions she received failed to meet her expectations, and who could blame her for feeling annoyed?

Seriously, it is not easy to engage beneficiaries in the business of contributing to project success, but that should be your expectation and your goal from the start of your project. Engaged beneficiaries:

• Make you aware of risk
• Accommodate your implementation strategies to the extent possible
• Are tolerant of project disruptions to their BAU world
• Provide knowledge base, resource, and political cover
• May help you with other beneficiary groups as good team players can
• May contribute corporate assets in the event of unanticipated obstacles

Unengaged beneficiaries can be counted on to be less than enthusiastic in these and other areas, so your efforts to engage instead of alienate them by what you do or fail to do are clearly significant. Let me warn you that appealing to their sense of corporate loyalty is not going to work for you, although you are welcome to give that a shot. What does work is this carefully orchestrated set of steps outlined a few pages back. If you review the steps, you can see that one result of following the script is that the beneficiary is educated about your implementation strategy. They will obviously immediately start thinking about the ways you can foul up their environment and what needs to happen to indemnify against that. If you give the impression that they should stay out of your way while you do your thing, they have little if any incentive to share that information with you, let alone partner with you to ensure a relatively pain-free implementation.

I believe that most of the ten steps outlined for beneficiary planning are self-evident or are covered elsewhere in this book; however, I do want to discuss three of them at this time. They are numbers three, six, and seven (i.e., roles and responsibilities, the development of a test plan, and service levels, respectively).

13.12 ROLES AND RESPONSIBILITIES

Here, your objective is quite simple. It is to transform the beneficiary's attitude from "what are you going to do for me?" to "how can I help?" As you outline your implementation strategy to the beneficiaries, you must identify the tasks for which you assume responsibility and those you clearly associate with them or are hopeful they will assume. I am not ashamed to say to a beneficiary, "It would really be a great help if your team could do tasks 15, 16, 19, and 25 because you are better positioned to do them based on your knowledge and experience. I could use your help on many of the others, but the way I see it, those four are really going to kill me to get done right unless you chip in. How can we work that out?"

That might sound presumptive, but as the old sales cliché goes: "You will not get the order if you do not ask for it!" Document these discussions candidly, ensuring everything is discussed, agreed upon, and published to the world. These are hard questions to ask and get answers for, but the consequences of not doing so leads to a lot more grief than the pushback you get when you do insist on specificity in this area.

13.13 USER ACCEPTANCE TESTING

Engaging beneficiaries in developing user acceptance test (UAT) plans is one of the best ways to ensure their cooperative, if not proactive, participation in your project. The UAT plan must have meat and potatoes, that is, it must be detailed. I am not an expert in testing methodology, so I will not go to that level of detail in this discussion. What I can contribute is this: ask the user what 10 or 20 parameters are good indicators that the technology or process being rolled into their environment delivers the value that has been agreed upon. Do not worry about the number of parameters. Focus on their definition of value. Technology is used to increase productivity, lower head count, eliminate error or manual rework, and so forth. Find out which of these apply to your beneficiary, and look for descriptors of them that will be evaluated as a part of UAT. Specificity derived through this process helps you by engaging them in the process of identifying success. Once that is done, they become more aware of the effort required to ensure success.

It makes them think about the value to be delivered in specific terms, instead of the old "it would be great if …." It becomes far easier to speak in realistic terms with beneficiaries about what your project can and will not deliver in this context. This is all part of expectation management. In this context you can tell them, "Yes, you are right. It would be great if in addition to X, Y, and Z, we were also delivering A, B, and C, but we cannot. Let me review the technology and financial reasons for not including A, B, and C."

In a vacuum, this conversation makes you sound inept, insensitive, or penurious. In the midst of planning sessions addressing real issues, your position sounds far more credible to those wondering why the project is not addressing each and every issue they may have about the corporation's technology.

Little or no specificity in this regard practically guarantees the noninvolvement of the beneficiaries. They are now set up to snipe at you as the project wobbles toward the finish line, because they were never challenged to think about the project the same way you do. And that, of course, is: "How do we get this thing to work without ruining everyone's careers?"

13.14 SERVICE LEVELS

You need to sit down with the appropriate parties to map out the operational aspect of your rollout. Beneficiaries need to be a part of this conversation. This is partly an educational activity, partly expectation management, and all business, particularly if the beneficiary is paying the bills. To be sure we are on the same page, let us define "service levels." In my mind, the term proscribes the operational parameters within which the project deliverable must function once it has been put into production. Exhibit 9 presents the appropriate components of service level agreements.

I am not too sure that project managers do a good job with this. Again, having these types of conversations with customers or beneficiaries puts you in a position of strength in terms of facilitating risk sharing, as well as work sharing, with the end-user community. In addition to the educational value, this provides an excellent opportunity for expectation management. Specifically, assumptions can be aired. For instance, the customer may wish to drag DR into project scope. You must take the opportunity to men-

Exhibit 9. Service Level Agreement (SLA) Components

SLA Component	Description
Availability	User access (e.g., 24/7), maintenance windows.
Authentication	Password and profile maintenance.
Access	Many applications have a user license constraint (i.e., only 50 concurrent users). Universal access is common but cannot be assumed.
Performance	May or may not be appropriate.
Backups	Frequency and type of backups, and the disposition of tapes for archiving.
DR	If required.
Business continuity	If required.
Escalation	Help desk numbers, response and resolution times, escalation lists.
Fault management	Specify monitoring tools, processes to be monitored, response and resolution times, escalation lists.
Links or dependencies	Support of automated data feeds (e.g., from mainframe to UNIX server).

tion that DR is out of scope and unfunded but that a plan can be negotiated whereby they can provide the incremental resources necessary to incorporate the implementation of DR into the overall plan. If this conversation is held early on, it is far different from the beneficiary asking, "Where is my DR?" about 2 weeks before the production turnup date. Therefore, having this service-level dialog with beneficiaries early in the project provides an excellent opportunity to avoid scope creep and engage the beneficiary in ways that help, rather than hinder, the project.

13.15 THROUGH THE LOOKING GLASS FROM THE OTHER SIDE

Just as you are sizing up the customers and beneficiaries, they are evaluating you. When you get assigned to complex projects, chances are that you will get involved with dozens, if not hundreds, of people previously unknown to you. If you are diligent by nature, your good reputation should precede you. Or, if you are lucky, customers remain open-minded until you prove your value, or lack thereof, to them.

As a consultant, I have had the opportunity to experience this with greater frequency and dramatic effect than most, and am perhaps more sensitive than most to this interesting aspect of the project world. Let me start out by relating a story about my father's funeral. I went to see the minister who was to preside over the affair, at her request because she did not know my Dad, to provide input on his life. After listening to my hopeful words, she asked if he was a miscreant. Despite my grief, I had to laugh because he had been a research scientist right out of central casting, a brainy but withdrawn and self-effacing man. She explained the seemingly insulting question by recalling the first eulogy she delivered immediately after graduation from divinity school. In it, she portrayed the departed in terms that could have shamed the Second Coming. She noticed that the congregation was less than enthusiastic or comforted by her kind words about the man, whom she did not know. She subsequently made enough inquiries to learn that the deceased had left such a legacy of mistrust and resentment that most of the funeral attendees were probably there to validate his demise!

The point of this tale is this: as you circulate among customers and beneficiaries, quite naturally you will find yourself in the position of wanting to talk up the competency of you and your team. Before you go down that road, however, see how the beneficiaries react to your team, who may not be known to you that well either. Some may have long and possibly unhappy histories with one another. In most corporations, people are far too polite to mention this publicly, but it can definitely color project activities. If you find a beneficiary looking for more reassurance than appears appropriate, this is an avenue to explore with them — tactfully and in private, of course. If they have been burned, they are clearly not looking forward to round two with certain members of your team. The project management organization, or even the entire IT department, may be viewed as incompetent, if not bumbling and dangerous.

Think about how you may be perceived as well. For some reason, many project managers do not handle this people thing very well. Ask yourself how true this may be about you, and be honest. It is my observation that:

- "Type A," that is, driven individuals, make great project managers from a task completion perspective. Those of us possessing that genetic code must ask ourselves whether being a human ramrod necessarily equates to having the right touch with people. Many project managers appear to adopt the dictator style of leadership, but with customers and beneficiaries, the dynamics require the softer skills of education, empathy, negotiations, and inclusion.
- Project managers with extensive hands-on technical experience do not always have the best social skills, possibly because they do not have to make nice with routers or case tools, despite some odd stories I have heard in this regard.
- Some project managers enjoy lording over customers because they hold the power of the budget and calendar and thus the ability to skew things in favor of those beneficiaries they feel comfortable with. Those project managers who are impressed with this temporary power may be setting themselves up for the eventuality some people like to call "what goes around, comes around."
- Customers and beneficiaries may put up with a project manager's bluster or posturing, but only to the degree that they must. People in

jail spend years brooding about revenge against the corrections offic-
ers for offenses, real or imagined, because they have nothing else to
do. Customers and beneficiaries can be assumed to have equally active fantasy lives. Do not underestimate the likelihood that your insen-
sitivity or grandstanding will be thrown back in your face. Be gracious,
be professional, and never throw the first punch. As for your own need
for retaliation, just remember that payback is a two-way street. We all
love to win, but our job is to win the war, not any randomly annoying
battle du jour.

13.16 BEARING BAD NEWS

One of the most common and egregious errors a project manager can make
when working with customers and beneficiaries is avoiding conflict. True,
it is normal to dislike incurring the displeasure of others or to knowingly
introduce controversy into these relationships. On the other hand, it is
highly likely that the bad news will get to them somehow, despite your
efforts to sanitize or bury it. Someone on your own team may let it slip by
accident or on purpose if they happen to enjoy stirring the pot. Customers
and beneficiaries make it their business to sniff out trouble and may, in
fact, uncover it before it comes to your attention. In large corporations,
relationships can go way back. So, you never know who used to work for
whom and who shares information even though they are presently on
opposite sides of the organizational fence.

If customers or beneficiaries come to believe, fairly or not, that you have
been stonewalling them, your troubles may just be starting. Therefore, it
makes sense to address potential controversies proactively and seek their
partnership in resolving them. It is best to take your pain in little doses,
starting as early as possible. If you do, there is a much-improved chance to
build good working relationships and avoid looking like Captain Smith
right after the Titanic crashed into that iceberg.

13.17 NEGOTIATIONS

Project managers should be skilled at horse-trading. The first rule of negotiating is that you have to give to get. Winning at all costs is a self-defeating
strategy. Sometimes, with all the demands and complaints that come your
way as the manager of a large project, it is very normal to feel harassed,
conned, and quite possibly, "ripped off." Turn that feeling around. You have
the power to help customers and beneficiaries, perhaps in ways that are
not as onerous and stressful as they may appear at first glance. That is why
these people are banging up against you. They need help and are trying to
leverage the dollars, resources, and cover of your project to get what they
need. As long as you avoid deleterious scope creep but keep the troops reasonably happy and nonobstructive, the judicious application of favors can

help. You do want to take care that you do not back yourself into the position of having to be Santa Claus to everyone just because you helped a truly needy party.

Once you throw something out there, however, the average beneficiary will probably expect more and will not be too bashful about expressing that expectation. In fact, they can start looking like demands instead of a polite solicitation of a favor, which is why many project managers feel that "no good deed goes unpunished." It is not unusual to do someone a favor and earn their criticism instead of their kudos because you did not meet their expectations perfectly.

Determining when to offer assistance, and to whom, is a judgment call that requires discretion. The lesson to be learned from this all-too-common experience is that people place value in an event to the degree that they contributed to it. Therefore, if the beneficiary contributes little, if any, money or sweat equity, then they perceive little value in it. Weigh the value to your project in rendering favors against the damage if the recipient turns insatiable on you. You solve this problem by finding ways, such as the following, to engage them before you start gifting anyone:

- If you hold meetings to plan how to do something for them, they must participate in agenda preparation and task planning.
- If the extra work you are doing for them requires an after-hours installation, be sure they provide staffing as well, for instance, for testing or server reconfigurations.
- If it costs you $7500 to buy that special piece of software to support scope creep, get one of their cost centers to charge it against.
- If you make any of these moves with reasonable forewarning and the beneficiary demurs, you should signal your commensurate loss in enthusiasm. The message to be delivered, however politely, is: "This work effort is no more important to me than it is to you, so I am happy to get if off my plate."

13.18 CONCLUSION

No hard and fast rules apply equally to each situation you will encounter when dealing with customers and beneficiaries. A natural antagonism occurs in such relationships. The trap we fall into, as salespeople do too, is we feel vulnerable to beneficiaries and are quick to react to their negativity by trying to placate them. A smaller group of project managers react to this stress by trying to bully back. Either tactic creates its own set of problems. Hopefully, this chapter has presented the right approach to adopt so that, as unique situations arise, you know that you have the tools and the flexibility to steer the situation toward an outcome facilitating project success.

I do not want to leave the impression that the ideas advanced in this chapter are foolproof. Each new person you meet and each new situation in which you find yourself offers the opportunity to learn new twists on old clichés. The fellow you trusted and relied on previously may turn out to be difficult or unreliable. You may have created enemies that you thought were burgeoning friends. People's agendas are not easy to infer sometimes. Agendas are also likely to change. On this topic, I may sound like Pollyanna to some readers but Machiavellian to others. What I can state with certainty is that the approach in the chapter is based on my trials and tribulations as well as those of many individuals who came before me. If customized to your own sensitivities and environment, they should serve you well.

Notes

1. This situation is discussed further in the Chapter 9 (see Section 9.8, "Service Delivery and Cost Recovery").
2. She also wants to know the risk to which she will be exposed.

Chapter 14
Handle Your Management

Your effectiveness as a project manager, not to mention your job satisfaction, is somewhat linked to your relationship with your boss, whether he or she is your project sponsor or some other senior project stakeholder. To make the best of this relationship, you need to understand your manager's strengths, weaknesses, and predispositions in several areas, so that you can:

- Leverage the better qualities
- Learn how to tiptoe around any deficiencies

No disrespect for the management chain and those who occupy its higher levels is intended or implied by this chapter; however, certain conditions can impact the project manager's effectiveness that appear to spring directly from the personal attributes of senior managers, including sponsors, to whom we report and with whom we must interact. I do not want to get into a lot of the political or social byplay that typifies the modern workplace because I do not place much stock in those things myself. What I do want to address is how you can understand your boss to the degree that you do not get either one of you in too much hot water while doing your job as best you can.

As the project manager of a complex project, you have a tremendous amount of responsibility. In this role, it is not always easy to know when to involve your immediate supervisor, or how. This is because there is so much activity that decisions constantly beg to be made, seemingly each hour, at times. As a good project manager, you want to get them made as they arise. This is because one of your most critical tasks is keeping everything moving, given that time, along with everyone's good will, is your most precious asset. If, for whatever reason, you feel like you have to go running to your boss each time choices must be made, you are not adding much value to the process. This interim approval step can also elongate the decision-making process. How much delay this can introduce depends, of course, on how available your boss is, how quickly he or she responds, and other issues that will be called to your attention in this chapter.

14.1 HOW MUCH AUTONOMY DO PROJECT MANAGERS HAVE?

Left to our own devices, project managers will assume as much autonomy as possible. After all, it is our project, and we are paid to shepherd this thing as the sole proprietor. Of course, the ranking partner in this relationship, your supervisor, may wish to have his or her hand in everything of importance that transpires. In that case, you find yourself to be a junior partner with less than a whole vote. Part of the adjustment process you go through with a new boss is finding that level of autonomy both parties can be comfortable with. As the junior partner, it is generally up to you to figure that out by yourself because bosses generally do not make their expectations clear in this regard. Adding to the confusion is the fact that you and your boss are relatively accomplished and thus pretty far up the food chain. This means that both of you are likely to assume as much autonomy as you can get away with — egos and all being what they are.

Gauging the level of autonomy a project manager can expect to enjoy is not easy. The factors that influence a supervisor's decision about how much leeway they will grant you are:

- His or her management style
- The political nature of the project and the environment in which it will operate
- The degree of difficulty, or risk, inherent in the project
- The level to which this manager trusts:
  - Subordinates in general
  - You, based on the relationship existing, or emerging, between the two of you
- The senior manager's perception of the level of your:
  - Competency
  - Maturity
  - Reliability
  - Loyalty (to him or her)

Although I have been on both sides of the street on this one, this book is intended for project managers, so most of this chapter covers that side. A few words regarding the view from the top are worth casting out there first. I have built some large operations, and I ran some program offices as well. The stakes at these levels are a bit elevated from the political perspective. When you and I sit around the table as project managers discussing an issue, chances are we spend most, if not all, of our time understanding the issue and kicking around a solution or two before getting down to the nitty-gritty of cleaning up the mess.

At the more senior level, the conversation is far shorter and, generally, less pleasant. The executive says to you, "What is this I hear about a missed date/unhappy beneficiary/cost overrun in the XYZ Project?" You had best be prepared to say, "Yes sir, we ran into a snag because of the ven-dor/operations/manufacturer/technology. This is what we are doing, this is when it will be fixed, and this is how we will insulate ourselves from further exposure."

That is it. No explanations take more than a sentence or two, no excuses, and no uncertainty as to whether you will facilitate timely resolution and effective damage control — period. Some senior managers are more gra-cious in these conversations than others, but they all want you to stick to verbs that are positive and unadorned with adjectives and adverbs that make them suspicious and "knee-jerky." Needless to say, the program man-ager or sponsor does not want to have those conversations with the senior vice president or chief information officer, so they try to avoid that by care-fully watching you, their subordinate.

Unless you are totally dense, you already know this, and you make every effort to have nothing but good news for your boss. This is precisely so that he or she will not have to endure the bushwhacking I just recounted. But, here is the problem. You are managing the project, which by default is going to be at times somewhat unkempt. Unless your boss understands this and appreciates and trusts your efforts to minimize these unpleasant "optics," you get the stress of covering up that which cannot be disguised.

Some of this goes with the territory, and some of it can be eliminated by understanding in more precise terms what your manager's various thresh-olds are on key personal attributes. Now that we have painted the back-drop, let us take a more detailed look at these qualities and see what we can do with, or about, them.

14.2 BE ON THE LOOKOUT FOR SPECIFIC MANAGEMENT TRAITS

Chances are, as the project manager of a large or complex initiative, your immediate supervisor is a career manager. They may have a technical background, but it is probably dated not only by the passage of years, but also by the churning of technology and changes in the project world as well. What we now deploy, how it is done, and the sensitivities a good project manager must have to be effective, are likely unknown to your supervisor. This is because they have been behind the lines for so long they can no longer tell the caliber of a bullet whizzing by their ears like we can, simply by the sound that it makes.

I have a list of attributes I apply to the process of acclimating myself to a new boss, much like I use the Big Thirteen to get up to speed on the envi-ronment. My "boss-o-meter" provides clues as to how best to interact with my boss, who in truth could be a far greater liability than asset when it comes to me doing my job. These are the key characteristics I recommend you observe in your supervisor, and formulate a relationship management plan once you have him or her pegged.

- Management style
- Problem-solving skills
- Political style
- Procrastination
- Conflict avoidance
- Risk aversion
- Grasp of theory and detail
- Communications skills

14.3 MANAGEMENT STYLE

The first thing you want to understand is the degree of involvement you can anticipate from the boss in your own daily affairs. From a rating perspective, the extremes are "control freak" and "laissez-faire." Micromanagers are very difficult to have hovering over you, especially when you have a lot on your plate. The quickest way to spot them is to watch how they react to project documentation or lack thereof. I had a supervisor who went over all my documentation like a cranky high school English teacher. This included Gantt charts, scope documents, issue logs, and so forth. Managers who spend a lot of time going over your documentation are control freaks who are going to give you little free reign in any aspect of the job. In other words, you will function more like a project administrator than a manager. A struggle between you can ensue, almost immediately, because you feel your supervisor:

- Cramps your style with constant scrutiny
- Has too rudimentary an understanding about project management in general
- Has a poor understanding about your project in particular

The natural fear a project manager experiences in this circumstance is that deferring to a demanding boss like this threatens the project. That being the case, the project manager goes into stealth mode, at least as far as that snoopy boss is concerned. Managing all the documentation "by the book" is incredibly time-consuming, wearying, and, at some point, counterproductive. For project managers, building and managing the interpersonal relationships with team members, customers, and beneficiaries is key to project success. If too much emphasis is put on documentation,[1] you spend an excessive amount of time:

- Tweaking it
- Explaining the gaps between it and the chatter around the water cooler

The bind you find yourself in is that, to meet the micromanager's incessant demand for detail, you interrupt stakeholders so often for new information they are likely to start handing you nonsense, just to get rid of you. As a consequence, the paper you are managing becomes worthless because no one, except your boss, takes it seriously. You may also appear weak and thus lose points on the relevancy scale discussed in Chapter 7.

The other extreme in this regard is the "hands-off" manager. This type can be perplexing and frustrating as well, particularly when you need their support and discover it may not be forthcoming. One wonders why some managers appear to be asleep at the switch. Although ignorance may be bliss for some, others may be cultivating deniability. In other words, should you crash and burn, they can deflect blame onto the next project manager (i.e., your replacement). Look carefully at the laid-back manager, because it may take a while to determine whether they are paying attention, could care less, or are keeping their hands clean, at least until you run into trouble. The way I tend to sniff out the "dumb as a fox" persona is viewing overall behavior for evidence of passive–aggressive tendencies, in other words, sneakiness. Listen to stories they tell about their past endeavors, either personal or professional. This tendency, or lack thereof, reveals itself pretty quickly, usually because the sneaky ones brag about it.

14.4 PROBLEM SOLVING

The second attribute you should understand about the boss is the level of his or her problem-solving skills. Presumably you are accomplished at this, so as they say, it takes one to know one. Your supervisor's problem-solving skills should be readily apparent. He or she might be accomplished in some areas, whether it is technology, purchasing, process, or politics. Or, he or she may have relationships with other highly placed individuals that can open closed doors, or raise your request to the top of someone else's to do list.

Take advantage of any of these talents you find when it is appropriate. On the other hand, if the boss is a "leaper," keep him away from those areas where his instincts or behavior could lead to unwanted outcomes. Your team will be watching how you handle your boss, so your credibility with them, and hence your power, will to some degree be influenced by whether you can turn the boss into an asset or "allow" him or her to become a liability. By the way, fairness to you in this regard does not pertain.

Be very careful how you do this, but do it. I had a sponsor whose favorite thing was pontificating about his prowess in resolving the impossible. Unfortunately, his anecdotes were ancient history and rarely mapped to our current issues. He was apparently aware of this compulsive verbosity, but did not resist the temptation to go on and on, particularly when he was the ranking meeting attendee. Whenever possible, I kept him out of meetings with compelling agendas because, once he was done sharing, there was never enough time left to conduct business. There was another program manager in my past who was equally capable of bringing meetings to a screeching halt, although her specialty was making those around her feel incompetent. Some people just have the knack.

Once you assess the problem-solving skills of the boss, the real issue becomes which problems you elevate to him, and when. It is generally a good idea to ask your supervisor for help with problems, even if you do not really need it. This strategy keeps the person involved and busy. It also helps them gain a better understanding of the personalities and issues you face every day. Showing that you need or trust your boss is generally a good idea too, even if that is not necessarily the case. I believe you need to give respect to get it in all cases, but particularly with supervisors, customers, or beneficiaries, even if extending that courtesy has not been earned.

Some issues you elevate may be undoable by you for many reasons. You need to be honest with yourself about that. The upside to this approach is that once such issues are elevated to the boss, you have handed them off, and thus have less exposure down the road should that problem turn sour. This is particularly important with bosses who have a tendency to meddle. Assigning them tasks, particularly those of a dicey nature, can also minimize their ill-advised interference because you have them busy with these other tasks.

Whatever your motivation, it is best when asking for their help to go about that in a very specific way. If your project is complex enough, the typical senior cannot be assumed to properly grasp the issues, and may therefore jump in exactly at the wrong time, or with an improper or uninformed agenda. That is his or her privilege, of course, but I have had numerous experiences where the boss's intervention creates dissonance with team members, vendors, or beneficiaries. Here is what I do when my intuition tells me there is a pending "gotcha" and my boss is going to be involved no matter what.

Start briefing your supervisor on the issue as early as possible, being careful to feed him at the pace he or she can absorb. Having done this, should crunch time arrive, the boss will not feel blindsided. If he or she does, the boss may become suspicious of your competence, or worse, your loyalty. Feeling blindsided tends to diminish his or her trust of you, which is never a good thing and is a difficult, if not impossible, condition to repair. On the other hand, being proactive in this manner is one of the best ways I know of to gain that supervisor's trust and respect.

Before involving your supervisor, be fully prepared with a solution and one or more alternates. Make sure that the "Is" are dotted and "Ts" are crossed to the best of your ability. This means you have:

- Lined up willing resource
- Quantified incremental costs
- Mapped out a timeline

Nothing is better than being at your boss's side with a bucket of wet sand when he or she first smells trouble. Then, all you have to do is hand him or her the bucket and point to the fire. Let your boss take credit for extinguishing the blaze. By way of contrast, nothing is worse than saying, "what fire?" when your boss inquires as to the nature of the conflagration in his or her wastebasket.

14.5 YOUR MANAGER'S POLITICAL TENDENCIES

Many information technology (IT) project managers have a technical background, and thus are likely to be suspicious of, if not unskilled at office politics. It is equally probable that your manager is immersed in internal politics, perhaps to the practical exclusion of everything else. When you find yourself confused by the prima facia evidence of corporate politics, keep in mind what is probably going on, because that makes it easier to understand why certain decisions are made, alliances struck, or issues ignored. Organizational politics spin around people jockeying to get as close as possible to the perceived nucleus of power and to stay there. That basis is really no more sophisticated than high school cliques. The trappings certainly are, and the more successful players are often, but not always, far more adept at disguising their motives than the adolescent in-crowd.

The upshot is that the chief goal of a politically motivated boss is to cultivate an upwardly visible reputation of defect-free performance and incredible managerial skill. Just like an elected public official does not want morals charges on his record, your boss does not cherish having the reputation of overseeing untidy or disastrous projects. Chances are excellent that the people higher up the corporate ladder than your boss probably understand the roller coaster nature of big, complex projects even less. As a result, this turns into a game where mistakes and controversy are glossed over, or stuck in the back pocket of some unsuspecting competitor or fall guy. By the way, project managers are organizationally well suited as sacrificial lambs, so this scapegoat could turn out to be you!

Even the most sincere senior manager is prone to this self-protective behavior. Although you cannot guarantee that the scent of pending disaster will not waft from your cubicle up toward the penthouse, you need to understand that your boss's intervention into your working world will most likely be motivated by the desire to quell bad press reflecting negatively on him, not you or the project. I hope you will agree that this does not necessarily accomplish the same as fixing the problem. In fact, from a project perspective, this intervention from above may be as helpful as pouring gasoline on a fire, despite your supervisor's belief that this intervention is politically astute and necessary.

Some IT projects are ugly during implementation, even those that are run well and bound for glory. Beneficiaries may leverage the bad aura of the moment to launch complaints, however, knowing full well your manager, who feels politically vulnerable to this presumably short-lived bad karma, will blow them out of proportion. I have seen beneficiaries do this even when they risk exposing deficiencies in their own organization. Finger pointing has an element of brinksmanship to it, in that these brazen ones are taking a calculated risk that those who they criticize are too genteel, passive, or timid to respond in kind. You may also want to consider that there is no guarantee that senior managers are consistently lucid or clever. People do illogical things when they smell the blood of a wounded competitor, or fear their own demise.

14.6 PROCRASTINATION

Everyone procrastinates and then rationalizes inaction with some pretty amazing excuses, including claims of political acuity. Whatever is in your supervisor's head, however, loses relevance once you have escalated something to them, and nothing appears to be happening — other than the fact that time is perilously slipping away. Your issue could be:

- A question of ownership or turf
- A purchasing or budgetary item
- A basic change in scope where you need the boss's assistance to steer through the maze

Let us hope that you involved your manager in this issue proactively, and thus allowed him or her ample time to obtain a higher-up's blessing, consult his or her spiritual advisor, or get a piece of paper signed. If instead your manager drops the ball, it can cause discord, delay, or even a project jeopardy if the issue is serious enough. I have heard some pretty interesting theories regarding the root cause of procrastination, but the simple fact is that the business world waits for no one. Compounding your exposure is that the boss, in a wily application of the waiting game, sometimes rationalizes procrastination. Unfortunately, this often leads to unpredictable results, because you cannot always be sure which dormant issues will turn hot and ugly at any given moment. In such cases, appropriate, not to mention face-saving intervention may no longer be possible. As a result, working for a procrastinator can be as confusing as working for a micromanager and can yield equally poor results.

On the other hand, you cannot afford to be too much of a nudge with the person who signs your timesheet. Hounding the boss about something he or she clearly does not care to address is not the best impulse to give in to. After years of pounding my own impatient head against this wall, I have come to the conclusion that the boss gets as many (or few) chances as anyone else does on the project before I go to my own Plan B.[2] I would no sooner go around my boss to his or her boss than I would let my children play in traffic. I take heart in the knowledge, born from successful experience, that other paths can always be pursued by the politically cornered project manager. Discretion is the key to any remedy you may elect to pursue when you feel compelled to circumvent your nonresponding supervisor. The best approach is to stealthfully engage a team lead's manager, or a critical customer or beneficiary. Perhaps you intimate that both you and your boss are hogtied on this issue and leave open the opportunity for this individual outside your own chain of command to pull a few strings, make a few calls, or even approach your boss with an offer of help, or demand for closure. As with any act of aggression pointing up the food chain, you must be very careful. Be sure that your name appears nowhere along the audit trail this sort of thing creates. Also, I console myself with the knowledge that by the time I push this button, the whole world probably knows where the roadblock is, anyway.

There is always the option of invoking the "it is better to ask for forgiveness than permission" rule. This means you forge ahead with the right action, without the boss's knowledge or blessing. Even I will not take unblessed or politically uncovered moves all that frequently, though, because I need that pay check as much as the next person. So, at certain times, you are just going to be stuck. In that case, I let the team know that the matter has been bumped upstairs and engage them in contingency planning (i.e., next steps to take if the escalation goes for naught). That way everyone knows you have tried to do your job. As I intimated in the Jeopardy section of Chapter 7, some jeopardy situations are actually caused by the boss, or ended up in jeopardy because, for whatever reason, you and the boss failed to share the same sense of urgency regarding an unwanted project development.

14.7 CONFLICT AVOIDANCE

A chronic distaste for conflict or controversy infects a huge class of corporate managers who believe that "rocking the boat" is unacceptable behavior under virtually any circumstance. That is too bad, because every project has moments crying for spontaneity, especially when stakeholders cannot come together on strategy, budget, timelines, or sign-offs. Project managers have to deal with this. As was pointed out in Chapter 12, this sort of circumstance should be handled without choosing sides or advancing one's own agenda or prejudice. Anyone who has been there will also acknowledge that remaining neutral and dispassionate during these moments is far more easily said than done.

Your boss may get involved in these rhubarbs by trying to quell the uproar without actually closing out the issue. That is to say, he or she intervenes without adding much value. This is not surprising given that keeping a lid on things is a basic instinct of the highly political supervisor. If your boss is this sort, you should adopt a strategy that gets things resolved without generating any noise. This allows your supervisor to be comfortable with the "no news is good news" condition you have choreographed for him. This may require discrete offline lobbying on your part so that consensus is built without much public posturing or scrutiny. In other words, your goal should be to get a problem solved without drawing attention to it, your part in the fix, or the path to redemption.

This last paragraph may sound like the confessions of a sneak, but I deny that emphatically.[3] If you are being paid to be a project manager, then manage your project. If every issue that confronts you gets up to your boss, then you run the risk of appearing transparent (i.e., adding little value), and of possibly being quite the wimp, too. One of the occasionally scary responsibilities of being a project manager is being the project's sole parent, especially during those moments when selfless and fearless leadership are in order. To be honest, there have been times when I wanted the boss to intervene, but he or she was nowhere to be found and, I am certain, quite deliberately so. This is a balancing act, to be sure, with no hard and fast rules around it other than this one. Do the best you can to resolve issues without your boss's assistance. Understand that anything you kick upstairs may come back in unrecognizable form or create conditions or additional work that is neither appealing nor helpful.

14.8 RISK AVERSION

Creativity and flexibility are excellent traits for project managers to possess. The ability to think responsibly out of the box is helpful in resolving the various technical, logistical, and administrative challenges that are bound to crop up every now and again. The problem is that when you go down this road, you will probably step on someone else's toes. Here are two common examples of this.

1. A technical issue may require introducing a nonstandard product or vendor into your environment. This can upset product managers, vendor managers, or the operations people who are entrenched supporting Product A or Vendor B, when you and the team feel that using Product Y or Vendor Z is the only way out of the bind.
2. Typically, a project like yours would engage Mike's team to move customers. The problem is that Mike cannot meet your specific

timeframes or technical specifications. The minute word gets to Mike that you are thinking about using someone else, he will feel his turf is being violated. He will probably go to your boss. If your supervisor is risk aversive, he is likely to insist that you use Mike, based on the boss' professed concern that nobody can do it as well as Mike.[4]

Other, similar scenarios can boil down to this. Thinking out of the box represents a change to business as usual (BAU) thinking and process. Your boss may fight you on this and insist that you follow BAU process, no matter how illogical, inconvenient, or inappropriate you sincerely believe this to be. Despite your protests that your solution is better than BAU, the risk-aversive boss is thinking that if you eschew BAU and the alternate plan fails, the finger pointers will wonder aloud why you did not go with BAU. This is, of course, the old management philosophy known as: "Better the devil you know, than the devil you do not."

There is some truth in this because of the learning curve associated with any deviation from BAU. An alternate technology means new commands, possibly different vendors from a procurement or support perspective, and unknown quirks. Replacing Mike's implementation team with an alternative may require more work on your part, because Mike has keys to the freight elevators, knows all the security passwords, and has internal relationships unbeknownst to you that makes the job easier from an overall project management perspective.

Do your homework, make your case, and live with whatever decision is made. One of the conundrums of our business is juggling the passion for doing what is best for the project and living to lead another day.

14.9 GRASP OF THEORY AND DETAILS

The older I get, the more complex the task of assessing the intelligence of other people becomes to me and the less relevant it appears, too! In the boss management department, however, there is a requirement to make a judgment about how well he or she grasps theories and details. Why is this important, you ask? Well, among other things, this becomes a communications issue. Project managers can, and generally do, go on and on about anything vaguely related to the project. Not that this is necessarily a good thing, despite the human desire to show what a fine grasp you have of your job. Talking to the boss, however, should not be a social exercise in spewing forth all the information in your head, as much as it targets these goals.

- *Education.* I want the boss to understand the project the way I do.
- *Status.* I want the boss to hear the news, good or otherwise, from me.
- *Escalation.* I want to control when and how the boss learns that he or she has to do something special for the project.

In short, I want to control as much of the boss's knowledge of the project as possible, because, quite frankly, I seek to maneuver him or her as required to protect or enhance my project. I cannot put it any more simply than that. I definitely do not want the boss being unduly influenced by others, or worse, have him or her trying to manipulate me. So, I must communicate effectively. To do that, I have to find the right level to aim at.

I once had a boss it was easy to explain or educate in a conversational way and let draw conclusions at her own pace. I have also had others who stared out the window as if pondering a Super Bowl bet. Most are somewhere in between, so it behooves you to know how much detail the boss needs and how theoretical you can be regarding technologies, implementation strategies, or even the gory details of project management itself as you try getting the boss up to (your) speed. Either overloading or undershooting a supervisor can lead to confusion, distrust, and other results that do not assist you in accomplishing these boss communication goals I just rattled off. Take care not to patronize your boss, however, because the smarter among us tend not to show off in that way. In fact, more often than not, I play dumb myself, because that generally causes others to show their cards, sometimes recklessly. I guess the thinking is that I am too dull to really catch on!

14.10 COMMUNICATIONS SKILLS

Although the cognitive skills outlined in the previous section may not be readily apparent, the level of your supervisor's communication skills should be quite clear. Why is that important? Perhaps because I have been at this for a long time, I take a somewhat proprietary view of projects I am on and work hard to ensure that they look and feel as professional as possible. Similarly, I want my boss, whenever he or she reaches out to the community, to effectively escalate, evangelize, or advocate that which we are looking for. Not everyone knows how to do these things all that well.

If your boss fumbles at the keyboard with e-mails or does not show well in big meetings, find ways to overcome these deficits without being arrogant, presumptive, or embarrassing about it. In the end, you may have to write e-mails or speak for him or her. Chances are, your boss is aware of any shortcomings of this nature, so if he or she trusts you, it will be arranged for you to be the mouthpiece in a way that no one loses face and no one forgets who is the boss, either. Of course, you do not want to end up being an administrative assistant doing all such work, but unless you are terribly clumsy, you can find ways to avoid this annoyance.

Exhibit 1. Rules of Boss Management

- Understand your boss's tendencies or skill level in the critical areas of management style, problem solving, political style, procrastination, conflict avoidance, risk aversion, ability to grasp theory and details, and communications skills.
- Engage the boss as required while staying mindful of these strengths and weaknesses.
- Never let the boss get blind-sided. Give him or her a heads up even if it makes you or your team look bad.
- It is better to ask forgiveness than permission. Use this wisely, but understand that if you go to the boss every time a decision has to be made, what value are you providing?
- "Ask me no questions, and I'll tell you no lies." At certain times, silence is as effective as engaging your supervisor in an issue. This has no hard and fast rules, other than your best guess once you have seen your supervisor react under pressure and have been able to gauge the relative thickness of his political skin.
- Offer solutions, not problems. When you escalate an issue to the boss, present it in terms of impact, with at least two possible solutions, even if one is unrealistic. Again, presenting problems without solutions is failing to add value to your role.

14.11 BASIC RULES OF BOSS MANAGEMENT

Exhibit 1 summarizes the few, simple rules you should keep in mind when juggling the boss along with the other sharp objects with which you come in contact.

14.12 CONCLUSION

When asked about the most difficult part of my professional life, I sometimes respond by saying it is not always easy to tell whether the bullets are coming at me from the front or from behind. If that is taken as a criticism of the seniors, even though it is said somewhat in fun, then so be it. The fact of the matter is that every boss you have will be a mixed bag of pluses and minuses. I have worked for some super people and drawn my share from the ranks of the less blessed. I make a point of learning from each one, the better of whom have reciprocated, which is nice. Do not forget that having a boss can be leveraged as a resource or as a shield in the event that things are not going well and the stakeholders are heaving rocks at you. Hopefully, my lessons learned in this area are presented concisely enough that you can use them to address this perplexing aspect of the project management experience.

Notes

1. This kind of emphasis should not be confused with the use of documentation as discussed in Chapter 8.
2. Yes, you may even need a Plan B or two for senior management.
3. Well, sort of.
4. Even if there is nothing special about Mike and his team.

Chapter 15
Lessons Learned

Before your project team disperses and those fond memories fade, it is standard practice for the project manager to facilitate the "lessons learned" exercise. I do not know how often this happens in reality, other than my own experience in which the frequency is low. This is partly because the employees move on to new assignments and consultants head out to new environments. Still, a wealth of opportunity for personal and professional growth can be realized by spending time reviewing the project from the simple perspective of "how could we have done things better?" This process should not to be confused with rehashing the more glorious or silly moments over beers with your buddies. Instead, this should be treated with the same honesty and sense of urgency as the other key tasks you sweated out during the life of the now expiring initiative.

Why? Well, unless you just won the lottery or joined "project manager's anonymous," you will live to guide more extravaganzas. That said, now you would do well to reflect back on the chaos while it is still fresh in your mind and before it transforms itself into a useless war story.

15.1 HOW DO PEOPLE LEARN?

A few years ago, my boss and I were looking to temporarily augment our project office with a senior project manager. It had gotten to the point that we could not keep our arms around everything. I certainly felt like I was trying to capture greased pigs. We sent a clear list of desired attributes to several agencies and reserved a whole day to interview the candidates who seemed worthy of consideration.

Amazingly, one of our questions stumped the candidates, namely: "Is there anything about your most recent project you could share with us in terms of things you did extremely well, things you now wish you had done differently, or anything else you learned?" Neither my boss nor I thought this question was particularly tricky or cruel, even if it was intended to get a peek at the individual's character. We wanted to make sure that whomever we hired was a conscientious self-starter, someone who could be trusted to ferret out issues and react appropriately. In other words, we wanted to engage someone who did not require much oversight. Anyway, to our amazement, four of the six interviewees tap-danced around this

255

question without answering it, whereas the other two stared at their shoes so long we had to suppress our own embarrassed laughter.

Obviously, it was not fair to conclude, based on their nonresponsiveness, that none of these people had ever learned anything during their careers. To answer the question fairly, each of them would have had to admit to mistakes and other imperfections, which admittedly is not common practice in the job interview situation. Still, one has to wonder how much people really do learn in the workplace or if most people recycle experience without really questioning how things could be done better next time. It is my contention that project management is somewhat ritualistic, meaning that a great deal of the job never changes from project to project. If this is true, it stands to reason, then, that one should assess one's performance to see what kinds of tweaks to approach and demeanor could hopefully lead to better results in the future.

I certainly am no expert on how people learn, but I have some ideas worth considering. As my grandfather used to say, "Anyone can make a mistake, but it takes a knucklehead to repeat it." Surely, cognitive psychologists have a far more elegant way of putting this, but in essence we learn because we want to avoid repeating previous hardships and believe we can find ways to do just that. One of the most painful but simple ways to accomplish this is to review past incidents, especially the more unpleasant or messy ones, and ask the following "did I ... " questions:

- Make things worse by something I did or said or failed to do or say?
- Miss a harbinger of trouble and therefore suffer the consequences?
- Articulate my expectations effectively?
- Not ask for clarification to avoid looking dumb?
- Listen and react professionally to negative feedback?
- Misread a situation as "not my problem?"
- Spend enough time and energy preparing for an upcoming event?
- Correct a hastily made decision upon further reflection?

The answer to these kinds of questions can provoke some very interesting dialog — even if it takes place in front of the mirror in the absence of witnesses. Be fair and remember that no one, not even you, is perfect and that past actions or reactions taken out of context can look worse in retrospect than they deserve to. Still, we must be willing to accept those indelicate moments as real stinkers and ask of ourselves, "what's up with that?"

Before getting too carried away on the personal front, however, let us take a look at how you should orchestrate a meaningful lessons learned exercise for your team. To do that, you first need to establish some goals, before engaging the team. Obviously the nature of the project will shape the dialog and the document that should emerge from this process. Lessons learned for a project focused on the development, integration, or rollout of a singular system will be far more detailed from a technology perspective than a project that had multiple deliverables, diverse beneficiaries, and few universal dependencies. In my own experience, this latter project type includes building a corporate campus, integrating a monorail system with a commuter railroad line, and Y2K.

The difference between single- and multideliverable projects from a lessons learned perspective is that the project manager and team leads assigned to the multideliverable project interact differently than when everyone is focused on a single thread. From a project manager perspective, the delta is somewhat akin to the contrasting duties of coaching a team versus individual sports:

- A team sport coach (e.g., field hockey or football) is similar to a single-thread project manager focused on coordinating everyone all the time.
- Multiple deliverable projects require an approach more like that of a tennis or wrestling team coach who has to worry about each team member's "issues" to ensure that in the end the team succeeds, because success in this case is an aggregation of mostly unconnected, individual performances.

15.2 SETTING THE GOALS FOR YOUR LESSONS LEARNED

You want to produce a document that:

- Reviews the project's relative success in implementing scope
- Notes significant positive and negative contributing factors
- Makes recommendations that ensure greater success for any sequel

This last piece should include constructive observations regarding BAU processes that impacted the project significantly, whether the influence was salutary or not. Operations and Procurement come quickly to mind as line functions that can be anticipated as sources of great help or hindrance for most projects.

Before holding the lessons learned session with the team, give some thought to these questions yourself. That way, you can steer the conversation, or at least keep it on track. Not that your views are necessarily in line with team thoughts, but at least you can give them examples specific to your project, based on your own analysis, as a means of stimulating meaningful conversations. We will look at some do's and don'ts later, after examining the meat and potatoes of the desirable dialog.

15.3 HOW WELL WAS SCOPE IMPLEMENTED?

This question has three components:

1. *Requirements as a reflection of scope.* Suppose the team developed a dozen requirements from scope and delivered them. It is possible that in hindsight you recognize you should have produced two or three more, or that one or more requirements were misidentified if not totally blown. Hopefully, you picked this up along the way and managed to recover, but in big projects this is not easy to do well. If the project was complex enough, it is also possible that a few requirements were either dropped or deferred to Day Two. This would require analysis as well, with a discussion of resources, feasibility, the maturity of technology, original assumptions, and funding as possibly relevant areas to explore. In other words, should they have been requirements to begin with? If requirements were dropped or delivered late, was that a good thing or a bad thing?

2. *Requirements delivered.* How well were the requirements fulfilled? Earlier in the book, I strongly urged you to develop success metrics beforehand as a means of honestly being able to declare victory after the fact. It was further recommended that these metrics be "hard" or quantifiable to the extent possible, even though it was acknowledged that anecdotal metrics are the norm.

   The delta between intended and actual results can be most instructive. This may be the one area where you must allow detailed technical conversations, because the cause of less than perfect results may have a technology component. The tricky thing here is that most of us are worldly enough to understand and tolerate the shortcomings or drawbacks of even the biggest name products and services we rely upon to do our jobs. Having said that, if part of the project's shortcomings are directly attributable to known deficiencies in Product X or Service Y, do not let your lessons learned exercise turn into a redesign of that product or service.

   In other words, the point to this process is to look for things you can fix and, unless you are a project manager within a big software, hardware, or integration shop, your chance of repairing things of this nature is nil. Do, however, encourage the team to examine the test, piloting, and risk processes as part of this conversation that specifically addresses how well you delivered. In my experience, this is an area where the professionals, as diligent as they may be, can use some "out of the box" assessment and mentoring. This last statement, by the way, is an observation, not a criticism.

3. *Exposure to perception.* From the moment a project is announced to perhaps years beyond its completion, there can be a wide range of interpretations regarding how well it did what it was supposed to do. The debate can be as much about what it was supposed to do, but did not, as about how well it delivered whatever it did. Obviously, if some observers believe you should have done X, Y, and Z, even

though your interpretation of scope did not lead to the same conclusion, you may be criticized as having under-delivered or failed.

Although negative press may be deserved, it could also be the result of politically motivated criticism. It may also come from people unfamiliar with your team's valiant struggle to make sure that key deliverables were implemented. Knowing this should help you temper whatever you choose to publish in your lessons learned document.

The scope of a campus project I was associated with was to develop and implement state-of-the-art technology to pilot the next generation buildings this client would occupy. As a result, the original design included some deliverables that it turned out, unfortunately, were too:

- Immature from a technical perspective to meet production standards
- Difficult to successfully assemble and integrate within calendar constraints

As project manager, would you dive into the latter scenario from a lessons learned perspective, knowing full well that the significant dollars invested in this piece of the project did not lead to useful products or services? With this one, I was tempted to invoke the "ask me no questions, and I'll tell you know lies" rule. In other words, because harm could come to many for resurrecting this dyspeptic chapter in an otherwise successful project, it seemed expedient to go into denial on this piece of it.

The argument can be made that whoever coined the phrase "Honesty is the best policy" was either incredibly wealthy or terribly reckless. On the other hand, the problem with being disingenuous is that this sort of unpleasant memory is likely to be unearthed when the "recollector" finds it politically expedient. Therefore, whatever you put on paper can be used as a club against you later. Thus, it should be addressed. In a few pages, this particular issue will resurface in an example. You can judge for yourself whether this is the way you might wish to handle your own missed requirements at future postmortems.

When you formulate lessons learned, be sure and capture any rationale that serve as "mitigating circumstances" and that might moderate second-guessing. The more lethal attackers will probably dismiss your rationale as excuses, so do not overdo it. If you had a good reason for shaving scope, clearly and honestly document the rationale and impact, and move on. By the way, there can be times when you can say, with pride, "At least we did not throw good money after bad."

15.4 POSITIVE CONTRIBUTING FACTORS

There have to be reasons that explain the degree to which you and your team were successful, besides, of course, your brilliant leadership. Again,

259

you are not nominating anyone for the Nobel Peace Prize but are putting into the record any techniques or approaches that others, including yourself, could benefit from applying, or avoiding, the next time they climb into the ring. Although some factors may be tricks of the trade specific to your project or a technology, and that is okay; what we are really looking for here is process. The following are areas you would like to be able to highlight as keys to your most recent success.

15.4.1 We Developed Excellent Requirements

The best projects do a great job of this. When this happens, implementation is much smoother and thus much more likely to succeed. This is because you know what you need to do well in advance of implementation time, and thus have the time for careful and thorough planning. The opposite of this, of course, is that you have to constantly make adjustments as you stumble across inconsistencies or gaps in previous assumptions or decisions. From the point a misstep is taken, getting back on track is a rough prospect, particularly given that it may take a while to realize you have wandered off the reservation. Mistakes, especially those early ones, tend to trickle down and compound the error rate as time passes.

Remember that the feasibility of implementing requirements should have been reviewed as early as possible. Clearly that analysis, or lack thereof, may require specific scrutiny now that you recognize how your handling of this process caused significant issues during the implementation or operational handoff phases of the project. Had I chosen to write a chapter titled "Famous Last Words," there would have been a section in it titled "Yeah, we can make that work!"

If that sounds familiar, perhaps now you can see how you did not effectively drive the requirements process, because you assumed those reassuring words from a team lead were based on competent preimplementation modeling or analysis. It is human nature to think optimistically and believe that any unanticipated or highly improbable problems can be dealt with when they arise. Information technology (IT) project history suggests otherwise.

Remember the idea of formulating success metrics in advance of implementation? From a lessons learned perspective, success metrics can be considered a significant piece of your requirements package. Had that been the case, not only can we say that the project produced Deliverable X, but that its performance characteristics were Y and Z, as desired. Consider analyzing the results of your project from this viewpoint, and reflect on how that approach really helped, or how helpful it should be the next time around.

15.4.2 We Got the Big Picture Early

Complex projects are just that. Components must work well together or not interfere with each other, depending on the nature of your project. From a practical standpoint, this means that you and your team understood:

- What the parts should be
- How they needed to fit together
- What, if any, sequencing would be required to achieve the desired results

The implementation strategy approach described in Chapter 4 is, to my way of thinking, the only way to do this effectively. Did you gather key team members around and find a way to articulate how everything would come together?

Look back at that process and discuss whether those strategies worked as well as you would have liked or if you would significantly modify your original implementation strategies based on the genius of hindsight. Take care with this conversation if the project scope or deliverables underwent transformation as a result of unforeseeable political, environmental, resource, or budgetary events. Every project, no matter how well conceived, will undergo one or more periods of winging it, because they just do. I contend that a great deal of project management competency stems from aggressive but informed anticipation. This does not require the powers of a psychic so much as enough humility to allow past surprises to teach you new wisdom.

15.4.3 We Understood Our Starting Point

No sane project manager believes he or she has been handed a *tabula rasa* (i.e., that blank canvas upon which you can exercise total creative freedom). Your deliverables must map into so many legacy processes that it can be confounding. Applications deployed to the desktop can have issues with existing operating systems or browsers. Going beyond corporate standards to implement "best in class" networking or computing platforms can wreak havoc with security or operations. You are not always free to select a vendor or product simply on merit. Not if the "standards police" are doing their job, that is.

The true practicality of your design can be an extremely serious matter, particularly in projects where there is a high degree of change or risk associated with an aggressive interpretation of scope. The problem is, this dynamic is not always as obvious as these examples indicate. It may not turn up until you start testing your new toys in the environment, and lose half your hair before remembering that you are injecting new technology into an already kluged and somewhat unstable environment.

There can be a more concrete, business-like aspect to this as well. For example, in our large campus project, we did not read the lease that our real estate department signed with the landlord. As a result, we learned very late in the game that there were certain hard dates regarding permanent power and legal occupancy that were in direct conflict with our plans to:

- Build power-hungry computer rooms in the facility
- House dozens of technicians and engineers for development and testing long before the legal authorities would allow

Because we neglected to read the lease, we were unaware that no cable entry facilities were being provided by the landlord through which we could bring high speed fiber optic cabling onto the campus from nearby telecom points of presence (POPs). The impact of this lack of knowledge led to an initial and totally incorrect assumption that networking infrastructure design and planning needed start up in the computer rooms, not down at the street a few blocks away.

15.4.4 Risks Were Correctly Identified

It would be great to include in your lessons learned document these words:

> We knew if the vendor did not turn the customized system over to us by July 5, then the system would not be able to go live for the quarter-end close in September. In recognition of this potential risk, we entered into a short-term agreement with a service bureau to process the data offline to our specifications so that the production output as mandated by Statute would not be compromised in the event that our vendor did not have the new system ready for testing by July 5.

The following words would have been a bit more horrifying to write:

> We had no reason to suspect that the vendor was incapable of meeting our deadlines.

The other significant point to be examined regarding risk is how things went if you had to face the decision of pulling the trigger on one or more of your Plan Bs, especially if that contingency was radical or expensive in nature. Sometimes pride, or fear of political retribution, keeps us from making hard decisions that attack risk but simultaneously make us feel like we failed because we had to push the risk panic button. This can also be categorized as stubbornness, which even a project manager can have too much of.

Of course, you should review risk in a general way, including whether what you anticipated turned out to be not so terrible or if risk that now looks so obvious never crossed anyone's mind. During these postmortems, an honest assessment may well be "stuff happens," but again, the wise among us learn to be a little more diligent or dig a little deeper the next time we consider what dire consequences may await us.

15.4.5 The Budget Worked Out

If you have millions to spend, you probably have room to maneuver. In this section, I have mentioned two real world overruns that were very costly and posed significant, jeopardy-level risk. In both instances, we escaped public humiliation from a cost perspective because we saved compensating amounts in other ways. Some savings occurred because the items were finally revealed as fiduciary fluff and thus cancelled. Other creative ways were identified to reduce costs based on an enlightened, midcourse change in a few implementation strategies. Did you let your project be like the custom-built home that has to cut corners at the end because you splurged on a pool table and jukebox in the walnut paneled basement before the roof had been raised? Did you neglect to hoard funds for that costly risk mitigation such that you could not afford to roll out Plan B when you needed to, without having to go begging for more project dollars?

15.5 NEGATIVE CONTRIBUTING FACTORS

No project is perfect, no matter how hard you try. In my view, you look equally foolish taking credit for serendipity and dismissing poor results as the inevitable consequence of undeserved misfortune. The previous section presumed to reflect success against how well we did certain things, and how we would do them even better next time. In this section, I look at circumstances wherein you may find it appropriate to address the less heart-warming results that visit nearly any project of consequence.

Let me give this some perspective. I am a relatively accomplished cabinetmaker, and have received some generous compliments about my work. Not only is that somewhat embarrassing, but it takes me some time after I finish a project to stop obsessing over the mishaps and blemishes that can be found in all my work. Apparently, those who compliment the work do not see the imperfections that gnaw at my gut, or they appreciate the overall value in the work, and are thus gracious enough not to mention my faux pas.

Put another way, success is somewhat binary. Either you basically succeeded, or you did not. When you look for the downside in your project, and you should do so aggressively, do not confuse style with substance. Poor results are basically the degree to which your initiative had a negative impact on the business. Those who go crazy about how messy or difficult your project was either do not get it or are disinclined to give you the benefit of the doubt anyway. Because you cannot change that, make your case honestly without being defensive.

Having said that, go ahead and develop a list of project issues that require serious discussion from a lessons learned perspective. Look for things you could have done differently that would have:

- Created more satisfied customers
- Driven actual project costs back toward the budget
- Achieved the dates and deliverables once touted as practical and desirable

15.5.1 Missed Dates

Included in Chapter 9 is a laundry list of date slippage opportunities you might want to review in support of this conversation. When you get into the scheduling postmortem, however, start by ascertaining what missed dates, if any, impacted scope. If Fred was 3 weeks late and that forced Mary to scramble to make her deliverable, which may be irrelevant today, unless it was more of a train wreck than an inconvenience. Even some customer, beneficiary, or sponsor angst over a missed date is regrettable but unimportant unless someone in the audience chooses to make it "Custer's Last Stand." There is a section in Chapter 7 (Section 12) titled "When Late Matters." From a lessons learned perspective, being late matters when:

- A costly or unacceptable workaround is required. Examples include staff augmentation, temporary facilities, manual workarounds, and buying supplementary hardware or software to effect a workaround that cannot be recycled once their project usage is complete.
- An expensive and embarrassing penalty fee from a landlord or government oversight body, for instance, is levied because you could not leave a building or print reports on schedule.
- The beneficiaries' business as usual (BAU) process is severely interrupted for an unacceptable time span. That could be hours, days, weeks, or even months.

15.5.2 Missed Budget

Only a few avenues can be explored:

- The original budget was too optimistic (i.e., insufficient).
- A poor job was done comparing the final plan against the budget.
- You did not keep a close enough eye on ongoing expenditures to contain profligacy or apply for relief well in advance of surprise expenditures. This area is especially vulnerable if you have an irresponsible subteam or vendor.
- Previously unthinkable disasters actually happened and proved quite costly.

15.5.3 Missed Requirements

Two possibly fertile grounds can be plowed:

1. A requirement could not be delivered and this was not good. The most likely cause is a bad bet made on a solution. I recounted experience with this in the first two chapters with the Integrated Services Digital Network (ISDN) project. By "bad bet made on a solution," I mean that the wrong technology, implementation strategy, or resource was mistakenly applied. This does not necessarily imply neglect or malfeasance, although a manufacturer, team lead, or vendor might look good for the role as fall guy. My personal takeaway from the ISDN project was to question all assumptions, walk through the implementation strategy with a jaundiced eye, and validate the feasibility of the solution well in advance of a "go/no go" date by which you could take another direction, issue a jeopardy, or recommend scrapping the whole thing while it looks like, but has yet to become, a waste of time, money, or a career's good will.

2. A requirement is inadequately delivered. Among other things, this could mean that:
   - Parts are missing.
   - Performance is not optimized or haphazard.
   - Beneficiaries do not take kindly to it.
   - It is a beast to support.

These are all very common symptoms of the unfortunate project outcome. Many of the comments just made about missed requirements can apply to this scenario as well. You also have to investigate whether or not the proper amount of discipline was applied during the design, risk planning, build, and testing phases for that requirement. Early on, true professionals worry if a proposed solution will work. At some point that changes to worrying if it is showing signs of working.[1]

The word discipline was used to flag the need for constant surveillance. Assuming all will go well without enough eyes on the process and resources with a willingness to escalate the moment one senses things are not going well is an absolute responsibility of all stakeholders. This includes beneficiaries, once they are looped into the project. I am amazed all too frequently at people who sense impending disaster but turn away in disgust, helplessness, or apathy. Do not fall into that trap yourself, or the equally counterproductive trap of assuming that someone else is watching carefully. You are better off assuming that nobody is, unless you are.

Remember this too. In today's world, your real or apparent inattention can be construed as disinterest, which can deincentivize those less than professional types who can be found in any crowd. So inspect early, often, and with a little public posturing such that even the project laggards get the idea that "big brother" is watching.

15.5.4 Operational Handoff Miscues

I really struggled writing about this in Chapter 11, just as I wrestle on every project with the prospect of getting the legacy support teams to help bring the deliverables into BAU operations. I am admittedly quite strident and detailed with so many project management tasks, but on this topic I can only say that your best approach is to cozy up to the operations people and do practically whatever it takes to get them to adopt your project offspring as their own. Understand that they can spend a lot of your energy in the hopes of avoiding as much of your project, and its output, as they can. Seriously, the issues here are predictable.

- Did you fill out all the required documentation in a timely manner, review it with them, and get their sign-off?
- Did you provide dollars for additional resource, training, or tools such that they felt comfortable adopting your project's deliverables?
- Were you able to demonstrate to everyone's satisfaction that:
  - The processes you deployed are stable in the legacy environment?
  - A ritualized fault management process is feasible?
  - Manufacturers, vendors, and internal groups will stand behind your deliverables to the degree that the legacy support teams can partner with them to resolve future glitches or outages after you vacate the premises?

Most project managers could write long essays on these questions. You may have to one day, also.

15.5.5 Ownership

Also known as "roles and responsibilities," this is a very likely opportunity for miscommunication and ensuing chaos. In large projects, it is not unusual to find unrequited ownership of deliverables spanning work groups. What tends to happen in this circumstance is that Joe and Marie, let us say, share a deliverable, but somehow do not fully coordinate the ownership and execution of every detail. This disconnect can be the result of factors that range from work or risk avoidance to someone, possibly you, simply dropping the ball in terms of accounting for everything. The implementation strategy walkthrough touted in Chapter 4 is the best way to identify and work through any gaps, in advance of implementation.

Should you identify this gap in your postmortem, do not be afraid to revisit it with the troops so that by the time your next project turns up everyone will be more educated, vigilant, and proactive regarding this potentially deadly challenge. I can cite many examples from my past on this one. The most recent instance had to do with the implementation, or lack thereof, of a telecom standard for electrical grounding of equipment racks for servers, routers, and switches. We specified this standard (TIA607) to the electrical and cabling consultants who did the detailed drawings and provided oversight of the electrical and cabling contractors who constructed these systems. There was a gray area, however, in which it was not clear which consultant and which contractor owned certain pieces of the grounding system in this huge facility.

In other words, although there was only one grounding system per se, it was divided between "base building" and "branch" systems. For whatever reason, the two consulting companies saw fit to mentor their pieces in the strictest of interpretations. The project team, myself included, failed to take responsibility for ensuring that the complete grounding system met spec, even though individual parties alleged that their parochial territories conformed to TIA607. It literally took months to complete the finger-pointing phase and subsequently enter and complete the problem resolution phase. We endured a lot of messy discussions to affect, at project's end, what we should have done at start up time. That was to identify:

- Who would own the deliverable of TIA607?
- Roles and responsibilities for components thereof
- An escalation process for territorial disputes
- Testing procedures
- Remediation
- Final certification

Pulling this together at the backside of the project was messy, if for no reason other than the sheer volume of players, which included the electrical and cable plant consultants, the project office, the two telecom team leads, facilities engineering, facilities management, the project architect, the general contractor, and the electrical and cabling contracting firms. Looking back, we are quite certain that had we driven the TI607 implementation ownership issue through the gauntlet 18 months earlier during the planning phase, we would have long since stopped gnashing our teeth.

On a personal note, this incident reminds me for the umpteenth time that I can never ask, "who owns this one?" too often, as annoying as it sounds.

15.5.6 Culture

As a consultant who changes environments every year or two, I am particularly attuned to the cultures of my clients. By this, I do not mean the kinds of things that human resources types speak about, such as diversity and empowerment, but the reality of how people interact. I spent my earlier IT

267

years in the more congenial worlds of Dallas and Tampa, compared with the most recent decade slugging it out in Manhattan; however, do not think this is a regional conversation, because it is not. It is an observation regarding the different ways that corporate cultures are manifested in terms of cooperation, competition, problem solving, work ethic, civility, quality assurance, morale, and other institutional behavior. I have noted sometimes amazing disparities in:

- How much public arguing is tolerated, versus backstage lobbying
- Whether or not people show up to meetings on time (i.e., take them seriously)
- Whether or not holding grudges and taking retribution are tolerated
- How much real work, and positive results, are encouraged and rewarded
- Whether or not unprofessional work or behavior is sanctioned

It is hard to give guidance in this area in terms of lessons learned because you do not want to get into a sociological analysis regarding poorly delivered requirements, but cultural dysfunction does impact project results. As with other negative contributing factors, be honest and fair about corporate culture, but use it more for tempering your remarks than as a bulls-eye.

15.6 GATHERING THE TEAM TOGETHER

Now that we have cycled through the kinds of analysis that can be useful, you are ready to pull the team together and talk this through. I promised a few do's and don'ts for this meeting, so here they are:

- *Your role.* You should assume the role of teacher and mentor regarding lessons learned. You may or may not work with this unique combination of people on future projects, but you want the group to disband with a positive feeling about the benefits of teamwork. Why? Because you want those kinds of players on all your future projects. If you are not promoting the attitude, who do you expect will do so within your organization?
- *Criticizing individuals.* You want to discourage personal issues from surfacing in this process. Even if it is true that Joe was always late with his deliverables, and that Maria bogged down team meetings with endless discourse, everyone already knows that, so why go there? I would never advise you to take Joe or Maria aside and "coach" them on such traits, because in today's world that can be turned against you. Therefore, you should not allow such observations to surface in your lessons learned activities either.
- *Body counts.* If you have been in the big time project world long enough, you have seen attrition, planned or otherwise, from the ranks

of stakeholders. Perhaps you have initiated or even been a victim of this sacrificial rite. In the end, however, the project's degree of difficulty, and any collateral damage suffered from a personal standpoint, is not fodder for lessons learned. Most project participants are drawn from the ranks of BAU employees and consultants and are thus probably unsophisticated, if not uneducated, in the mysteries of project management. So, interpersonal struggles and the sadly inevitable loss of face or employment is part of the detritus one might expect. A review thereof adds little value to the lessons learned process.

- *Criticizing the corporation.* Anything beyond passing comments about the dysfunctional nature of your organization is not very productive either. Numerous project problems can rightfully be attributed to convoluted process, political infighting, or the lack of cooperation among stakeholders and BAU line functions (e.g., procurement). I can assure you that this is typical of all large organizations and, therefore, can always be assumed to cause trouble. So, instead of belaboring these issues, make note of them, if appropriate. Solicit positive recommendations regarding future reparations to such processes that can be passed along to those who might be in a position to do something about them.
- *Dreams of a better world.* In a similar vein, it is important that the reality of the project world be taken into account. There is no such thing as a perfect project or the penultimate environment into which rollouts are deployed. There will always be issues with people, places, and things. That should be your expectation and that of your team as well. Part of your job is to promote a positive attitude about overcoming any such obstacles. A big part of the lessons learned exercise is addressing the peculiar aspects of this in regard to your project, and taking the "knowing what you now do, would you still have handled situation X the way you did fourteen months ago when the project was still on the drawing board?" If the conclusion is "we will never try this again!" the value of your lessons learned process is highly suspect. This is so, even if the assessment that the project was pointless is basically true. If that is true, then you face an even more interesting question (i.e., How in the world did this ill-fated idea become a funded project?).
- *Awards.* Some projects are doomed to succeed. How? Everything can, and sometimes does, come together. This is particularly likely if the scope is good, funding is adequate, executives pitch in, and the team is sound. "Impossible!" you say? Actually I have experienced those conditions several times. Even in the best of times, however, the absence of good project management in these no-brainers will practically ensure self-destruction.

Throughout this book, I have been quite clear about my view that humility and self-effacement are imperative components of the project manager's makeup from a leadership perspective. It would be fantastic if your team leads followed suit. Until such time as self-promotion disappears from the workplace, however, you will probably have to combat hubris that surfaces during the lessons learned process. If something clever or heroic did occur, by all means commend the event for someone else's future use. As a means, however, of advancing the careers of you and your merry band of pranksters, lessons learned is not the right vehicle.

15.7 SAMPLES

I have been quite frank about prior experiences that, although instructive, were not necessarily too successful. On the other hand, I have alluded to personal experiences, and, humility aside, I think I added tremendous value. Quite naturally, the tougher battlefields are far more fertile grounds for exploration from a lessons learned perspective than those where you had the sun in your face and the wind at your back. Let us try to remember what we are trying to do here. We are not looking to explain away the eyesores anymore than we are looking to take credit for success. What we are really doing is reviewing the project just past, and asking ourselves, as well as our team, three questions:

1. Knowing what we now know, how should we have handled situation X to make it more in line with timelines, budgets, or expectations?
2. What did we do in this project, either in general or specifically, that we must keep in mind as useful strategies for future projects?
3. What basic assumptions can we acknowledge we made about our work that require adjustments, of any sort, as we go forward?

This last question is perhaps my favorite. As I mentioned at the beginning of this chapter, many people appear to recycle their experience without learning very much. The most common symptom of this lethargy is the reiteration of past project strategies with statements such as: "When we (I) did the so and so project, we did process A this way. That is how it shall be done this time." That may sound like a lessons learned approach being applied, but I would caution you against taking statements like that on face value. Ask a few questions so you can deduce whether or not the past and present situations are similar and whether the results from the past were in fact all that great. Sometimes you will find that:

• What is really going on here is a power play.
• What is really being said is, "I decide on how these things are done, so butt out!"

Surely, you have the rectitude to ascertain whether or not that past tactic is something you want associated with your current project. Experience and growth do not automatically equate to one another. I learned that the hard way, too. Now, it is time to wrap up this subject matter with the example promised to illustrate the points made in this chapter.

15.8 EXAMPLE: SOUTHPOINTE LESSONS LEARNED

One of the key drivers for the SouthPointe project was to implement state-of-the-art technology in the new campus. The rationale behind this vision was to demonstrate how the newest generation of voice, video, and data communications and processing platforms could be rolled out and supported with off-the-shelf products, using in-house expertise. The intended benefit of deploying these tools was to make the workforce more mobile and productive by making data and applications globally accessible in a high performance, but secure, manner. These values became more compelling as a result of the World Trade Center disaster on September 11, 2001, which sadly occurred during the planning stage of the project.

Although we originally intended to deploy 16 technologies, by project's end, 3 were not deployed. We omitted the wireless local area network (LAN), thin client computing, and Internet Protocol (IP) desktop video conferencing. These deployments were deferred for the following reasons.

15.8.1 Wireless LAN

- The current generation of this technology supported a throughput of 400 kilobytes per second, a bandwidth that compares quite unfavorably with campus-wide, 100-megabyte-per-second connectivity from data jacks to the switched gigE backbone.
- Current technology was not considered adequately "hack proof," given the sensitivity of data routinely transmitted across the network.
- Customer demand was not adequate to offset these potential product liabilities. We did complete the data-cabling infrastructure to prepare for future deployment of the technology. It still holds great promise in future iterations.

15.8.2 IP-Based Video Conferencing

- The proof of concept process validated the utility of this product on a campus-wide basis; however, it was determined that the product presented interoperability challenges with existing desktop video conferencing products currently in use elsewhere, most notably with the critical function of call origination.
- Because current users moving to the campus are high profile, it was deemed prudent to install compatible legacy systems for these known users at the new site and defer deployment of the IP-based product until such time that product maturity advancements make that more ap-

propriate for universal deployment, and user demand reaches critical mass.

15.8.3 Thin Client Computing

- Due to a variety of technical and product integration issues, the engineering team was unable to meet a twice-extended go/no go decision date on the rollout of the ambitious new distributed computing model intended to provide numerous user productivity and operational maintenance benefits.
- Some targeted beneficiaries were disinclined to adapt the proprietary portion of their legacy environment, which included business critical applications, to the proposed new model. The key objection was a very limited prerollout test window due to their preexisting business schedule that could not be changed. The project had equally hard but incompatible dates, so there was no opportunity to mutually define agreeable milestone dates.

15.8.4 Analysis

Threads common to these postponed deliverables are instructive enough to merit a closer look. Whereas the potential benefits of each requirement were significant enablers of project goals, both of the following conditions contributed to the decisions, made independently for each deliverable, to postpone their deployments:

- The project schedule could not accommodate the longer than anticipated timeframes required to resolve issues regarding product maturity or interoperability with legacy systems and processes.
- User demand for each deliverable was lower than originally believed. This fact put in question the business value to be received in return for the continued, significant investment in each of the technologies as part of the SouthPointe project. This conclusion is particularly compelling because from an overall corporate perspective, the project was driven as much by real estate requirements as it was by the decision to implement technological innovation.

It is clear that beneficiary management should have been included in the planning conversations far earlier than was done to give them adequate time to evaluate the proposed products and make a commitment to support their implementation, or to request the products not be deployed on their behalf. Regarding the product maturity and fit issues, the project office could have benefited from a more proactive stance on pressing for a go/no go decision on each of the ultimately postponed deliverables.

Because each of the three technologies had relatively long development cycles, the project office elected to be patient with the process. In retrospect, the engineering team and project office, together, could have addressed feasibility of each deliverable within the context of overall project objectives and constraints sooner than was actually the case. Put simply, applying a triage-type approach to these technologies would likely have lead to quicker exclusions from scope of this particular project. This would have allowed the redirection of resource to other aspects of the project or back to the corporation for other pressing needs.

15.9 CONCLUSION

So there you have it. Honesty compels me to report that some of what you just read has been highly sanitized. In fact, a significant amount of rancor existed in some of the relationships described. Considerable time and energy was consumed by skirmishes among key players before uncomfortable truces could be orchestrated. I lost confidence in the feasibility of certain deliverables remaining compatible with the overall project calendar. Some engineers were vested in their development for reasons other than project goals. That led to their pressing us to keep their agenda on our docket far longer than made sense from a business standpoint.

As noted earlier in the chapter, however, this is all quite immaterial from a lessons learned perspective. That is why the eventual exclusion of these deliverables was couched in terms of degree of difficulty that although true, hardly described the pickle we sometimes found ourselves in. There will always be folks advancing their agenda, even if it eventually fails the relevancy test as far as your project is concerned. What is important in regard to this chapter's topic, however, is this. The bottom line to these experiences, and most others I have been associated with, is that most project problems arise when we fail to play the shepherd's role well enough. By that, I mean you must count the sheep hourly, be sure your Border Collie keeps the herd intact and scares off predators, and do not doze off for too long.

Quite frankly, regarding one of the deliverables cited in the foregoing sample, if I were the sole decision maker, it would have been taken out of scope long before entropy caused its demise. Keeping it on life support longer than I felt necessary was a political decision that, like many, was someone else's CYA-type thing than a sound business, technical, or project decision. My desire to cancel it was CYA, too, although in retrospect it is clear I was playing to the wrong audience.

The longer I do this job, the more flexible and less opinionated I try to appear in the political arena. That is a terrific lesson learned no matter how tough such admissions might be. Not all decisions made further up the management chain make much sense, except in the context of an executive's agenda. This is one mud puddle you do not want to land in with both feet, or head first, for that matter. As a result, at certain times, you feel like your project is getting distracted, if not damaged, by these kinds of issues. The problem is, the individual who does not share your viewpoint may sign your timesheets or purchase requisitions, so you may have to go with the flow to continue adding value where you can.

Note

1. Perhaps you could think of this as pre- and postnatal care.

Chapter 16
Becoming the Project Adult

In this book, we have stepped through the basic responsibilities of a project manager. We have looked at how you start out with little or no understanding of the mission handed to you. From there, we discussed how to discover your requirements and then arrange for their birth. Last, we offered tips for guiding you, your team, and your deliverables through the challenges that the targeted environment will present to you during deployment and their subsequent handoff to operations.

My professional and technical boundaries have expanded greatly from the diversity of technologies, work environments, and project types I have experienced as a traveling professional project manager. Still, I find myself learning the same lessons over and over, only at more depth, or to better effect. Another way of putting this is that with each new project, one has the opportunity to gain greater insight into the process, and refine one's outlook and demeanor. I thought it would, therefore be useful to examine the characteristics that make an effective project manager. You can use this list to:

- Appraise yourself and build an effective self-improvement plan.
- Do a great job hiring a project manager for your next cumbersome initiative.

16.1 A DAY IN THE LIFE

Whenever I look back at past projects and compress those six to eighteen month spectacles into a single day, I am always struck by the bipolar nature of the job. At times I felt omnipotent. I was so busy setting direction, hiring and firing, dueling with the client, pushing back when someone yanked my chain, chastising some vendor, or doling out project dollars to curry favor or pacify the restless. On other occasions, I have been reminded of the intermittent powerlessness of the job, like when a boss stepped in to grab the helm,[1] the customer ran roughshod over me or the team, or some other ill wind blew through my office.

There have been times when being passive seemed appropriate. Other times, I had to drive the team toward success, or I had to solve a problem that did not belong to me but loomed nonetheless as a certain showstopper. Then, I had to contend with all the scut work. I have typed so many spreadsheets, documents, and project plans that at times I felt overpaid for those countless hours spent on administrative duties.

I have sat alone in a room full of hostile customers and negotiated a solution to an obstacle they might possibly have concocted. I was not always sure I was empowered to make the commitments I did to escape these meetings unscathed or that I could make good on those promises with the resources at my disposal. And, of course, those pithy moments always happen, like when a project activity rendered the personal computer (PC) belonging to the executive vice president's assistant inoperable minutes before her boss needed a printout of two dozen color transparencies someone spent weeks concocting for the board meeting.

Overall, I have faired well. At the very least, I have learned from my mistakes and have managed to avoid repeating most of the ill-fated stunts I have seen other project managers try out of desperation or for possibly less wholesome purposes. Reflecting on all this, it appears that the job calls for:

- A curious blend of toughness and wisdom
- The ability to swiftly shift gears, and the intelligence to know when to do so
- At least enough political smarts to stop leading with one's chin

None of these traits, at least in proper combination, sound typical of the average corporate soldier, but instead sound like something that comes from experience and the willingness to grow through honest self-appraisal. Things always look different in the rear view mirror, so it is a good exercise if you learn those lessons and move forward. Therefore, before I lead this discussion into psychological nonsense, I think we would all be better served by refocusing on the deliberate behavior model.

16.2 BECOMING THE PROJECT ADULT

Try as I did, I could not resist using the term "project adult" in this chapter's title, the subject of which is the more desirable attributes of project managers. To me, the term "project adult" is perfect because it implies both a condition and a responsibility that map perfectly to great project managing.

- *The condition is maturity.* Self-discipline, self-control, tolerance, and the knowledge and willingness to be empathetic and gracious toward others are all the marks of a mature person. Those who seek and achieve maturity also gain the ability to negotiate when an impasse is reached with an eye toward compromise and suppress the impulse to win every argument, no matter the cost.

- *The responsibility is parenthood.* Of its four goals, two of which are spiritual and cultural, the ones relevant to this conversation are learning how to:
  - Nurture and support the child.
  - Give the child the tools he or she needs to adapt to the world, to achieve his or her own maturity, and eventually assume the responsibility of parenthood.

After we look at how most engaged parents go wrong, we will be better prepared to understand how budding project managers err in a similar, albeit vocational manner. Suppose my wife is pregnant and I decide that our new child will be a professional hockey star. Even though my wife bears a brainy little girl who does not appear to be particularly athletic, I persist in my dream of having sired a "super jock." The only accommodation I make to reality is switching my child's burden from "winning the cup" to winning the Olympic gold medal in hockey. This minor concession is simply due to the fact that women cannot compete for the Stanley Cup. The child's life may turn into a living nightmare as long as I insist that she meet my expectations, no matter how unrealistic or inappropriate my dreams for her might be. An outsider might watch the ensuing struggle and be saddened by the irreparable harm I cause by insisting on my way, despite its misguided intentions.

As a loving and effective parent, it would be far more appropriate to discover and work with whatever unique sensibilities and talents emerge as our little girl takes on a life of her own. I may have to sit with her each night to do homework or force her outside to play with her pals when she would rather stay in her room reading and dreaming. Good parents carefully balance that which they insist on for their offspring, and which of each child's desires, sensibilities, and talent is allowed to develop. This does not mean we put the children in charge of their own upbringing. It does mean that expecting them to wind up exactly as we hoped is not only naïve, but, if acted out, can possibly be harmful to everyone involved.

Being a leader in the workplace is not unlike being a parent. You are looked to for protection, for setting expectations, for reassurance, for recognition, and occasionally for setting boundaries so people know how far they can go. You are anointed the "go-to" person, if not the lightning rod, when trouble erupts. A good parent tries to create this kind of environment but cannot live the children's lives for them. Likewise, a project manger may set the goals, the pace, and the rules of engagement for the team; but it is up to individual stakeholders to perform and react according to their mutually agreed upon roles and responsibilities. The project manager must not only allow but also encourage this, and adapt his or her own feelings to the project realities as they emerge. Similar to parenting, this is not easy to do and can be scary.

There is a direct relationship between your project's complexity and the accompanying levels of uncertainty and chaos. You face a mass of people advancing a profusion of agendas. You are also saddled with endless dithering while people circle around issues instead of bringing them to closure. Why is that? Well, it appears that in the absence of leadership, all groups wander aimlessly with a frustrating purposelessness. Have you ever stood on a street corner in a big city with a few friends or associates and wasted a half hour deciding which restaurant to pop into? Sure you have. Why should project teams be any different? If you do not assume the role of leader and become your project's adult, no one else is likely to. Sure, someone greedy for recognition or power may grab the reins, but that is not the same thing and cannot possibly be good. At least, it has never worked out that well the times I have seen it happen. It reminds me of the class cutup running the show, which simply guarantees the results will be skewed toward satisfying someone's emotional needs but probably nothing else.

So, your first personal act as a project manager is to adopt the persona of the project adult. To do this, you need to be self-assured but humble. You have to trust the process, but that is only after you understand what that process is. This is why this book has run down two parallel roads:

1. One road is the methodologies and processes that project managers are tasked with orchestrating or performing. You know the drill: gathering requirements, analyzing risk, and coming up with a plan that really works.
2. The other path I have tried marking out for you is the specific role the project manager must play, at least in my opinion, to ensure those results. This is the people side, the nontechnical but equally important role and responsibility that you as project manager must understand and execute. In this final chapter, I will pull this together with a review of the attributes, at the personal level, that if found in sufficient quantity will flag you, or who ever you are evaluating, as a likely candidate for the project manager's "Hall of Fame."

16.3 WHAT MAKES A GREAT PROJECT MANAGER?

There is, of course, more to professional competency than maturity, but that is not the worst place to start. For years, I have joked that good project managers are born, not made. Although not a qualified participant in the "nature versus nurture" debate, I do believe that competent project managers display certain characteristics in significantly higher doses than the worker of average knowledge. Although these traits, if left unchecked, do not necessarily make their owner the most charming, well-adjusted human being after hours, they clearly flag the possessor as being the shameless nudge and ruthless organizer one must be to excel in this field. Their order of appearance does not necessarily imply their relative importance, although I have tried to lump them together with a semblance of coherence.

When evaluating yourself or others against this list, keep in mind that it is the blend of characteristics that determines the potential suitability of any project manager candidate, instead of the weight of any single attribute. Also, try to separate style from substance. Being abrasive, for example, is to me a matter of style that does not necessarily indicate the appropriate level of aggression required to get the job done as much as it points to a possibly intolerant, if not uncouth, personality.

These significant attributes are divided into three categories:

1. Experience and training
2. Professional skills
3. Personal attributes

16.4 EXPERIENCE AND TRAINING

I will introduce this section with two quick stories. The first involves a fine man I did a project for. At the end of our 1-year association, he and many of his peers had the opportunity to take a very generous termination package, which he did. He asked me to review his resume, because he had decided to be a consultant and was interested in my take on how his background would play out there in the real world. After reviewing his 30-year effort on behalf of his employer, who rewarded him with many promotions, I had to find a nice way to tell him that his resume did not make clear what he could do. Sure, it was replete with names of initiatives and other buzzwords that had great meaning and significance within that corporation, but an outsider would have no clue what his contributions were. Perhaps we should all know about Project Apollo, but who knows what my boss's 3 years on The Diamond Project at XYZ Corporation meant in terms of scope, duties, challenges, and accomplishments?

The next tale occurred a few years later. I was managing a complex and demanding program and in the process of hiring three project managers to implement the plan I had spent months developing. One of the candidates had a very impressive resume that included top-of-the-line project management certification and an MBA. Similar to my former boss, he was testing the consulting waters after taking an early retirement package from another huge company. After scrutinizing this gentleman's resume, however, I could not really tell how much actual project management experience he had, so I asked him to drop in for a chat. In advance of this interview, I felt it unlikely that he had adequate hands-on experience and responsibility managing complex projects to meet my needs. Despite my misgivings, his education and recent employment stature caused me to give him a look. Sadly, the interview confirmed my fears. His project management experience was long on institutional process and short on management participation. He had not been in the trenches, and lacked the level of detailed experience that allows me, for instance, to write a book like this.

The point is this: I tip my hat to all of you who have committed the time and money to become well educated and formally certified in the methodologies that this profession espouses. These methodologies and certifications exist for a reason, but, as stated elsewhere, some of our tasks as complex project managers are not any easier to perform well based on academic accomplishments.

I believe it is relatively easy to evaluate prior experience. Simply ask what the candidate did. If I were to answer this question using my most recent project, my diluted response would look something like this:

- Planned and managed weekly project meetings
- Oversaw documentation of minutes, engineering, and operational planning
- Coordinated data center rack, power, and cabling design and installation processes with consultants, vendors, and users
- Oversaw the integration of the various technology designs into the rolled up implementation and operations plans
- Developed and managed the migration strategy for users to the new technology
- Developed the plan and managed the subsequent relocation of hundreds of servers to multiple sites

If you were interviewing me as a potential project manager, you could drill down into any of these activities to get a feel for:

- How many people, servers, or dollars were involved
- How complicated this was
- Whether I did any scheduling, risk analysis, or design work
- What my boss contributed and how much autonomy I had
- What my level of involvement was from a technology perspective
- What my level of involvement was from a leadership perspective

You should be curious about my contributions, in other words, the value I believe I added to the project through my participation. This last word's significance is sharpened when you reflect on the difference between attending meetings and participating in them. Project managers who participate in their projects, as I have tried to illustrate throughout this book, learn innumerable valuable lessons that help them grow the critical skills. Those who summon enough "chutzpah" to get down into the trenches like this are far more experienced and, thus, capable of plying our trade effectively.

When you do this, you are not writing code, patching network connections, or racking servers. What you are doing is basically making yourself available to team leads while they struggle to get their jobs done. I cannot tell you how many subteam meetings I attend as a mostly silent partner. I am always available to answer project questions or to field issues thrown my way. I am also there to learn and to look for issues that could turn into trouble for me because I am the project manager.

Remember, these people who are the heart and soul of your project are technologists and operations staff. They may be unbelievably talented in their specialties, but they are probably not too adept at project management. As a consequence:

• They may wait too long to escalate issues.
• They may make poor decisions on resource utilization.
• They may not be comfortable getting a disappointing vendor on the phone and making whatever demands are appropriate.
• They may shy away from confrontations with beneficiaries or any other stakeholder because of the politics.

If you are not a participant, you will not be aware of these things — at least not until they snowball into major problems if not jeopardy situations. If you are participating, you will recognize these and similar conditions as opportunities for further analysis or escalation that project managers with great skill and a wonderful sense of timing use to the advantage of their project.

16.4.1 Project Management Methodologies

Any top-notch specialized professional is effective because he or she has adequate if not impressive academic credentials, proven successful experience, and a passion for the work. Other than standing on the level of familiarity with project management methodology as implied by this book, I am not necessarily the authority on the right level of certification an individual should possess to be an effective project manager. There is no such thing as too much education, but that is equally true of the other two parameters of prior success and passion as well.

From an interviewing perspective, a discussion of a candidate's familiarity with the proper procedures is important. At the very least, it is important to ask each individual how he or she approaches a project from a process and organizational perspective. There is no correct level of knowledge other than the basics that were covered in this book.

16.4.2 Technical Background

A background with multiple technology experience indicates a general comfort level with technology. Without that comfort level, project managers tend to get hung up on singular technical issues and then lose their perspective and probably control of their projects as well. I once took an assignment because it was a chance to do an ambitious Web site project, something that my network-centric background lacked. The challenges of technology are naturally quite diverse, but it is the willingness to take on any technology that is key.

Being a consultant, quite naturally I peruse the Internet want ads more often than most employees (I hope). I always get annoyed when I see requirements for project managers stating unequivocally that the right candidate must have 15 years of experience using Product X, or building trading floors, for instance. Although this is somewhat understandable, it is, in the end, rather uneducated on the part of the hiring individual. Project management is not about knowing how to deploy Product X or rebuilding Trading Floor Y. Project management is about knowing how to develop and manage a project that will successfully deploy Product X or rebuild Trading Floor Y. If you need expertise in Product X or Trading Floor Y, then go hire experienced analysts, people we once called subject matter experts, in Product X or Trading Floor Y. The expertise of competent project managers is project management, not these specific technologies or product types.

I cannot resist taking one last look at this scenario of requiring previous success with Product X or Trading Floor Y. The reason this is so common is, quite frankly, because good project managers are few and far between. They are a rare commodity — just as it is rare to have a good understanding about what it takes to be a good project manager in the information technology (IT) world. By insisting on demonstrable past success, the hiring manager can check and see if you did a good job with Product X the last time around. In his more honest moments, however, any project management expert will tell you that previous success with Product X is not a foolproof predictor of equally satisfactory results the next time around. That would be somewhat analogous to expecting the same team to win the baseball World Series year after year after year.

But I digress. As mentioned in the preface, fully half of the project managers assigned to complex projects that I have known through the years had a nontechnical background. I rationalized this by saying that strong interpersonal management skills are important in our specialized profession, too, so lacking personal technical expertise should not, by definition, exclude that individual from spearheading complex technical projects.

As an interviewer, however, I would expect this individual to have processes, similar to those laid out in Chapter 3, to attack their lack of specific knowledge of the project's technologies, have a terrific track record, and possess excellent skills in the areas covered in this chapter. I would definitely ask them how they handle unfamiliarity with the technology, and business processes that your project will address. If you are not satisfied with their answers, you can always reach for the next resume from the pile in front of you.

16.4.3 Quality Orientation

In my admittedly lengthening career, this was once called process reengineering, then Total Quality Management (TQM), then quality assurance (QA). The more common methodologies in place today include Six Sigma, International Organization for Standardization (ISO), and Capability Maturity Model (CMM). I am neither unlearned nor agnostic about these processes and their fine goals and expect those with whom I work to have an equally high commitment to the disciplined pursuit of quality.

A word of caution is in order, whether the application of any of these methodologies, or one of their cousins, is a project requirement, or discretionary. I am not an expert in any of them, but have observed that they complicate the project from an implementation perspective. I would look for additional resource, longer timeframes, and considerably more tasks to manage if:

- Project output must be in compliance with any of the standards described.
- Their methods (e.g., Six Sigma) will proscribe your implementation strategies.

These conditions add significant cycles to the project and should be planned for accordingly, despite the fact that adopting high standards and incorporating a process that assures the attainment of these standards is a noble thing.

Experienced complex project managers are aware that:

- Perfection is not always possible.
- Error and misfortune are part of the landscape.
- Quality methods cannot be emphasized to the degree that business and functional requirements are sacrificed or overlooked. A project

can sustain just so many deliverables without becoming overloaded and, ultimately, become bogged down by the sheer weight of them all.

The quest for quality from an academic perspective is laudable, but from a "down in the trenches" standpoint is not always possible to the degree that these methodologies demand. Part of the project management experience is treating poor results as a risk and looking for ways to mitigate that, sometimes after the fact. Quality is not simply a matter of following the right processes. Were that true, as I have asked before, what do we need project managers for? I designed two programs in which a major sub-team was dedicated to quality. Each team's mission was to apply strict methodologies to all project phases and synchronize handoffs to operations.

We need to understand how to manage poor quality in the same way that we need to ensure that the right processes are in place from the outset to, hopefully, obviate inadequate results. I have found that error reduction is an ongoing affair, not just a certification you can earn for the way a project's deliverables were crafted. The attainment of quality is, to some degree, dictated by the environment, so project managers cannot be unfairly saddled with the burden in a demonstrably dysfunctional environment. Expecting projects with specific, detailed deliverables to significantly uplift the quality of dependent legacy systems and processes is a somewhat unreasonable expectation, when, in fact, it is more likely that the environment will dilute the quality of the new deliverables. This is why so much space is taken up in the early chapters of this book offering details on how to hunt down these opportunities for failure, and proactively circumvent them to the degree that is humanly possible.

I recognize that some of these thoughts are politically incorrect, but, as always, I offer a defense for my posturing. The way I see it, the aggressive introduction of quality methodologies into the project environment have two potential downsides:

1. Processes like Six Sigma originated in the manufacturing environment, where the principles of identifying and remedying systemic error are a near-perfect fit and certainly long overdue from a perspective of productivity, profitability, consumer satisfaction, and the health and safety of producers and consumers alike. Not too many complex IT project activities fit this model.
2. The second caveat I would use to temper enthusiasm for this process, at least a little, is that its utilization sometimes strikes me as a proxy for common sense.

Using a technology to implement business goals is far more art than science, and requires as much experience and skill as it does process. To the degree that quality methodologies can enhance success, I fully agree that:

- Each component of the project experience should be subjected to the best available quality management tools.
- The goal to eliminate error in all phases of the initiative, including the automated processes that result from any complex IT project via such methodologies, are similarly welcome.

One wonders if the quality scrubbing processes take precedence over other management techniques and ignores the human factor, exactly where does the point of diminishing returns reside along the project's critical path? I am most comfortable with the application of these quality methodologies as coaching and modeling tools, not as filters through which all project activities and output must be strained.

Those are my thoughts on the topic. You are equally welcome to your own. In the interview process, each candidate's views on this topic are critical, whether or not their skill with, or certification in, any given methodology is important to you and your organization.

16.4.4 Business Acumen

The selection of this section's title is unfortunate if it implies expertise in finance, marketing, and whatever products or services your corporation is best known for. I use it in the far broader sense. After years of working in the corporate environment, one should have learned how to act, how to think, and how to contribute. I mention this because, sadly, I encounter many people who appear to lack this basic footing that good, competent corporate soldiers are supposed to have. It is a kind of common sense born of reacting to and learning from your environment, so when you earn the chance at your first big IT project, you have some political and interpersonal skills that are far, far better than what little you probably brought to the table when you came into this world from college or the armed forces.

16.5 PROFESSIONAL SKILLS

These are skills we should possess because we make use of them every day to be productive project managers. Some of the items in the list may surprise you, and are offered as areas you may choose to explore within yourself, or with candidates for that project management position you are looking to fill.

16.5.1 Leadership Skills

A project manager who takes credit for a winning project is either on an ego trip or has low self-esteem. Leaders get hard jobs done with minimal collateral damage. Good leaders put their charges in the position to be successful. Success rolls up hill, not down. The top-down leadership success model does not work because gravity causes failure if selfless mentoring does not counteract it. I wrote this book mostly in the first person, but would have preferred saying "we" most of the time in recognition of the many good people who have worked with me through the years to achieve team goals. I always try to think "we" at home and in the workplace.

To be honest, I counteract my own high-handed tendencies in the leadership arena by envisioning the hapless army lieutenant, sword in hand, scrambling over the hill shouting, "follow me, men!" As the machine gun fire rattles overhead, those he would lead remain in the safety of their foxholes, apparently not convinced that their lives are worth risking for this disrespected, if not feared and reviled, so-called leader.

Leadership is about leading, not about exercising power at the expense of others. It is also about setting a good example and about helping those in your command be successful. When I was a line manager of a sixty-person work group, I had power built into my role from the simple fact that I could fire people and hand out raises and plumb assignments.[2] Now, even as a senior project manager, I can do none of those things. Today, I can do team members little harm and no good at all except to the extent that I help them succeed and be recognized for their accomplishments. I treat them as though they can do more for me, or harm to me, than I could possibly dream of reciprocating, in either direction.

Testing for leadership in the interview process is not easy. I do ask for anecdotes sometimes, if for no other reason than to count how many times the candidate says "I" or "we" when recounting past experience. I have no rule on this except that if everything is "I," I cannot say that I was not forewarned.

16.5.2 Advocacy Skills

A good salesperson makes you feel like:

- You need whatever they are pitching.
- They will personally ensure your satisfaction.

Likewise, a good project manager gets people to buy into the project, and applies the same skills to negotiate consensus when conflicts arise. A good advocate is sincere and can explain things without making speeches. Understanding the "feature, function, benefit" approach described in Chapter 13 is an invaluable tool in this regard.

Remember that practically every aspect of your project represents something new to the legacy environment. As a rule, people do not like change because it creates more work or new stress for them. This is understandable. It also creates an ongoing challenge to the project manager, who must enlist all kinds of help in an environment that is not change-friendly, and, therefore, is not project-friendly either. As discussed throughout the book, being able to proselytize the benefits of your initiative is the only way out of this jam. Any such presentations should be principled, not slick or shallow. Keep in mind that your audience recognizes the sound of bluster and the scent of baloney, and will consequently dismiss you as a blowhard more quickly than you can ask, "what did I say wrong?"

This talent, or lack thereof, should be easy to test for during the interview process. After all, we assume each candidate is there because they seek the position, so it makes sense that they advocate their candidacy. Ask yourself how well each one made his or her case. If an interviewee fails to say why you should pick them or indicate a strong interest in the position and the reasons behind that, what does that say about their advocacy skills?

16.5.3 Solicitation Skills

Can you pick up the phone, introduce yourself to a stranger who may not know you and be unfamiliar with your project, and enlist the stranger's support? This takes audacity, even when you are under the gun. I know people who are loath to do this, but then again, project management is not for everyone. If you have done this, what is your batting average? Have you gone back to a previously helpful individual and found that door closed the second or third time around, like you went to the well once too often?

I am no shrinking violet in this regard, but I have certainly mellowed over the years. One reason is that I finally asked myself why people should buy into my problems and raise a finger to help me. The only answer I have come up with is that those who are willing and able to assist have a reason to do so. Some want to look good for the purpose of advancing their careers or raising their self-esteem, while others enjoy doing the right thing. Another group wants to avoid looking bad, particularly if you, your boss, or your project have a high enough profile. Then, these potential allies may want to be seen as contributors, not roadblocks.

On the other hand, certain individuals will decline the opportunity to contribute to your success. Many motives can be attributed to this crowd, too, not the least of which are sloth, and not being a fan of yours.[3] In the end, though, it is best to let those in your path, either as enemies or allies, manage their own motives. Forget evangelizing and manipulation, and focus on getting the help you need. Here is what works for me:

- Approach your potential ally with humility.
- State your case briefly, but in candor.
- Be very specific about your requirements.
- Be clear about any peril you face.

- Remember that overplaying the gloom and doom makes people suspicious.
- Listen very carefully to the response.
- Be very proactive and cooperative with those offering help.
- Be polite with the recalcitrant, but make them aware that you do not have the luxury of accepting failure as an option.
- Request their guidance on how best to remedy what, from your perspective, is an impasse.
- Be explicit about your intent to escalate in a nonthreatening manner, if that is your likely course of action.

You will also be confronted with what must honestly be called "maybes," or "I wish I could, but ...." These are clearly signals of a willingness to negotiate. You have to be acute enough to hear this and smart enough to slow down and negotiate. Project managers often forget that what is so important, possibly even earth-shattering to us, is a curiosity or nuisance to our potential allies.

"Maybe" has so many nuances, and I have yet to see them all. Once detected, I address them by digging out the objection without anyone losing face. This may sound silly, but it is not. For example, it is not unusual to find out that a legacy process in your organization — one you are counting on to support a requirement — is so rigid, antiquated, or dysfunctional that it cannot accommodate your needs. This could be a resource issue, for instance, in terms of availability or skill level. Compounding this problem is the fact that the owners of those processes may choose to fight you or confuse you, instead of helping you understand where the gaps exist, so that together you can reach an accommodation. It is for this reason that I recommend taking great care with these conversations, because you may have stepped on a land mine without knowing it and do not need to exacerbate the situation with bellicosity or some other impolitic if not impolite response.

What does all this have to do with negotiating? The basic rule of horse trading is that you want to live to trade again, so you:

- Do not cheat.
- Do not bully.
- Never lie.

Your goal should be "win–win." Remember, this is not a garage sale. It is a corporate environment where career advancement, a clean conscience, and getting home early are all coin of the realm for the people you are dealing with, so you must be willing and able to make trades in kind.

When interviewing candidates on this subject, I ask them how they approach internal obstacles, which these things almost always are. Ask for specific examples and listen closely. As with many personal traits, I try to imagine a particular candidate trying to be effective in this way in my environment. Keep in mind that nobody I know will earn a perfect score, either during the interview process or during actual project activity, because the truth is that sometimes roadblocks are not only unmovable but also sacred.

16.5.4 Grace under Fire

I am not much of a poker player because I am too darned earnest, but I agree with Kenny Rogers that "you gotta know when to hold 'em, and know when to fold 'em." In a complex project there will be scenarios, either public or private, when what you say, or do not say, creates what the dramatists call "defining moments." These will be painful and probably quite heated times in which it may, or may not be, wise to hold your tongue. During that instant, you may need to protect a team member or deliverable, or hang that project element out to dry. It is hard to get very far into this without wandering too far off the reservation, so I will leave you with the following thoughts.

In those heated moments, can you disassociate yourself from the scrum enough to avoid misapprehending the heat of the moment as the issue? Can you leverage that moment with generosity or by saying "No!"?

Regarding interviewing project manager candidates, the only way to test for this quality is to ask yourself if:

- You can envision the candidate finessing his way though these moments.
- Under these circumstances, is he more likely to be dense than deft?

16.5.5 Relationship Building

Throughout this book, I have cited examples where knowing people and having their respect sets the table for solving problems by ensuring their cooperation. Some of these tough moments fall into the "do or die" category, or so it appears at the time. This is why I pride myself on collecting friends and allies from Day One, because you never know when a relationship will come in handy. This may sound mercenary, and it is, but it is also the right thing to do.

In fact, being comfortable with and interacting with many different kinds of people is very smart, because the key component of "doing business" is social commerce. As a project manager, you are a businessperson first, then a project manager. People that you do business with are in the same boat as you are. They too are looking for allies because, at times, they need help or recognition from others, possibly even you. It is not that friendships, enjoying the company of others, and gossiping in the cafeteria are bad things. They are fine, but consider this. Friendships tend to spring from like-mindedness in sensibilities and other things that do not necessarily contribute to workplace success.

You cannot restrict who you do business with to people you would enjoy spending time with away from work. You need to forge relationships with people you may have little in common with. You should be able to cross lines of ethnicity and culture and personality types, too. It is rare that you cannot find some common ground with everyone with whom you come in contact.

For instance, I am not a golfer, so I miss a major bonding opportunity with many co-workers. Still, because it is important that I get along with everyone, I even get along with golfers. I actually know a joke or two they seem to enjoy, and I am able to do business with them despite the fact my Saturday mornings are spent at the home improvement center, a location most likely unknown to the "hook or slice" crowd. How you accomplish this universal friendliness is basically a matter of style or personal comfort and is not all that hard. Once, that is, you adopt the attitude that it is best to be friendly, empathetic, and respectful, as a matter of course, with everyone with whom you come in contact.

16.5.6 Organizational Skills

This is a tough one. Complex projects have so many pieces and parts that it is difficult, if not impossible, to superimpose a rigid superstructure over it such that:

- Everything runs smoothly.
- Unpredictable or unwanted surprises are minimized.
- Few errors result from confusion or miscommunication.
- Stakeholders always know what is going on and what is expected of them.
- Significant changes in the game plan are communicated effectively.

At the beginning of this chapter, I offered the grandiloquent phrase "shameless nudge and ruthless organizer." Clearly, I place high value in sophisticated organizational skills. In fact, particularly with complex projects, if the project manager adds little more value than a strong sense of organization, that should be practically enough to ensure success. To resort to the vernacular, this translates into:

- Staying on topic
- Keeping on top of things
- Watching the donut, not the hole

The two pieces to this key attribute are how you keep yourself and the project organized. It is a safe bet that the better a job you do with the former, the more effective you will be with the latter. Being organized is a state of mind, a somewhat reflective one at that. Soon after takeoff, a complex project will dissemble into far too many meetings, personalities, issues, and e-mails to stay manageable with any approach that focuses on the details (i.e., with a "bottom up" strategy). Sadly, this is how micromanagers work, scurrying from event to event with ever thickening file folders. They initiate and receive far too many e-mails to make sense of. Sadly, they soon lose sight of the forest for the trees and rarely find their way back from that wilderness.

It is far better to shield part of your mind from the project hubbub. Keep that mental partition focused on the core project values, which are essentially the output of the Big Thirteen interrogatory. I subsequently use those values to filter out the ambient project noise that would puncture my eardrums if I let it. I have the ability to absorb and leverage a tremendous amount of detail, perhaps more than most, but not as consistently as I would like. This is one reason, for instance, why I am not much of a note taker. When I am scribbling, I am not listening, and when I am not listening, I am unable to seek value in that which is swirling around me. It has taken many years of practice to get good at this, but for me, at least, the effort has been well worth the discipline it requires.

I focus, from Day One, on the Big Thirteen deliverables, and I let them congeal into a meaningful vision of the whole project, including the goals, environment, and people that will shape our final outcome. As the project progresses, I keep steering everyone and everything in this way. When I first adopted this approach, I fell into the trap of insisting that the original vision remained valid and sacrosanct from the moment it became clear to me. Eventually, I learned that setting my feet so firmly in wet concrete had the unwanted consequence of making my views irrelevant, because project truths are bound to change. So, I learned to reassess the project every few weeks and adjust my project truths accordingly.

This may not be the best way for you to approach these challenges, but I hope we can agree on the absolute necessity of putting a framework together that gives you a consistent means of:

- Communicating with stakeholders
- Running meetings
- Building consensus
- Addressing problems
- Interacting with management
- Interacting with the team's members
- Interacting with customers and beneficiaries

It is consistency in these areas that will help frame an organization. Consistency is key, because people are most comfortable when they know what to expect when they approach you for help or attend your meetings. The advantages from being organized in these ways will be not only to help them, but you and the project too.

The manner and means you choose are a matter of style, taste, and comfort. As I said, I keep a running tab in my head during meetings (i.e., take mental notes) and write them down later, if necessary, for future use or dissemination. Perhaps you prefer to capture everything and reflect on it later. If that works, that's great. Just keep in mind that you are the one who has to get things organized and steer everyone back toward the middle of the road when you see the car wandering toward the shoulder or median. If you do not do this, who will?

When you are testing for these skills during candidate interviews, ask them how they approach beneficiaries, for instance, regarding their involvement in the project. What would they tell them? What would they ask them? The answers you get will go a long way toward showing how each candidate has grasped the role and whether they can assume responsibility for packaging everything in such a way that people understand what they are supposed to do. In the final analysis, that is what a project manager's organizational responsibilities are all about.

16.5.7 Attention to Detail

This is another cognitive skill allowing one to remember many small but significant things and reprioritize them as project knowledge and circumstance change, as they surely will. Requirements, risk, and dependencies are generally detail-driven. These critical project realities have at their heart subtle issues one must be keenly aware of as decision points keep flying by at a high rate of speed. If you do not adequately understand detail, you will miss the nuances they suggest and either make bad calls or rely on others presumably more knowledgeable than you to make them for you. From a leadership perspective, this reliance on others introduces the risk of being manipulated by them. I have also found that having a command of project detail is an effective way of keeping stakeholders honest. This is so because, if I am perceived as very much in tune, I am also seen as rather difficult to "snow."

As mentioned in the Organizational Skills section (16.5.6), you do not want to manage at the detail level because that is a far too easy way to get lost. In other words, it is best if you can operate at both levels, from 30,000 feet and at ground level. I try to avoid getting overwhelmed with details by applying the simple relevancy test, which is "why do I need to know this?" This takes a little practice, but you have time. It is not a lesson one learns on the first try, or ever stops learning for that matter. Just do not be afraid to take it on, because as an old mentor once told me, "Son, I forgot more than you will ever know."

16.5.8 Work Ethic

Either some people are allergic to work, or they confuse filling out a timesheet with productivity. Everyone occasionally skates, either when off one's feed or to take advantage of a lull in the action. Similar to a good plow horse, project managers should stay with it and make steady progress, even when everyone else appears to have drifted off into the ether. I spend downtime mending fences, building new relationships, and cleaning up documentation. I like to goof off, too, but I generally stay busy preparing for upcoming challenges or catching up on my technical education, which can always use an upgrade. This last task has become so easy that it is shameful not to indulge in it on a regular basis. Simply load the browser on your computer, hit the Internet, click on your favorite search engine, and type in your question regarding technology, certification, quality management, or whatever you find deficient in your personal knowledge base.

When I interview people, I am very concerned about work ethic. I do not expect people to be as task-hungry as I am, but I do expect them to take a reasonably proactive view of their workload. A few follow-up questions on any project story they tell will indicate the likely truth about their professional character in this regard.

16.6 PERSONAL ATTRIBUTES

Professional characteristics appear to come as much from adapting to prior experience as from those attributes one might clumsily call "built-in." This next class is personal and, as such, may not be the result of intentional learning. Still, they are quite interesting to look at with an eye toward self-improvement, despite my earlier joke that project managers are born, not made.

16.6.1 Builder's Mentality

Projects are all about building new systems or remodeling legacy processes. This almost sounds like a general contractor in the home construction industry, does it not? If you were planning on remodeling or building a new home, how would you pick your general contractor? After going through the phone book, evaluating references, and possibly reaching out to someone whose work impresses you, in the end, you probably select someone one you can trust, someone who just appears to be competent at what he does for a living. Not everyone can read a blueprint and turn it into a valuable asset. Can you?

16.6.2 Problem Solving

Most people's knees buckle when the obstacles begin to pile up. The key to problem solving is being able to see that mountain as a big pile of dirt you can move one shovelful at a time. If the hill is really big, the problem solver shrugs his shoulders and ponders whether he needs:

- More shovels
- More time
- Dynamite

We all panic when the enormity of a new issue strikes us, but the more competent among us soon turn analytical. For some, that may indicate the blessing of composure, but for most of us, it is the challenge that motivates us to see things through. If you are interviewing, ask your candidate for an example of a difficult scenario they were able to turn around. Listen for how they analyzed and facilitated resolution. If they cancelled a vacation to write code, this sounds like a dedicated worker, not the capable leader we are seeking. Good problem solvers go all the way back to the beginning and take a sharp look at the assumptions underlying the path to the problem. Oddly enough, therein lies the most probable key to success. More, even, than devising a brilliant workaround, although that is not too shabby, either.

16.6.3 Common Sense

Leave the rocket science to NASA. Although it is nice to know that you can plug local area network (LAN) and analog connections into the same network switch, the "whys" surely do not matter. What does matter is having the common sense to ask whether the switch going down cripples your network, phone, and fax communications all at once, or what. The answer might surprise you and definitely could matter.

I encourage people to ask common sense questions in the face of complex technical or logistical issues. If you look back at the Big Thirteen interrogatory, I doubt there is one question a neophyte in technology or big projects could not ask. Sometimes I feel out of my depth, but I remind myself that if the answers to my simplistic questions fail to make sense, perhaps it is the answer, and not me, that is wanting. Persistence in follow-up questioning will solve this riddle.

Common sense, to me at least, is closely linked to problem solving skills. Have you ever sat in a project meeting when the team is trying to come up with a solution to a serious problem, and had to stifle exasperation over some of the ideas that get advanced, ideas that were impractical if not over the top? Testing interview candidates for the quality of common sense is not easy unless you go right after it. I find the hypothetical scenario best, and I usually ask how they handle projects where the technology is new to them. This will give you some insight into how close to the ground their feet truly are.

16.6.4 Maturity

It is all about learning from your mistakes and growing as a person and a professional. That implies a capacity for tolerance, self-examination, and humility. Given the current youth movement going on in the workplace, whence the more experienced, pricey employees are "taking the package," we cannot all be temperate and sagacious, but it would surely be helpful if someone was willing to assume the role of Project Adult. Getting everyone home safe and sound is far more important than getting an award for the accomplishment.

Maturity is not necessarily age-related, just as tenure does not ensure skill. I test for it in strangers by assessing how comfortable they appear to be in their own skin. Do they look you in the eye, are they self-effacing, is their humor pleasant, do they speak warmly of family or associates without prompting? Maturity is a quality that should not be inferred from sophistication in dress or speech.

16.6.5 Equanimity

True, this is but one sign of maturity. It is singled out because although it is understandable that I raise up on my hind legs in the heat of battle, might I consider it better to react to everyone else's stress by managing the chaos back toward harmony? If I cannot do that for myself, how do I propose to settle down the team ?

16.6.6 Tolerance

In the business world, tolerance is the ability to be even-handed when dealing with the diversity of people around us, even though we are more comfortable with, and appreciative or trusting of, some kinds of people over others. That is your business with after-work friendships, but shortsighted and self-limiting on the job. In the workplace, we must interact effectively with those we do not like, or possibly cannot understand, whether those differences stem from ethnicity, culture, lifestyle, or personality.

16.6.7 Self-Confidence

Can you look someone in the eye, give them bad news, and enlist their partnership in making the darkness go away? Can you tell your boss about a team triumph without dwelling on your personal contribution? Can you take your hunches seriously and act on them before they turn out to be true?[4] What self-confidence is about in our business, ultimately, is your willingness to pull the trigger the minute it is appropriate, based on decisions that others might find risky or presumptive.

Projects are special in that way, particularly when you compare them to the operational side of the IT world where quick, proactive decisions are hardly the norm. Implicit in this aggressiveness is, of course, the willingness to expose yourself to second-guessing, ridicule, or worse if you happen to be wrong. I have defended myself after such inglorious moments by reminding the kidders that if the job was that easy, then anyone could do it! Seriously, you need to do your homework, and trust the right people before going out on these limbs. On the other hand, lacking confidence wastes these assets that you undoubtedly worked hard to accumulate.

Self-confidence is critical for another reason. In Chapter 12, I carried on a bit about gaining team members' trust as a key to opening up honest and useful communications pathways. I also warned you that this could also lead to you getting buried under an avalanche of other peoples' problems. There is one more potential exposure with this open door policy that I failed to mention.

Being open and accessible leaves you vulnerable to manipulation, because you are relying on others to keep you enlightened. There is a subset of corporate citizenry who will use this as the opportunity to influence you for the purpose of their agendas, particularly in the realms of funding, assignments, and recognition. You must have enough self-confidence to not only recognize that which we do not care to perceive in others, but to get over the disappointment you naturally feel after discovering you have just been bamboozled. I used to get angry with this. Now, I make note of the offender and in the future handle them in a more circumspect manner than I would generally find necessary.

16.6.8 Energy Level

It is quite all right to need a cup of coffee in the morning before you can function effectively, just like a freight train needs time to rumble up to speed. Project managers need to be one step ahead of the pack, be eternally vigilant, and pounce at the right moment. You might find it interesting that many times the appropriate initial response to unhappy news is to project a calm and reassuring demeanor. That prevents others from panicking and buys you time until you can conjure up an attack of brilliance. Being alert and engaged is key to that, which, in turn, requires a fairly high energy level.

Some people, when assessing others in this regard, can mistake high anxiety as positive high energy. We all know this type: the "nervous Nellie" who is, in fact, about as productive as a dog chasing its own tail. The other trap you can fall into is to not give the more composed enough time to loosen up during an interview. If you chat with someone long enough, his guard will come down if he truly is full of it and raring to go. If the interviewee remains dispassionate for too long, however, that placidity might actually be a woodenness that is a desirable trait for a Buckingham Palace guard but not for a project manager.

16.6.9 Goal Orientation

We all run into managers who occupy a box on the organization chart without contributing all that much. Of course we want polish, good manners, excellent communications skills, and all that, but in the end, it is the desire to dive across the goal line with the ball in an outstretched hand, possibly having lost one's helmet in the process, that shows the passion for success that good project managers possess. A disdain for winning is wonderful for intimate relationships, but a bit troubling in our profession.

Having made a big deal about maturity, however, induces me to hedge a little. An apparent or professed thirst for winning at all costs is not necessarily an indication of goal orientation so much as it indicates a desire to win at all costs. The truth is that we must sometimes acknowledge and accept defeat, not as a habit or an expectation but as a concession to reality.

Effective business leadership has a give and take component to it. Sometimes we must partner with past, present, or future adversaries. Most people are uncomfortable doing this, so engaging potential adversaries is a skill people must cultivate. Having said all this leads me to the conclusion that seeking goals is not exactly the same thing as chasing victories, which can be Pyrrhic. Such was the case after World War I when the sanctions imposed on the losing Kaiser's Germany by the victorious Allies caused disastrous Teutonic financial ruin and patriotic resentment. Hitler's subsequent rise to power was fueled by his gruesome oath of vengeance for these humiliations, despite the repugnant goals he espoused and tragically achieved. I have never met a project manager of this ilk, thankfully; however, I have been associated with a few individuals who consistently ran roughshod over others — almost is if it were a sport.

16.6.10 Superman Factor

If you are interviewing prospective project managers or thinking about how to present yourself, it is wise to be on the alert for those statements that allege infallibility, invincibility, or omnipotence. The truth is that we imperfect human beings toil in an imperfect world. So it does not make sense to suggest otherwise or to be drawn to those who make such claims. I generally take them as an indication of insincerity and other traits too indelicate to mention in a professional book.

There is another piece to this. A dear friend of mine loves to talk about an interesting lesson she learned from her therapist when her long marriage sadly found its way into divorce court. She felt a lot of guilt over the break-up, despite the fact that most observers felt her soon to be ex-husband was demonstrably more culpable. Her therapist tried numerous ways to help free her from this misguided shame, but did not fare too well. Until one day, that is, when he challenged her by saying, "Well, then fix it!"

"Excuse me?" she responded.

"Sure, if you made it go wrong, then make it right!"

The point is that imperfect project results will result despite the best of intentions. All projects have bad moments and many underachieve, to say the least. Those of us who are conscientious take these as our own fault and resolve, "never again!" I am a big fan of self-examination, out-hustling the next person, and so on, but I need to get a life on this point myself.

There is no Superman, even though many of us should admit that we would like to be that powerful. In fact, none of us is Superman. Appreciable honesty, humility, and humor indicate that the possessor has a good handle on this. In contrast, the danger with the Superman complex is someone with that self-image can become obsessive and brutish. This type of person tends to manage projects in a way that no one wants to suffer his meetings, return his calls, or read his e-mails.

16.7 ABOUT CONSULTING PROJECT MANAGERS

I have labored in the IT environment as an employee, as an outsourced service provider, and as a consulting project and program manager. Each role has its interesting attributes, most of which I have commented on throughout the book. What I want to do now is to mention a few observations I think are valid for those of you who are learning this demanding profession or who are hiring or managing a consulting project manager as we speak.

Consulting project managers can be extremely effective because they are not plugged into the subliminal power struggle that typifies the corporate environment. Not that they are immune to it, but consider the attitude one adopts after doing this for a while. Experienced consulting project managers suffer few illusions about the tenure of their engagement, which may last for three months or three years but rarely longer. As a result, they try to earn their wings every day, motivated by the goals of:

- Building that perfect resume
- Earning great references

Intelligent consulting project managers do not try to show up anyone or steal jobs, either. Nor are they protecting the last 2 years that they need to become fully vested in the retirement plan. So, if they possess good judgment, they will take chances necessary for project success without undue obsessing over political fallout, not to mention career jeopardy. This can have an incredibly positive impact on the team and the project.

A good consulting project manager is there to behave responsibly, teach and mentor where appreciated, demonstrate a good work ethic, and share insights or knowledge gained prior to joining your environment. From a personal growth perspective, consultants seek to become experts in project management, not in the arcane skills of career advancement at Global Behemoth Ltd. Those are noble aspirations for employees, but these aspirations probably do not generate the skills and attitudes this tricky business of complex project management requires.

Not all consulting project managers follow this script, any more than all employees add consistent, selfless value to their job slots either. That is the nature of the world we live in. Most of the consultants I have known through the years are sincerely dedicated to doing a great job. Sometimes they must practice the patience of Job, because they must occasionally pause to let clients catch up with themselves. As a rule, the corporate environment does not encourage or reward lightning fast decision-making and execution. Nor are the indigenous rules of accountability and consequences all that clear or helpful from a consulting project managers perspective either. That is okay because the business of business, even in the IT world, is more about process, politics, and culture than it is about relocating active volcanoes overnight.

16.8 AND FINALLY ...

To paraphrase Conan Doyle's detective Sherlock Holmes, viewed in groups human beings are highly predictable, but with individuals one can only guess at what comes next. The guidelines presented in this chapter, as well as insights sprinkled throughout the book, are intended to sensitize you to the dynamics you can anticipate in your role as project manager. Understanding the culture and individuals where you work, having an undiluted sense of purpose, and being patient and tolerant of all circumstances create an attitude that will appreciably enhance your effectiveness as project manager. The better practitioners of our craft remain focused on the taxing and sweaty business of:

- Gathering information and keeping it current
- Constantly rallying the team around scope
- Delivering a quality product on the customer's behalf to the beneficiaries

It is an extremely satisfying yet anonymous and frustrating job. Just when you think you have it all figured out, new information or changing conditions give you cause to doubt previous beliefs or assumptions. This does not mean you missed something. In fact, you will make yourself dizzy worrying about that, even though it is often true. This profession is a one-day-at-a-time occupation, so what was true yesterday matters only if it is true today, and remains probable for tomorrow. I have come to understand that:

- Adjusting to changes, in reality, is my primary focus.
- Analyzing why a condition changed, or if it was misperceived to begin with, is a great lessons learned exercise to be taken up when the project is completed.

This is why I recommend being agnostic about technology, as well as ever curious about stakeholders' motives, because the guiding facts of your professional duties are subject to change from the day you sign on to the day you sign off.

I feel responsible for representing the project, but I sometimes struggle to make sure it is the project's agenda, not my own, that I advance. You must be prepared to adapt to changes you may not like, as would be the case if something you resisted as scope creep gets blessed by senior management as a new or revised requirement. It is best to stay mindful of this. Do not emotionally invest too heavily in project specifics. This includes relationships with stakeholders, which are sure to blow hot and cold over the long haul.

Do not expect much in the way of accolades. If you need them, this is not the job for you. One of the sports television clichés states that a well-officiated sporting event is one during which you hardly notice the referees. This means they do not interrupt the flow by turning the game into a personal showpiece of rulebook enforcement. Even when they step in, hopefully it is to tag someone for unfair or inappropriate behavior that, if left unabated, would unfairly influence the outcome.

Similarly, the project manager has to be all eyes and ears; he or she has to get the project back on track when the project's integrity is threatened by the dysfunctions of the team, the institution, or the technologies. A significant challenge to the project manager is to know when and how to intervene but, for the most part, as they say, just "let them play." The other trick is to recognize that it is your coaching, as described throughout the book, which minimizes your need to be the referee, too.

If this author's intent counts for anything, you will benefit from many of the ideas presented in this book. I enjoyed putting this together with that outcome in mind, and learned quite a bit myself while doing so. And finally, best wishes on your current or next adventure in complex IT project management!

Notes

1. Sometimes behind my back!
2. Those were the days!
3. Or your project, or your boss.
4. If hunches about good things really worked, we would all hang out at the racetrack.

Index

Note: Italicized pages refer to notes, tables, or illustrations

A

Access, 227
Accounting closes, 16
Acquisitions, 16
ADA (Americans with Disabilities Act), 34
Addressing information, *202*
Advocacy skills, of project managers, 286–287
Agendas, 5
   documenting, 152
   in meetings, *158*
Air conditioning, 16
Airport construction project, 31; *see also* Projects
   Big Thirteen interrogatory in, *32*
   feasibility of implementing requirements in, 39–40
   feedback in, 37–38
   issues list, *33*
   milestones in, *120*
   wheel of dependency in, 34–36
Alpha test, *61*
Alternates, *98*
Americans with Disabilities Act (ADA), 34
Analog cards, 141
Answer Man, 130–132
Anti-virus protection, 21, 51
Apollo Program, 5–8
Application overview, *202*
Applications, *53*
Application servers, 51
Artificial intelligence, 40
Asset management system, 19, 152–153
Assumptions, 3–4
   in budget management, 162–164
   documenting, 151
   in risk analysis, 91
   socializing, 37
   turning issues into, 36–37
Attributes of project managers, 278–279
   business acumen, 285
   experience and training, 279–285
   personal attributes, 293–298
   professional skills, 285–293
   quality orientation, 283–285
Attrition, 269
Authentication, *236*
Autonomy of project managers, 242–243
Awards, 269

B

Back-end processing, 12
Backing out, *98*
Backups, 21
   in runbooks, *202*
   in SLA (service level agreement), *236*
Backward compatibility, 13
"Bad car mechanic" scenario, 144
Bad news, 128–130, 238
Bandwidth, *46*, 47
Base building, 267
Basic needs, for technologies, 48
BAU (business as usual) process, 14
   error rates, 19
   identifying support for, 164
   and missed dates, 264
   and risk aversion, 251
   support requirements, 199
   in workflow disruption, 227
Belt and suspenders strategy, *98*
Benchmarks, 162
Beneficiaries, 11; *see also* Customers; Projects
   in budget management, 167
   vs. customers, 217–219
   dealing with, 219–220

expected behavior of, *218*
joint planning with, 232–234
negotiating with, 238–239
objections of, 226–229
and project timelines, 16
risks of, 86, 91–92, 229
roles and responsibilities of, 234
scope creep from, 89
service levels, 235–236
sharing assumptions with, 37
in technology design reviews, 59
in UAT (user acceptance testing),
   234–235
in vendor management, 80–81
Beneficiary tasks, 214
Benefits of projects, 8–11
Big Thirteen interrogatory, 3; *see also*
   Projects
in airport construction project, *32*
beneficiaries: who benefits?, 11
benefits: what are the benefits?, 8–11
chart of, *4*
costs: what is the cost?, 15
customers: who is the customer?, 11–12
dependencies: what are the key
   dependencies?, 16–17
legacy environment: what is the fit?,
   12–15
risks: what is the risk?, 17–18
scope: what is to be done?, 5–8
shelf life: what is the shelf life?, 21
sponsors: who is the sponsor?, 12
success metrics: what are the success
   metrics?, 18–20
support: how will we support this?,
   20–21
timeline: what is the timeline?, 15–16
Billing records, 1
Body counts, 269
Boss management, rules of, *253*
Bouncing ball, following the, 4, 214
Brainstorming, 11
Branch systems, 267
Browsers, compatibility issues in, 13, 41
Budgets, 4; *see also* Costs
approval of, 175
assumptions in, 162–164
common processes in, 161–162
and cost recovery, 174–175
documenting, 152
estimates, 169–171
laundry list, *172*
missed, 264
overruns, 175–176, 177–178

reviewing, 172–173
and service delivery, 174–175
shortfalls in, 173–174
source data, 164–169
tracking expenditures in, 176–177
working out, 263
Builder's mentality, 293
Buildings, delay in occupancy of, 147
Business acumen of project managers,
   285
Business drivers, *46*

C

Cabling, *46*, 267
Calendars, 14, 120
Call centers, 79
implementation pyramid for, 112–113
support for, 203–204
in vendor management project, 107
Call detail reporting (CDR), 14
Capability Maturity Model (CMM), 283
CDR (call detail reporting), 14
CD-ROMs, 14
Certificate of occupancy (CP), *120*
Certification process, 200
Change control, 203
Channel service units (CSUs), *167*
Client-server architecture, 12, 41
Closure rates, 145
CMM (Capability Maturity Model), 283
Coaching, 211–213
Comfort zones, 27
Common sense, 294–295
Communications skills, 252
Communications strategy, 153–155
Compatibility, 13
Completion schedules, *143*
Conflict avoidance, 249–250
Construction, and slippage of project, *141*
Construction module, 28–29
Consultants, 162, *172*
Consulting project managers, 298–299
Contingencies, 123
expenditures, 162
funds for, 95
Contracts, 22
"Control freak" managers, 244–245
Corporate backbone, 16, 102
Corporate network, *103*
Corporate risks, 86, 92
Corporate standards, 41
in design assumptions, 163
in selecting technologies, 48

Corporation, criticism of, 269
Costs, 15; *see also* Budgets
    moving, *172*
    objections to, 222
    overruns, 175–176
    recovery of, 78, 174–175
    of risk management, 95–97
    turnover, *172*
    of using technologies, 49
Countertop installation project, 65–66; *see
    also* Projects
    design details, *72*
    implementation details, *70, 72*
    implementation strategy, 67–68, *72*
CP (certificate of occupancy), *120*
Creativity in management, 250
Critical paths, 117–119
    and disconnects, 4
    tracing, 93
    in vendor management, *116*
Criticism of individuals, 268
CSR (customer service representatives), 1,
    28
CSUs (channel service units), *167*
Culture, 267–268
Customer management, 23, 220–222
Customers, 11–12; *see also* Beneficiaries;
        Projects
    vs. beneficiaries, 217–219
    in budget management, 167–168
    dealing with, 219
    expected behavior of, *218*
    and project timelines, 16
    relationship with project managers,
        236–238
    relationship with vendors, *180*, 186
    in resolving project issues, 146
    in technology design reviews, 59
    in vendor management, 80–81
Customer service representatives (CSR), 1,
    28
Customer site dispatch module, 29
Customer tasks, 214
Customized BAU support, 199–200

D

Database administrators, 203
Data centers, 79
    in budgetary laundry list, *172*
    moving applications servers in, 51–52
    risk management in, 96
    support types, 202–203
    in vendor management project, 107

Data circuits, 78
Data jacks, 141
Data packets, 1
Dates, 15, 264
Day One vs. Day Two strategy, *98*
Decision making, 209–211
Deliverables, 3; *see also* Projects
    in call center project, 112
    compatibility within the legacy
        environment, 12–15
    objections to, 222
    in project plans, 121
    quality of, 147–148
    target state chart for, *53*
    workflow analysis, 42
Deliverable view of projects, 73
Delivery, late, 146–147
Demilitarized zone (DMZ), 133, 203
Demographic data, 22
Dependencies, 16–17
    in implementation strategies, 67
    in project plans, 123
    in SLA (service level agreement), *236*
    workflow analysis, 42
Design, 10
    assumptions, 162–163
    changes, 230
    details, *70*
Desktop support, handoffs to, 195
Details, 29; *see also* Requirements
    attention to, 292–293
    getting ready for, 119–120
Digital service units (DSUs), *167*
Digital subscriber line (DSL), *46*
Directories, *53*
Disaster recovery, 20
    in application platform, 88–89
    cost of, 96
    facilities for, 79
    in runbooks, *202*
    in SLA (service level agreement), *236*
    support for, 203
    in target state chart, *53*
    in vendor management project, 107
Disconnects, 4
    in customer-vendor relationships, *180*
    RFP (request for proposal), *185*
Discovery process, 3
    techniques in, 22–23
    workflow analysis in, 43
Divestitures, 21
DMZ (demilitarized zone), 133, 203
DNS (Domain Name System), 59, 227–228
Documentation, *122*

guidelines, *152, 155*
types of documents, 151–153
Domain Name System (DNS), 59, 227
Draft runbooks, *61*
DSL (digital subscriber line), *46*
DSUs (digital service units), *167*
Duplication of effort, 74

E

EDI (electronic data interchange), 80
Education, 251
Egos, clashing of, 209
Electric power, 16
Electronic data interchange (EDI), 80
Elevators, 16
E-mail, 155
Emerging model, 197–198
Encryption, *46*, 47
End computing devices, 50
End users, *see* Beneficiaries
Energy level of project managers, 296–297
Engineering, and slippage of project, *141*
Equanimity of project managers, 295
Error codes, 29
Error rates, 19
Escalation, 128–130
and boss management, 251
in runbooks, *202*
script, *130*
in SLA (service level agreement), *236*
Escrow account, 95
Estimates, in budget management, 169–171
Evaluation, in selecting technologies, *49*
Expenditures, tracking of, 176–177
Extensible Markup Language (XML), *46*, 80
Extranets, *134*

F

Facilities, 79
in call center project, 112
delay in occupancy of, 147
handoffs, 195
in vendor management, 107
Factory design, 10
Fault management, 20, *236*
Features, functions, and benefits strategy,
220–222
Feedback, 37–38
Fibre Channel (FC) Protocol, 183
File servers, *138, 139*
File Transfer Protocol (FTP), *61*
Firewalls, 112

in increasing security, 47
upgrading, *46*
First road, in airport construction project, 35
Fit, in using technologies, 49
Flexibility in management, 250
Flight of fancy, in projects, 10
Football team management, 207–209
Forward proxy servers, 47
FTE (full-time employees), 162
FTP (File Transfer Protocol), *61*
Full-time employees (FTE), 162

G

Gantt chart
defining tasks in, 116
in implementation strategies, 77
percent complete feature in, 135–136
in validating assumptions, 125
Goal orientation, 297
Go/no go decision points, 85, *100*, 140

H

Hand-held computers, 50
Handoffs, 195–196
in implementation strategies, 74
miscues in, 266
in project deliverables, *3*
"Hands-off" managers, 245
Hard metrics, 19, 50
Hardware
architecture, *202*
implementation, 203
information, *202*
repair, 203
vendors, 180
Head coaches, 207–209, 257
Headcount, 20
Help desk, 20
in budgetary assumptions, 163
handoffs, 195
Hijacking of computers, 83
Historical precedent model, 161
Historic model, 197
Home directories, *53*
Host systems, 51
HTML, *46*
Human resources, 79

I

Impacted sites, number of, 163
Implementation

costs, 166
details, *70, 72*
issues, *143*
manager, 202
Implementation strategy, 63, 65; *see also*
   Projects
   alternative view of nine planning tasks
      in, *69*
   in budget management, 166
   building, 74
   components of, *75*
   and disconnects, 4
   Gantt chart in, 77
   gaps within, 74–75
   in LAN printing project, 75–77
   need for, 68–69
   nine high-level planning steps in, *68*
   as positive contributing factor, 261
   reviewing, 93
   risk planning in, 97
   risks in, 17
   using, 69–73
   vendor management, 77–81
Incompetence, 132
Indemnification plan, 88
Industry benchmarks, 162
Ineffectiveness, 132
Infighting, 211
Information management, 151–158
   communications strategy in, 153–155
   discovery techniques in, 22–23
   documentation in, 151–153
   meetings in, 155–158
   for public consumption, *129*
Information technology (IT) projects, 8–11
Infrastructures
   in budgetary laundry list, *172*
   in call center project, 112
   and slippage of project, *141*
Instant orange drink, invention of, 7–8
Insurance, 95
Integration issues, reviewing, 58–59
Intelligence, 251
Internal project managers, 168
International Organization for
   Standardization (ISO), 283
Internet, 1, 51
Interviewing techniques, 23–24
Inventory, documenting, 152
IP (Internet Protocol) addressing, 47
IP Telephone project, 55
   feature/function/benefit sell, *222*
   objections in, *225*
   Plan B strategies, *98*

ISDN (Integrated Services Digital Network)
   project, 1; *see also* Projects
   benefits of, 9
   deliverables, 3
   feasibility of implementing requirements
      in, 40
   requirements, 28–30
   workflow for, *2*
ISO (International Organization for
   Standardization), 283
Issues, 4
   assigning, 34–36
   documenting, 151
   eliminating, 33–34
   list, 33, 143–146
   reviewing, 58–59
   turning into assumptions, 36–37

J

Jeopardy of projects, 132–135
Job aids, documenting, 152

K

Key dates, 15

L

Labor, in budget management, 162,
   169–171
LAN/desktop platform, 57, *58*
LAN printing, *53*, 75–76
Laptops, 144
Late deliveries, 146–147
Late status of projects, 146–147
LCD (liquid crystal display), 7
LDAP (Lightweight Directory Access
   Protocol), 54
Leadership, 206
Leadership skills, of project managers,
   285–286
Lead times, *85*, 98
Leap of faith, 27
Legacy systems, 29
   compatibility of deliverables with,
      12–15
   databases, 41
   replacing, 8
   risks in, 93
   stability, 227
Lessons learned process, 255–257; *see also*
   Projects
   implementation of scopes, 257–259

negative contributing factors, 263–268
positive contributing factors, 259–263
pulling project teams together, 268–270
setting goals for, 257
SouthPointe project, 271–273
Life cycles, product, 21
Lightweight Directory Access Protocol (LDAP), 54
Liquid crystal display (LCD), 7
Load balancing, 51–52, 58, *62*
Loaners, documenting, 152
Local area networks (LANs), 50, 144
  authentication process, 58–59
  eliminating legacy protocols in, 93–94
  handoffs, 195
Long distance calls, 14, 78

M

Mainframe access, *53*
Mainframe printing, 76
  feature/function/benefit sell, *222*
  target state, *53, 221*
Mainframes, 16
Maintenance contracts, 153
Majority, rule of, 209
Management information bases (MIBs), 153
Management style, 244–245
Management traits, 243–244; *see also* Senior managers
  communications skills of, 252
  conflict avoidance, 249–250
  rasp of theory and details, 251–252
  management style, 244–245
  political tendencies, 247–248
  problem solving, 245–247
  procrastination, 248–249
  risk aversion, 250–251
Manufacturing cycles, 16
Master plan, 119–120
Maturity of project managers, 295
Meetings, 155–158, 213
Mentoring, 211–213
Mergers, 16, 21
Methodology, in budget management, 162
MIBs (management information bases), 153
Micromanagers, 244–245
Microwave technology, 7
Middleware project, 16
Milestones, 15
  in implementation strategies, 67
  and scheduling of projects, 140
  in vendor management, 116
Minutes, documenting, 152

Miscellaneous costs, *172*
Missed budget, 264
Missed dates, 264
Missed requirements, 265–266
Monitoring tools, 203
Move schedules, documenting, 152
Moving costs, in budgetary laundry list, *172*
Multideliverable projects, 257
Multiplexers, *46*, 112
Murphy's Law, 89–90

N

NASA (National Aeronautics and Space Administration), 6
Negative contributing factors, 263–264; *see also* Positive contributing factors; Projects
  culture, 267–268
  handoff miscues, 266
  missed budget, 264
  missed dates, 264
  missed requirements, 265–266
  ownership, 266–267
Negotiations, 20, 238–239
Network address administration, 195
Network migration project, 164–169
Network security, *46*, 47
Network/telecom support, 202
Network transport, 180
Network turn-ups, 15
New construction project, 16–17
New products, 16, 20
Nomenclature, standardization of, 19

O

Objections, 222–225
  of beneficiaries, 226–229
  emphatic response to, *225*
  resolving, *226*
Obstacles, 5
One-on-one meetings, 155
Online database, 22
Operating systems (OS)
  support for, 203
  upgrading, 13, 142
  vendors of, 180
Operational runbooks, 22
Operations
  and slippage of project, *141*
  in vendor management, 79, 107
Order fulfillment time, 78

Organizational skills, of project managers, 290–292
OSP (outside plant engineering), 28–29
Outside plant engineering (OSP), 28–29
Outsourcing, 162
Overruns, 177–178
Ownership, 266–267

P

Parenthood, 277
Password administration, 21
PBX (private branch exchange) telephony, 49
    triggers for, 99–101
    vendors, 78
Perfect project, dreaming of, 269
Performance issues, root causes of, *212*
Permanent virtual circuits (PVCs), *167*
Personal attributes of project managers; *see also* Professional skills; Project managers
    builder's mentality, 293
    common sense, 294–295
    energy level, 296–297
    equanimity, 295
    goal orientation, 297
    maturity, 295
    problem solving, 294
    self-confidence, 295–296
    Superman factor, 297–298
    tolerance, 295
Personal computers (PCs), 50
    in budgetary laundry list, *172*
    replacing, 12, 144
Personalities, 5
Personal preference, in selecting technologies, 48–49
Phased rollout, *98*
Pilot, *98*
Plan B, 84–85
    documenting, 151
    pulling together, 101–102
    and risks, 58, 85–86
    strategies in, 97, *98*
    triggers in, 97–99, 140
    in WAN (wide area network) implementation, 102–104
Planning process, *see* Project plan
Points of presence (POP), 261–262
Politics
    in budget management, 163–164
    and senior management, 247–248
POP (points of presence), 261–262
PO (purchase order), *134*

Positive contributing factors, 259–260; *see also* Negative contributing factors; Projects
    budget, 263
    developing excellent requirements, 260
    implementation strategy approach, 261
    risk identification, 262–263
    starting point of projects, 261–262
Pricing, 185–186
Print servers, *138, 139*
Print services, 144
Private branch exchange, *see* PBX (private branch exchange) telephony
Problem solving, 245–247, 294
Procrastination, 248–249
Procurement, 15
    dependencies, 115
    and slippage of project, *141*
    tasks in, 213
    vendors, 180
Product identification, 30
Production support models, 197–198
Product life cycles, 21
Professional skills of project managers, 285; *see also* Project managers
    advocacy skills, 286–287
    attention to details, 292–293
    leadership skills, 285–286
    organizational skills, 290–292
    relationship building, 289–290
    solicitation skills, 287–289
    work ethic, 293
Profits, 10
Program managers, 12
Project administrators, 127
Project adult, 276–278
Project jeopardy, 132–135
Project managers, 241, 299–300
    as Answer Man, 130–132
    autonomy of, 242–243
    bad news, 238
    communications strategy, 153–155
    consulting, 298–299
    day in life of, 275–276
    dealing with beneficiaries, 219–220
    dealing with customers, 219
    experience and training of, 279–285
    implementation strategies, 67
    internal, 168
    interviewing techniques, 23–24
    managing objections, 222–225
    negotiations by, 238–239
    personal attributes of, 293–298

in politics of bad news and escalation, *130*
professional skills of, 285–293
as project adult, 276–278
in raising project jeopardy, 132–135
relationship with customers, 236–238
roles and responsibilities of, 2, 206–209, 268
rules of engagement, 127–128
in selling the critical path, 117–119
in understanding benefits of projects, 8–9
working with people, 205–206
Project plan
checking status against, 135–137
details of, 119–120
mapping requirements to, 42
objectives in, 105–106
steps in, 106–107
team leads in, 121–124
for vendor management, *109, 114, 121*
Project planners, 127
Project pyramid, 110–115
Project risk, 86, 90–91
Projects, 2–3; *see also* Big Thirteen interrogatory
agendas in, 5
assumptions in, 3–4
benefits of, 8–11
costs of, 15
customers of, 11–12
dependencies, 16–17
disconnects in, 4
exposure to perception, 258–259
failure of, 51–52
implementation strategy approach in, 261
information discovery techniques, 22–23
issues in, 4
and legacy environment, 12–15
negative contributing factors to, 263–268
obstacles to, 5
personalities in, 5
positive contributing factors to, 260
risks, 17–18
shelf life of, 21
sponsors of, 12
starting points of, 261–262
success metrics, 18–20
support for, 20–21
timeline of, 15–16
views, 73
Project teams; *see also* Team management
coaching and mentoring in, 211–213

decision making, 209–211
following the "bouncing ball" in, 214
infighting in, 211
leadership, 206
lessons learned, 268–270
ownership, 213–214
table manners, 214–215
timelines, 16
Proof of concept, *61, 98*
Provisioning module, 29
Proxy servers, *46*, 47
Public presentations, *223*
Public projects, 8
Public telephone network services, benefits of, 9
Purchase order (PO), *134*
Purchasing documents, 152
PVCs (permanent virtual circuits), *167*

Q

Quality assurance (QA), 19, 283
Quality orientation, 283–285

R

RAG (Red Amber Green) statusing methodology, 133
Random access memory (RAM), 133
Reengineering, 19
Relationship building, 289–290
Remediation, 88
cost of, 95
in server migration project, 145
Reporting module, 29, 115
Request for proposal, *see* RFP
Requirements, 5; *see also* Scope; Specifications
Apollo Program, *7*
cost elements of, *167*
and cost overruns, 176
delayed, 118
delivery of, 258
and dependencies, 16
deriving, 30–31
in detailed scheduling, *122*
developing, *31*, 260
and disconnects, 4
documenting, 151
feasibility of implementing, 39–40
following the, 27–28
implementing, 39–40
mapping to project plan, 42
missed, 265–266

vs. scope, 7, 27–28, 258
vs. specifications, 7
turning into specifications, 40–42
universal sign-off on, 38–39
validation of, 6
and workflow analysis, 42–43
Reserved requirements, 30
Resolvers, 146
Resources
  allocation of, 123
  availability of, *170*
  issues, 227
  skills, 123
Revenues, 10
Reverse proxy servers, 47
Revision level, 13
Rework, 75
RFP (request for proposal), 78
  disconnects in, *185*
  support of work (SOW), 113
  techniques in, 187–189
  in vendor selection process,
    184–187
Risks, 17–18
  analysis of, 86–87
  aversion to, 250–251
  avoidance of, 226
  beneficiary, 86, 91–92, 229
  corporate, 86, 92
  identifying, 87–89, 262–263
  in implementation strategies, 67, 74
  management of, 95–97, 195
  Murphy's Law, 89–90
  and Plan B, 85–86
  planning, 97
  project, 86, 90–91
  reviewing, 57–58
  types of, 86
Robbery, 83
Roles and responsibilities, 266–267
  documenting, 152
  in implementation strategies, 67
  in managing customer and beneficiaries,
    234
Rolled-up implementation strategy,
    107–110
Roll up view, 73
Routers, 21, *46*, 112
RPF (request for proposal), 77
Rule of majority, 209
Runbooks, 201
  contents of, *202*
  draft, *61*
  operational, 22

S

Sales entry module, 28
Sales management, 23
Salespeople, 168
  dealing with customers, 219
  managing objections, 222–225
SAN (storage area network), 173
Satellite video, 103
Schedules, 107–110; *see also* Status of
    projects
  adjusting, 141–143
  changes in, 230
  documenting, 151, 152
  drafting, 115–117
  elements of, *122*
  handling challenges to, 140
  logic, 123
  objections to, 222
  planning tools, 124–125
Scope, 5–8; *see also* Requirements;
    Specifications
  Apollo Program, *7*
  and budget management, 168–169
  documenting, 151
  implementing, 257–259
  progress to design specifications, *6*
  vs. requirements, 7–8, 27–28, 258
  and risks, 17
  vs. specifications, 7–8
Scope creep, 89
  managing, *232*
  in project accounting, 161
  reacting to, 230–232
  recognizing, 229–230
Second road, in airport construction
    project, 35–36
Security, 203
  in budgetary laundry list, *172*
  handoffs, 195
  and slippage of project, *141*
Self-confidence of project managers,
    295–296
Self-promotion, 206
Senior managers, 241
  communications skills of, 252
  conflict avoidance, 249–250
  grasp of theory and details, 251–252
  management style of, 244–245
  political tendencies of, 247–248
  problem-solving skills of, 245–247
  procrastination of, 248–249
  risk aversion, 250–251
September 11 attacks, 96

Servers
  in budgetary laundry list, *172*
  changing, 144
  delay in testing of, 147
  migration, *58*
  monitoring tools, 51
Service bureau, 79–80
Service level agreement, *see* SLA
Service levels, 235–236
Shared directories, *53*
Shortfalls in budget, 173–174
Shrink-wrapped software, 180
Shutdown processes, *202*
Silicon chips, 7
Simple Network Management Protocol
  (SNMP), 203
Single-deliverable projects, 257
Site availability, 15
Six Sigma, 19, 78, 283, 284
Skillsets, 20
SLA (service level agreement), 19
  components of, *236*
  and contract budget, 80
Slippage, 264; *see also* Schedules
  date-constrained tasks affected by, *142*
  factors in, *141*
SNMP (Simple Network Management
  Protocol), 203
Soft metrics, 19
Software
  in budgetary laundry list, *172*
  information, *202*
  releases, 15
Software development manager, 12
Solicitation skills, of project managers,
  287–289
SONET, *46*
Source data in budget management, 164–169
Sources of information, 22
SouthPointe project, *138*
  lessons learned in, 271–273
  meeting agenda, *158*
SOW (support of work), 107, 113, 116
Specifications, 6; *see also* Requirements;
    Scope
  Apollo Program, 7
  documenting, 151
  progress from scope to, *6*
  vs. requirements and scope, 7
  turning requirements into, 40–42
Speeds and needs approach, 220–222
Sponsors, 12
Staff
  augmentation of, 180

change in, 230
headcount, 20
Stakeholders, 3
  assessing critical paths with, 118
  inducing buy-ins from, 31
  sharing assumptions with, 37
Standardization of nomenclature, 19
Standards, in design assumptions, 163
Starting points, 261–262
Start-up processes, *202*
Status of projects, 127; *see also* Projects
  adjusting schedules, 141–143
  Answer Man, 130–132
  and boss management, 251
  checking against project plan, 135–137
  documenting, 152
  generic reactions to, 140–141
  guidelines, *140*
  handling challenges to schedules, 140
  issues list, 143–146
  late, 146–147
  monitoring tool, *136*
  politics of bad news and escalation,
    128–130
  and quality of deliverables, 147–148
  reports, 137–139
  rules of engagement, 127–128
Storage area network (SAN), 173, 183
Storage management, 203
Stress test, *61*
Success metrics, 18–20
Superman factor, 297–298
Supervisors, 242–243
  communications skills of, 252
  conflict avoidance, 249–250
  grasp of theory and details, 251–252
  management style of, 244–245
  political tendencies of, 247–248
  problem-solving skills of, 245–247
  procrastination of, 248–249
  risk aversion, 250–251
Suppliers, and slippage of project, *141*
Support, 20–21
  for legacy systems, 14
  of vendors, 180
Support groups, 145
Support requirements, 198–201
Swing space, 87
Switches, 21, *46*, 112
System design and architecture, 30, *61*

T

Table manners, of project teams, 214–215

Tape backup and archiving, 195, 203
Target state, 28
    chart of, *53*
    listing elements of, 53
    in planning process, *68*
Task forces, 162
Tasks, 213–214
    dates, 15
    and slippage, *142*
TBD (to be determined), 30
TCP/IP (Transmission Control
            Protocol/Internet Protocol), 47,
            76
Team leads, 5
    assessing critical paths with, 118
    dumping work on project managers,
            207
    in managing plan details, 121–124
Team management, 205–215; *see also*
            Project teams
    coaching and mentoring in, 211–213
    decision-making in, 209–211
    following the "bouncing ball" in, 214
    of football teams, 207–209
    and infighting, 211
    leadership in, 206
    ownership, 213–214
    and roles of project managers, 206–209
    table manners in, 214–215
    working with people, 205–206
Team sport coaches, 257
Technical background, 282–283
Technical projects, common defects in, 27
Technical sales, 23
Technologies, 50–51; *see also* Requirements
    and business drivers, *46*
    failure of, 49–52
    plan, *53*
    selecting, 48–49
    standards, *49*
    understanding, 54–56
    using, 45–48
    validation process, *61*
    in vendor management, 79–80, 107
Technology review board, 59–60
Teleconferencing, 78
Telephony, *53*, *221*
Telex, 78
Testing, and slippage of project, *141*
Test plan document review, *61*
Thin client computing, *46*
    analyzing feedback in, 38
    as front end in LAN/desktop platform, 56
    lessons learned in, 272

Third road, in airport construction project,
            36
TIA607 standard, 267
Tier pricing, 185–186
Timeframes, 74
Timelines, 15–16, 30
Timing, in project plans, 123
Tolerance, 295
Tools, in design assumptions, 163
Totally customized support, 200–201
Total Quality Management (TQM), 283
TQM (Total Quality Management), 283
Training, 19
    risk planning in, 97
Transport logs, documenting, 152
Triaging, of unanticipated project disasters,
            146
Triggers
    dates, *100*, 140
    in IP telephony implementation, 99–101
    in PBX (private branch exchange)
            telephony implementation,
            99–101
    in Plan B, 98–99
    test, *85*
Turnover costs, in budgetary laundry list,
            172
Turnover management, 195
    handoffs, 195–196
    negotiating support in, 201–204
    production support models, 197–198
    runbooks, 201
    support requirements, 198–201

U

Unit pricing, 185–186
Universal sign-off on requirements, 38–39
Unix boxes, 41
Upgrading, *3*, *46*
Usability, 13
User acceptance testing (UAT), 234–235
    in detailed scheduling, *122*
    in technology validation, 60, *61*
    timelines, 15
    in vendor management, 80
User census, 152
User functionality, 163
User guides, 152
Users, in design assumptions, 162–163

V

Validation process, 56–57, 60–63

Vendor management, 179–180
  critical path, *116*
  definition of, 78
  of existing vendors, 180–182
  general guidelines in, 190–192
  implementation pyramid for, *111*
  implementation strategy, 77–81
  of new vendors, 182–183
  project plan, *109, 114, 121*
  RFP (request for proposal) in, 187–189
  rules of engagement, *181*
  scheduling in, 107–110
  steps in, 190–192
Vendors, 179–180
  existing, 180–182
  new, 182–183
  pricing by, 185–186
  relationship with customers, *180*, 186
  in rolled-up implementation strategies,
    78
  selection process, 183–187
  services of, 179
  support by, 20
Ventilation system, 66
Video conferencing, 78
  lessons learned in, 271–272
  target state, *53*
Voice mail provisioning process, 20
  workflow, *44*
Voice services, 78
Voice/telecom support, 203

Web masters, 203
Web servers, 47, 51
Wedding reception, Plan B for,
    84–85
White papers, 22
Wide area networks (WANs), 50, 93
  in budgetary laundry list, *172*
  budget planning worksheet for,
    167
  connectivity, *103*
  Plan B for, 102–104
Wireless LAN, 63
  feature/function/benefit sell,
    222
  lessons learned in, 271
  target state, *53, 221*
Wire transfers, 78
Workdays, 169–171
Worker productivity, 169–171
Work ethic, 213, 293
Workflow, *2*, 29
Workflow analysis, 42–43
Work hours, 170
Workweek, 170–171
World Trade Center, 8, 89
Worst-case scenarios, 133

X

XML (Extensible Markup Language),
    46, 80

W

Watch design project, 9–10, 13

Y

Y2K projects, 161